READINGS IN ELEMENTARY SOCIAL STUDIES

READINGS IN
Elementary
Social Studies

by

Richard E. Frickert, Ed.D
Professor of Elementary Education
Assistant Chairman, Department of Elementary Education

Homer R. Pankey, Ed.D
Professor of Elementary Education
Chairman, Department of Elementary Education

California State College
California, Pennsylvania

KENDALL/HUNT PUBLISHING COMPANY
DUBUQUE, IOWA

*To our beloved wives and children
who have encouraged and supported
our professional endeavors.*

Contents

I. Introduction   1

II. History
  A. History for the Elementary School Child
     by Vincent R. Rogers   5
  B. History in the Social Studies
     by William H. Cartwright   11
  C. Numismatics in the Classroom
     by Paul W. Kane and Robert W. Marvin   24

III. Geography
  A. The Problems Approach to Geography
     by Marilee Jean Bradbury   29
  B. Geography: Sighted Subject-Sank Same
     By Gary C. Fox   33
  C. Maps, Globes and Children
     by Marlow Ediger   36
  D. Orienting the Child to His World
     by Rose E. Sabaroff   38
  E. Geography and the Contemporary Urban Scene
     by Michael E. Eliot Hurst   46
  F. Fourth and Sixth Grade Students' Knowledge of
    Topographical Terms
     by Arthur K. Ellis   54

IV. Economics
  A. Economic Education in the Elementary School
     by Robert M. Bruker   61
  B. Economic Education in an Age of Great Expectations
    and Instant Solutions
     by Albert Alexander and Edward C. Prehn   66
  C. An Economics Unit That Really Works
     by James Powell   81
  D. A "Blue Chip" Teaching Unit
     by Robert M. Bruker   87

V. Political Science
  A. Political Studies in the Schools
     by Robert E. Cleary and Donald H. Riddle . . .   93
  B. Teaching Law in the Elementary School
     by Joseph C. Johnson, II, and
     Henry L. Sublett, Jr.   96

VI. Anthropology
  A. The Role of Anthropology in Elementary
     Social Studies
     by Richard L. Warren 101
  B. Field Anthropologists and Classroom Teachers
     by Paul J. Bohannan 107
  C. Introducing Anthropological Concepts in the
     Primary Grades
     by Frances Emmons and Jacqueline Cobia . . . 118
  D. Building Anthropological Content into Elementary
     School Social Studies
     by Jack R. Fraenkel. 125
  E. Materials for Teaching Anthropology in the
     Elementary School
     by Marion J. Rice 132

VII. Sociology
  A. Ethnic Pride Begins at Home
     by Marjorie G. Unger 141

VIII. Skill Development
  A. The Role of Skills in Elementary Social Studies
     by Helen McCracken Carpenter 149
  B. Skills Teaching in the Primary Grades
     by John Jarolimek 156
  C. Using Learning Resources in Social Studies Skill
     Development
     by Clarence O. Bergeson 162
  D. Skills in the Elementary School Social Studies
     Curriculum
     by Clifford D. Foster 169

IX. Values and Attitudes
     A. Can We Teach Values
         by Robert Botkin 177
     B. Values Held by Teachers
         by James T. Hamilton 189
     C. Little Lessons in Spiritual Values
         by Augusta Graham 195

X.   Curriculum
     A. Social Studies Interests of the Primary-Grade Child
         by J.D. McAulay 203
     B. Encouraging Creative Pupil Behavior in
         Elementary Social Studies
         by Mary Lee Marksberry 208
     C. Why Inquiry Fails in the Classroom
         by Martin Laforse 215
     D. Projective Education for the Child's Need to Know
         by Barbara Ellis Long and David Wolsk 220
     E. Selecting Social Studies Testbooks: The Challenge
         of Choice
         by Ralph Adams Brown and Marian Brown . . . 231
     F. Toward Relevancy, Curriculum, and the
         Social Order
         by R. Neil Reynolds 246

XI. Media
     A. Understanding Technology and Media: A
         Curriculum Inperative
         by O.L. Davis, Jr. 251

I. Introduction

This book of Readings is designed to provide some of the most current writings in the Social Studies area of the elementary school curriculum. It is also designed to provide information on selected curriculum studies being conducted throughout the nation. Currently teachers of Social Studies in the elementary schools have advanced beyond the mere socializing process and are slowly recognizing the fact that a combination of disciplines is required to provide children with a program of study attuned to our most important commodity—man.

In an attempt to provide a framework for this belief we have designed the reader in a manner which includes the following disciplines: History, Geography, Economics, Political Science, Anthropology, and Sociology.

Skill development, values, and attitude development are primary concerns of the compilers, therefore, relevant writings pertinent to the areas are included in this work.

The classroom teacher, the college student, and professor can use these writings as a resource volume, a study guide, or a basic text. The availability of pertinent articles, as gathered, provides a base or framework from which many creative teaching techniques may be developed.

1. Introduction

II. History

HISTORY FOR THE ELEMENTARY
SCHOOL CHILD

by

Vincent R. Rogers

During this year's summer and fall quarters at the University of Minnesota's demonstration centers one might have observed the following "lessons" being carried out with various groups of elementary school children:

A group of seven-year-olds has just heard Virginia Lee Burton's engaging story, *The Little House*, as a part of their study of the community. The story has to do with a house in the country that is eventually engulfed by the growing city. Roads are built, trains roar by, and skyscrapers appear. Eventually the little house is moved back to the country again, and so ends the story. Following the reading of the story the children list all of the changes they can think of that have happened to them during the last year. They follow this by listing changes on their streets, in their houses, and "down town." When the list is completed the teacher suddenly erases it and asks this question: "Suppose none of these changes had ever taken place—would you like it or not? Would things be better or worse?" There is considerable disagreement, since some of the items on the list are (in the children's eyes) "good," some "bad." This discussion of change continues off and on during the next week, resulting in a collection of pictures on a bulletin board illustrating "good" and "bad" changes in the community, such as the construction of a new theater, the opening of a new busline, and the burning of a nearby school (this last was classified as "bad," incidentally).

A group of eight-year-olds is studying the First Thanksgiving and the coming of the Pilgrims and others to America. The hardships of the first winter here are discussed briefly. The children are then asked to imagine that they are going to make a similar voyage today to an unknown, unsettled wilderness. They would not get any help from anyone "back home" for a year. "What food and clothing would we need in order to live through a year? What should we take along?" A long list is made on the board, including many items that only one living in the 20th century might consider essential. The children are then shown a list of essentials that were actually taken by a group of settlers. The lists are compared and the teacher draws a line through the items on the children's list that do *not* appear on the settlers' list. A number of the children express the view that it would have been very hard to go with just those things; many say they wouldn't have gone had it been up to them. The teacher then suggests that

From *Phi Delta Kappan*, December 1962. Used by permission of the author and the publisher.

Mr. Rogers (Alpha Phi 726) is associate professor of social studies education at the University of Minnesota.

they imagine for a moment that they are living in London at the time the Pilgrims came to America. However, in this case they have no intention of moving—they like things in London. The children are asked to look again at *their* list. What items would not be available in London? They find that most of the items that had been crossed off their lists originally would have to be crossed off again. Life was hard (by 20th century standards), they conclude, both for those who went *and* for those who stayed. It is hard to tell what you would or wouldn't do unless you lived as the people did then.

During a study of the westward movement, a group of ten-year-olds is told to imagine that they are living on a rocky, rather unproductive New England farm during the year 1867. One evening an older brother bursts into the kitchen with a poster clutched in his hand. It says, in effect, that the Union Pacific railroad is offering new lands for sale in Kansas. The land is said to be cheap, abundant, and fertile. Schools and churches have been built and there will be no taxes for six years! The family is gathered around the fire. The poster is read.

Now the class is asked, "What do you suppose the family will do?" The quick and almost universal reaction is, "They'd move west to Kansas!" The teacher then suggests they try acting out the story, with different people in the class playing the roles of various members of the family. Each volunteer is given a 3 x 5 card telling something about his "character." For example, father knew the farm was failing and felt he had little choice. Grandfather had brought his family here from Scotland fifty years ago. His wife was buried here. He had had enough of travel; this was home to him. The oldest son loved adventure and wanted desperately to go, while the sixteen-year-old daughter was in love with the boy on the next farm. When the play is finally dramatized, the decision turns out to be far more difficult than the children had first imagined. In the final analysis the class is evenly divided on the issue of whether the family should go or stay.

Each of the experiences described above is designed to help children understand some element or strand in the "structure" of history. While the descriptions are brief and (of necessity) incomplete, they represent halting first steps in a long overdue attempt to strengthen and improve, to both "beef up" and yet make more meaningful, children's early encounters with history.

Those of us who read the journals of our profession regularly know that we have more than our share of educational diagnosticians, but that we seem to suffer from a serious shortage of therapists. Criticism voiced during the last decade alone would (and does) fill volumes, and programs in elementary school social studies have gotten their share and more. A good deal of this criticism has to do with an almost universally misunderstood and often mishandled area: the teaching of history to elementary school children. Critics have complained that history is generally approached at this level as a precise body of knowledge, proven beyond doubt and ready to be "mastered" by students; the textbook is still the basic teaching tool, and particularly at this level they (the texts) tend to be exceedingly unrealistic, overly idealistic, and often lack the stimulating detail so necessary to give meaning to the broad generalizations they so freely employ. One might add that children in current programs are seldom asked to use thinking processes characterized by Torrance and others as "divergent" (i.e., independent or original work that gives students an opportunity to discover ideas for themselves), or "evaluative" (i.e., work involving critical thinking, judging, selecting and organizing). Unquestionably, the reader may wish to add or perhaps subtract from this list. We are attempting, however, to proceed beyond diagnosis and enter the realm of therapy.

Bruner Not Much Help in Social Studies

A few short years ago Jerome Bruner tantalized many of us with the publication of his *The Process of Education.* On first reading it I felt that surely the solution to the problems associated with the teaching of history in the elementary school lay within its pages. A second, third, and even fourth reading left me with basically the same feeling, i.e., the answer was here somewhere; but somehow it was elusive, seeming to lie always on the page to come. A partial explanation has to do with Bruner's selection of examples and illustrations. Most of them, you will recall, were drawn from mathematics and physics. The humanities and the social sciences, if not ignored, were certainly treated sparingly. This should not be taken as a criticism of Bruner, who after all was not attempting to offer a detailed program of curricular improvement but rather to indicate a new direction. Nevertheless, the fact remains that the way seemed considerably clearer in mathematics than it did in history.

Bruner does, however, make at least two points that are vitally important to those seeking to improve the teaching of history in the elementary school. First, of course, is his concept of the structure of a discipline, i.e., the importance of a child's understanding of the underlying principles of a given field of knowledge. Second is the importance he attaches to presenting basic ideas to young children *in a form they can understand.* He is not willing (as are so many current critics of education in general and of the social studies in particular) to ignore the body of knowledge that exists concerning the nature of the child, his interests, abilities, and learning processes. He is obviously concerned with both the curriculum *and* the child. Bruner, however (and here he parts company with many educationists), feels that we have only begun to discover effective ways to help children learn.

He is well aware of the work of men like David Page at Illinois, Suppes at Stanford, and Karplus at California, in which elements of the structure of mathematics and physics have been successfully taught to elementary school children. He is also aware of emerging and related research in the social sciences, such as David Easton's work at the University of Chicago dealing with the political socialization of young children. Among other things, Easton's research seems to indicate that children often develop political attitudes and an awareness of political differences by the age of eight or nine. Easton also exposes the unhappy results of unreal, idealized programs in elementary school social studies.

If one accepts Bruner's assumptions that an understanding of the structure of history is of vital importance and that structure can be taught to young children, where, then, do we go from here? The first step, of course, is to decide what basic principles comprise history's structure. Apparently the physicists, the biologists, the chemists, and the mathematicians have been able to do this promptly and rather effectively in their areas. We are still waiting, however, for a similar treatment of history. This is, of course, understandable. Man's behavior is a complex thing and exceedingly difficult to classify. Nevertheless, the first steps must be taken, and I offer the following analysis as a possible beginning.

As I read the literature dealing with the nature of history, I find considerable agreement on at least one aspect of its structure. The methodology of history—how the historian works—is generally agreed to be an essential element of the discipline. Some would go so far as to say that the historian's method *is* the structure of his discipline, that once one has mastered the methodology of history one has gained an understanding of history's underlying principles. It seems to me, however, that ideas related to the structure of history tend to cluster around *three* major hubs: first, ideas related to the methodology of history; second, ideas related to the nature and goals of history; and third, ideas related to the content, the people, and events themselves that comprise history. The "sample" ideas stated under each heading below seem to me to represent important principles that form the foundation for a mature understanding of history. I am suggesting that much of this can be taught to and understood by young children. I suggest further that the content chosen to aid in the development of these ideas (a unit on the community, the westward movement, or colonial life, for example) is of secondary importance to the principles themselves.

Ideas Related to Nature, Goals of History

History attempts to delineate, assess, interpret, and give a relative place to the efforts of people, important ideas, and great national achievements.

History is *not* a body of precise, memorizable facts; history is, in a sense, constant controversy. Historians do not always agree.

Historical interpretations change as man examines events at different times and in different places.

History provides us with a series of case histories that may help us deal with contemporary affairs; history does not, however, offer us revealed unchanging laws or patterns of events.

All historical events were, at one time, "open questions," just as today's decisions (which will become tomorrow's history) are similarly open. We may only evaluate the choices made in the past and attempt to find meaningful alternatives or possibilities for today's decisions.

Ideas Related to Content of History[1]

Change has been a universal condition of human society. Change and progress, however, are not necessarily synonymous.

Races, cultures, and civilizations in various historical periods have made contributions to the growth of our present civilizations.

Mankind has been motivated by morals and ideals *and* by material wants and needs.

While physical environments in many places and regions have been altered, human motives or drives have remained nearly the same.

Peaceful cooperation is one of man's worthiest, earliest, and most persistent historical experiences. Conflict and hostility, however, are also within man's experience.

In the contemporary world, historical events affect people and places far beyond the limits of the place of their origin.

Men in every age and place have made use of basic social functions such as educating, transporting, communicating, etc., in adjusting themselves to their world.

Ideas Related to Method of History

The historian works basically with primary sources such as letters, diaries, traveler's logs, newspapers, and magazines. These are the "stuff" of history.

The historian draws conclusions, formulates principles, and makes generalizations on the basis of his study and interpretation of primary sources.

In evaluating sources, the historian is concerned with the authenticity of his material; he recognizes, for example, that the time that elapses between the occurrence of an event and the reporting of an event often affect the accuracy with which the event is reported; he is concerned with the author of the report, his interests, and qualifications, and biases.

---

1. The statements in this section were largely adapted from the *Report of the State Central Committee on the Social Studies* published by the California State Department of Education, Sacramento 14, California.

The historian recognizes that one's feelings and emotions, his drives and motives, may often affect how one interprets a given event.

The historian looks at historical events with an appropriate perspective. For example, one must gauge the real heartbreak and suffering involved in the Pilgrims' coming to America or the pioneers moving west in relation to the hardships of life in general at this time.

The historian is aware that advances in historical scholarship, discoveries of new sources of information, may necessitate a reevaluation of his conclusions and generalizations.

The ideas presented above are undoubtedly incomplete; statements of considerable importance may have been left out while minor points were included. This is, however, a beginning statement or working paper that has proven most useful to us in the development of new materials and techniques in the teaching of history to elementary school children. Each of the experiences described at the beginning of this paper is directly related to one or more of the basic historical principles described above. As new materials and techniques are experimented with, we are of course trying to discover whether children do begin to understand the method of history; whether they are able to apply generalizations to other problems and other content. We are analyzing children's written materials and their discussions, looking for evidence of deductive and evaluative thinking. We are also curious about the types of children who are able to work successfully with these materials. How important is IQ, for example? We wonder, too, whether so-called "average" teachers (with appropriate manuals and guides) will be able to work effectively with these materials. At the moment, precise answers to these questions are not yet available. We are, however, both encouraged with and enthusiastic about current progress and future possibilities.

HISTORY IN THE SOCIAL STUDIES

by

William H. Cartwright

My topic is the place of history in the social studies. To state my conclusion in advance, I believe that history should be the core and the unifying agent of the social studies. This is not to say that the kind of history that we have generally taught should be the core and the unifying agent of the social studies. Nor is it to say that other social studies should not have an important place in the curriculum. But this last matter is beyond the scope of this paper.

I am glad that scholars in the social sciences, as well as those in other fields, including psychology and physics, are showing great concern for the social studies curriculum. It is also gratifying that school administrators and curriculum generalists are giving our field more attention than they formerly did. It should be a cause for rejoicing that, at long last, considerable quantities of money are being allotted to the development of the social studies and that many large and potentially significant curriculum projects are under way, bringing together academic scholars, specialists in the social studies, and specialists in learning from universities in cooperative endeavor with school administrators, curriculum leaders, and social studies teachers in school systems. These developments are long overdue.

Nevertheless, I am troubled by much of what is being advocated in the social studies. Some wise man said recently that he measured his age by the degree of pain he felt upon encountering a new idea. And it may be merely that I am growing old. Yet, as I listen and read, I get the feeling that much of what is being advocated is not new—that earlier curriculum makers have been over this ground before, but that we are unaware of their endeavors and debates because we do not make effective use of history. Now I am not unwilling to retrace old paths; because of my historical training, I like to do just that. But I want to be aware that this is what I am doing; and I want to utilize the activities and knowledge of those who have been here before.

Several individuals and groups advocate the fusion of the social

From *Social Education*, March 1967. Reprinted with permission of the National Council for the Social Studies and William H. Cartwright.

William H. Cartwright, Professor of Education at Duke University, presented this address at the Annual Meeting of the National Council for the Social Studies held in Cleveland, last November.

studies into a single subject; some even call the field of the social studies a discipline. This idea is not new. We were over this ground in the 1920's and 1930's, not to mention Comenius. And no more cogent arguments are presented by the fusionists of the present day than those that were set forth by Rugg, Marshall, and Goetz. Now, as then, some would organize the social studies around social processes, some would organize them around social problems, some around expanding horizons, and some around narrowing ones. Now, as then, the lists differ. Now, as then, parts of the resultant curriculum proposals are fuzzy, and others are segments of traditional subjects. I see the same values in these approaches now that I did then. They are useful in the lower grades before children have the knowledge needed to appreciate the values of a subject approach. They provide valuable criteria for evaluating a secondary school curriculum, but they do not provide an adequate basis for organizing one.

Some individuals and groups, justifiably disturbed by the terrible problems of mankind, are urging that the social studies seek to attack these problems directly. This is not the first time that educationists have suggested that the schools should "reconstruct the social order." The confusion between social action and social education that this movement represents is not new. I expect that it will fail, as it has failed before. If it waxes to a point at which it threatens to take over the social studies, it will again bring down the wrath of the people and so, once again, facilitate a reaction that will destroy much that is good. School children cannot be expected to solve the great problems of the day, and they should not be led to expect that children can do so. Teachers and their professional leaders should not confuse their function of social actions as citizens with their function of social education in the schools. The function of the social studies is not to reconstruct society in the image of somebody's Utopia, but to help develop a self-generating, life-long process of social education that may give men and women such knowledge, skill, and motivation as will enable them to cope ever more successfully with their problems. History has much to contribute to that development. As my colleague, R. Baird Shuman, has remarked, the Red Guards of mainland China are a stellar example of what can happen when young people have a total commitment and a sense of destiny but no sense of history or time.

We hear often that a revolution is taking place in the social studies. I hope that there is no revolution. Surely, changes are needed, but revolutions are usually costly and wasteful. And the situations that follow immediately upon them are generally worse than those out of which they rose. Probably revolutions are necessary sometimes, but not in societies that are so organized as to encourage peaceful evolution. One of the reasons for the rise to pre-eminence and the longevity of the United States has been its ability to evolve through compromise and thus to avoid revolution. Only once in the history of our government, and it is one of the oldest now existing, has the ability to compromise really broken down, and the revolution attempted then was not successful. This process of evolution through compromise has extended into many areas of American life, including education. It is true that evolution needs to be hastened sometimes and that it may be hastened by rebellion. I think that what we have now in the social studies is not a revolution, but a considerable number of rebellions. I expect that some of them will be costly, but I trust that the ultimate outcome will be the hastening of the evolutionary process.

However, let no one think that there has been no evolution in the social studies. Those who proclaim this to be a fact either do not know what has taken place in the past few generations or choose to ignore it as damaging to their causes. Let me call attention to some of its salient features. In the first century of our national history, what we call the social studies had no firm base, not even a potential base, in either scholarship or pedagogy. During the last quarter of the nineteenth century both these bases were laid. This development was so rapid as to almost justify, in a sense, the term revolution. But because the obstacles were ignorance and lethargy rather than organized opposition, I do not consider the term wholly applicable.

Since 1900, the changes have been substantial. The social studies of 1900 consisted almost wholly of geography and history in the elementary grades and of history in the high school. The geography was mainly physical and gazeteer; the history was principally military and political chronology, and little of it dealt with either modern times or America. The textbook was almost the only tool of instruction and was designed with the expectation that such would be the case.

The situation is vastly different today. The elementary curriculum draws heavily on disciplines other than geography and history. The contemporary social sciences have made their way into the high school, whether as separate subjects or through civics and problems courses, to such an extent that half of the secondary school social studies program is something other than history, although enrollment figures show that we have been slow in requiring the study of nonhistorical subjects. For this reason, among others, the evolution that has taken place in the nature of geography and history may be more important than the introduction of the other subjects, and the future evolution of geography and history may be more important than the much talked of revolution. Both geography and history have changed greatly; both are changing rapidly; and the change must be hastened. It is history that is my concern here.

The much maligned history textbook has improved greatly over the past two generations. It is almost always a product of historical scholarship, pedagogical expertness, and editorial skill. The proportion of its social and economic content has grown almost steadily to a point at which that content now far exceeds the strictly political and military content in the elementary school and the junior high school and at least equals it in the senior high school. Its authors and editors have woven many elements into a pattern that scarcely resembles the stereotype of school history. They have suggested further teaching and learning procedures and materials that, if used, would both adorn the fabric and bring the pattern into bolder relief. School libraries, elementary and secondary, have grown phenomenally in both number and content. Classroom maps and the whole mass of "new media" of instruction are a development of the twentieth century. Beyond these considerations, the provision of substantial funds for the purchase of instructional materials has removed the last defense for employing only the so-called "textbook method" of teaching history.

And what of the history teachers? In 1900, only a tiny fraction of them were college graduates. Most of them were not graduates of normal schools. A large proportion had not graduated from high school. Most of them had never had a history course more advanced than those they were teaching and had had no formal work in the teaching of history. Today, almost all history teachers are college graduates, and a large proportion of them hold graduate degrees. They have studied history under history scholars. And both the depth of their historical studies and the breadth of their studies in other social sciences have increased decade by decade.

In all these matters, further and more rapid development is needed. But who, having considered the history of history teaching, can seriously contend that the social studies in general, or history in particular, are still in the nineteenth century?

I have not said all this because I think that school history is doing what I think that it should do. I have said it so as to put our present situation in historical perspective and to demonstrate the necessity for such a perspective. Indeed, I know that in many school class-

rooms history has not caught up with the advances of either historical scholarship or pedagogy. The social lag that takes place in education can also be documented historically. If we do not greatly reduce
the time of this lag in history instruction, I fear that history will, and
probably should, lose its leading place in the social studies.

In considering school history, I must also start with doubts about
some of the so-called "new ideas." Two of those that I see set forth
often are that we must teach "the structure of the discipline" and
that we must adopt the "inquiry approach." I must confess that I am
not quite sure what these terms mean, especially when they are
applied to the school curriculum. This uncertainty does not grow out
of lack of attention to them. I have read many of the recent books
and articles that deal with them, and I have struggled with something
like them for a third of a century. As I understand their present
advocates, I think that I have been over the ground before. This past
summer, a dozen social studies teachers and I struggled with them in
a seminar for six weeks. We had an enjoyable, and I think, profitable
experience, but, as I predicted at the outset, we emerged still confused but with the hope that our confusion was at a higher level than
it had been.

What is the structure of history? There must be many. From a
common-sense point of view, chronology is one, and a useful one. It
should even be taught, but this is no new idea. Another possible
structure of history consists of its major divisions, but I do not now
want to get involved in an attempt to make a list of such divisions to
which all distinguished historians would agree. I gather that those
who advocate that the structure of a discipline must be taught seem
to feel that it may consist of a list of generalizations or concepts or
ideas—I keep wanting to say speculations—that all historians would
accept. It is fun to toy with this idea, but I find it useless and
probably dangerous as a basis for organizing a curriculum that we
must all accept.

The institutional historians of the nineteenth century went over
this ground in their search for the laws of history, but few of their
descendants contend that those laws are likely to be found in this
generation. Considering our present state of knowledge and our pluralistic society, I am thankful for this development in historiography.
And I am skeptical of attempts to get the great scholars to agree on a
list of generalizations that all students ought to learn. If the historians come back to this approach, I shall be greatly interested in what
they do with it. In the meantime, I hope that we avoid the indoctri-
nation that would have to follow its adoption in the schools. For

further elucidation of these ideas, I commend to all David Potter's brilliant last paragraph in his essay on the background of the Civil War in the thirty-first Yearbook of the National Council for the Social Studies.[1]

Still another approach to identifying the structure of a discipline seems to be through its tools of inquiry. (Although some writers use this phrase so as to seem to connote values unrelated to structure.) Here, I am sure that I have been over the ground many times. The principal tools of inquiry in history are documents, and the principal methods of history have to do with the use of documents. But such a statement is woefully inadequate. As a matter of fact, the means of inquiry in any discipline have to do with words, numbers, relics, models, ideas, concepts, hypotheses, criticism—you extend the list. Some disciplines make more use of some tools than other disciplines do, but no tool of inquiry is the exclusive possession of any discipline. And, so far as school history is concerned, the adoption of documents as the sole, or even the principal approach is doomed to failure. This is not new ground.

One of the panaceas for history instruction in the 1890's was the "source method." It had strong advocates then who published articles and books, gave speeches, and developed programs of instruction. It was condemned out of hand by the Committee of Seven of the American Historical Association and has only recently reentered the professional literature under another name. No historical scholar, working as a scholar, comes to conclusions on even a narrow historical problem without trying to exploit all the documentary evidence that bears on that problem. And, for purposes of pedagogy as distinguished from research, the documents are no more important than the reflections of the scholars who have been through them—if indeed they are as important.

Of course, the documents are important. For example, every high school student of American history should consider the Constitution itself. But his consideration of it will mean little unless he also considers the reflections and decisions of those who have considered a myriad of documents that bear on it which are not available to the student and from the direct study of which he has neither the time nor the knowledge to profit. And it would be a terrible mistake for

1. David M. Potter. "The Background of the Civil War." In William H. Cartwright and Richard L. Watson, Jr., editors, *Interpreting and Teaching American History*. Thirty-First Yearbook. Washington, D.C.: National Council for the Social Studies, 1961. p. 87-119.

him to decide, on the basis of his superficial study, that he is a constitutional historian or a constitutional lawyer.

When I was a school teacher, my students used documents to advantage. For some simple questions they found answers in this manner. Upon examination of the Charter of 1606, they not only found that the textbook maps showing the boundaries of the grants to the London and Plymouth Companies were in error, but also that such boundaries could not be drawn. They wrote to one author pointing out the discrepancy between a textbook statement and a provision of the Preemption Act of 1841. These activities were useful, and they were fun. But the only time that my students ever had a right to feel that they were real historians was when they tried to run down the date of the fire that destroyed the heart of their village in the early 1880's. Here they were able to consider all the evidence that could be found, including newspapers, diaries, immigration papers, a wedding license, and the memories of living men and women. They had a difficult, time-consuming, but exhilarating experience. They did not establish the date, but they did gain first-hand appreciation of historical scholarship. I thought that the effort was worthwhile, but I would hate to justify building a curriculum around such insignificant events. Yet only in such cases can school pupils play the role of historians.

The purpose of the social studies is neither to solve social problems directly nor to train historians or other social scientists. It is, as Charles A. Beard said a generation ago, to develop rich and many-sided personalities and competent citizens. It is to get children and youth to understand, as best they can, themselves and their society and to help them develop the knowledge, skill, and motivation necessary to improve themselves and society. All fields of knowledge can be of assistance toward those ends, but history is the most promising medium for bringing them together.

History should be the core subject and the unifying agent in the social studies because it is the most inclusive of the social studies. Every social study makes use of all the others and of subjects in other fields, but history, properly conceived, takes a broader approach to man and society than does any other social study. There are no fixed boundary lines around any subject in our field; nevertheless, a definition of a subject is an attempt to place boundaries around it. To claim anthropology, economics, geography, government, psychology, or even sociology as all-inclusive would be to give up the claim for the subject's unique contribution. That unique contribution is the basis for placing, not a boundary line, but a shadowy boundary zone around a discipline. The one distinctive feature of history is that it treats of the past. It is otherwise all-inclusive.

And there are lessons to be learned from history. From a secular point of view—ignoring intuition, revelation, and prophecy—the most obvious distinction between mankind and other species is that mankind alone seems to have a history and to profit from it. All animals react with their environments and with other animals, and all have ways of making a living. Many species have relatively efficient forms of government and seem to have other social institutions. But, alone among the species, each generation of man seems able to build on the gains that previous generations have made. Except for history, every human being would have to start where his remote ancestors started. For all of the gloomy pessimists who assert that we do not learn from history, differences between our lives and those of our forebears are obvious, and could not have come about without the study and use of history.

We have not learned as much from history as we wish that we had learned. But to understand even that generalization, the study of history is required. The editors of the thirty-first Yearbook of the National Council for the Social Studies made this point by quoting from one of the most distinguished jurists of our time, Learned Hand, who said that history is especially well "fitted to admonish us how tentative and provisional are our attainments, intellectual and moral; and how often the deepest convictions of one generation are the rejects of the next." Judge Hand went on to say that this uncertainty "does not deny the possibility that, as time goes on, we shall accumulate some body of valued conclusions; but it does mean that these we can achieve only by accumulation; that wisdom is to be gained only as we stand upon the shoulders of those who have gone before."[2]

Historical scholars have not always conceived of history as all-inclusive. But there has been rapid evolution in their thinking on this matter. The institutional historians of the late nineteenth and early twentieth centuries did not all welcome the "new history." But the transition from history as past politics to history as everything that man has ever thought or felt or hoped or done has almost been achieved. The evolution can be traced from the work of Frederick Jackson Turner and James Harvey Robinson through that of a later generation, including Arthur M. Schlesinger, Charles A. Beard, Dixon

2. *Ibid.*, p. 4.

Ryan Fox, and August C. Krey to that of David Donald, Stanley Elkins, David Potter, Joseph Strayer, and a whole host of younger scholars.

Evidence that shows the great progress in this evolution is easy to find. Here are a few suggestions (I shall not take time to quote from them; they are easily available to teachers of the social studies): The 1954 report of the Committee on Historiography to the Social Science Research Council, included in Edwin Fenton's *Teaching the New Social Studies in Secondary Schools;* Joseph Strayer's chapter in *The Social Studies and the Social Sciences,* sponsored by the National Council for the Social Studies and the American Council of Learned Societies and published in 1962; Robert Heywood's article in the May 1964 issue of *Social Education;* Henry Steele Commager's article in the June 1965 issue of *American Education;* and Mark Krug's articles in the December 1965 and the October 1966 issues of *Social Education.*

The evolution of the new history is accelerating. When David Potter wrote *People of Plenty* in the early 1950's, he castigated his fellow historians for ignoring the lessons of the other disciplines. He appeared more optimistic about his colleagues last February, when he told the symposium conducted by the Center for Southern Studies in the Social Sciences and Humanities at Duke University:

> We have come into an era when, in the profession generally, historians are increasingly dissatisfied with the adequacy of their traditional methods, and are concerned to bring the knowledge, now at the command of other disciplines, to bear upon history. What do the sociologists know about the social structure of classes which historians might use in the study of specific conflicts between groups? What do economists know about the factors conducive to rapid development or to stagnation which historians need to know in order to understand the prolongation of poverty in one country and the sudden recovery in another? What do psychologists know about human motivation which will enable historians to understand what impels human action? For generations we have assumed that human motives were rational—the selfishly rational motives of self-interest or the altruistically rational motives of ideals. We keep talking as if this assumption were true, and yet we know that a great deal of human motivation is not rational, either selfishly or altruistically. We know, too, that an object of hate is sometimes hated not because of its own qualities, but because the forces of frustration-aggression can so readily shift their focus from a dynamic source of frustration which may not safely be attacked, to an object of aggression, which may be attacked, with impunity.
>
> Historians are aware of all these points and of others like them. They are aware too of the need for appropriate historical contexts within which to explore the relationship between traditional history as we have known it and these newer components.

To recognize that history must draw on other fields of knowledge to fulfill its own function is not to conclude that those fields of knowledge can be substituted for history or that they can be merged into history or history into them so that one or another field loses its identity. Indeed, as the traditional disciplines fragment and specialization grows, the unifying service of history is needed all the more. Professor Potter emphasized this need in a specific context of American history when he said:

> To deal with the history of Negro-white relations—the changes and the slowness of change—he [the historian] must know what a psychologist can tell him about the sources of prejudice but he must also remain aware that he knows certain things which the psychologist does not know.

The developments required to bring about the needed evolution in school history are under way. They must be nurtured and accelerated. One is a change in the nature of the history that teachers study in college and graduate school. As historians broaden their concept of history and research procedures, their own teaching changes. And the old adage holds: Teachers tend to teach as they have been taught. As the "new history" grows, as more and more professors of history hold broad views of their discipline and themselves exploit many tools in their own research and teaching, a larger proportion of beginning teachers of history have better models.

There is another kind of change taking place in the nature of the history that prospective teachers study. This is the increasing consideration of the history of other parts of the world than Western Europe and the United States. The growth of offerings in the history of the Soviet Union, Latin America, Asia, and Africa is desirable in its own right, for we can no longer afford only a provincial view of world history. But this growth is valuable for another reason; namely, that it is difficult to consider the history of the peoples of those areas without giving serious attention to concepts and procedures belonging to the contemporary social sciences, the behavioral sciences, philosophy, and religion.

The 1962 statement on the *Preparation of Secondary School History Teachers* of the Committee on Teaching of the American Historical Association laid stress on both these matters. It said that college history should deal with the problems of mankind and should teach "desirable ways of thinking and skills in reading and study . . . since teachers teach as they were taught." And the Committee recommended that the history of Russia and of the Far East should be required in the preparation of teachers.

Aside from the multifold change in the nature of history that teachers study, another development to be encouraged is the increased study by teachers of disciplines related to history. It is not enough for them to have considerable exposure to the "new history." Historians may be expected to use in their own endeavors the relevant concepts and tools of those disciplines. But historians cannot be expected to teach those concepts and tools directly for their use in work other than the study of history; yet such use becomes ever more necessary.

The study of social sciences other than history has had strong support. More than a decade ago it was recommended by the Committee on Teacher Education and Certification of the National Council for the Social Studies. The 1962 statement of the Committee on Teaching of the American Historical Association said, "Partly because the history teacher may be required to teach social studies other than history, but more because his teaching of history will gain perspective and support from social sciences other than history, such courses should be included in his studies." The Committee did not venture to prescribe the particular subjects, but it did recommend 18 semester hours or their equivalent drawn from cultural anthropology, economics, geography, government, and sociology. It should be noted that the Committee also recommended the study of psychology over and above the history and social science requirements.

James B. Conant, in 1963 and 1964, recommended that the prospective social studies teacher, in addition to 42 semester hours of history, should be required to study philosophy, sociology, anthropology, political science, economics, psychology, and geography, as well as educational psychology and the philosophy, history, or sociology of education. The requirements of the states for certification of social studies teachers and of teacher education institutions for their recommendations to teach social studies increasingly reflect these kinds of recommendations.

It is reasonable to expect that, with the continued growth of developments now under way, a time will come when beginning teachers of the social studies will be able to make history a truly unifying agent for the social studies. But that time will be a "long time coming" unless we can hasten it by doing something material for teachers now in service. That "something material" is a different kind of "in-service" education from the one we knew in the 1940's and the 1950's, but here, too, significant developments are under way. Although some of the evils of the past are still with us, less and less frequently do or can social studies teachers take courses unrelated to their teaching as a means of getting their salaries increased.

More and more, state and local school regulations require that in-service courses be related to the teacher's work. More and more, professors of history and the social sciences are involved in both in-service education and in curriculum revision. (And I might note that these two activities must be related for either to be effective.)

For a good many years, social scientists have been contributing significant writings for teachers. Publications of the National Council for the Social Studies and of the Service Center for Teachers of the American Historical Association are notable examples, but similar writings have come under various auspices in all the disciplines. Both privately and through Project Social Studies, scholars in all the social sciences, specialists in the social studies, and teachers are working together toward the improvement of social studies instruction.

The institutes in history, geography, economics, and civics that have suddenly become available under the recent federal legislation will increasingly bring thousands of teachers of the social studies annually into intimate contact with newer ideas and techniques.

The stimulus that will be provided by the growing number of state and local supervisors of social studies and by the ever-increasing materials of instruction should do much to bring about improvement.

I do not expect that the developments to which I have just referred will bring about the kind of history instruction that I described earlier as rapidly as I wish. There will be many obstacles to improvement. Many of those now teaching will not carry on the kind of in-service studies that I think they should; many of them will not want to. Perhaps this fact is the biggest obstacle. If all of us in the profession really had been captured by the idea that education is a life-long process, we would read and think more widely and deeply than most of us do, and our teaching would reflect our self-imposed study. Unfortunately, many beginning teachers will continue to be misassigned to courses that they are not qualified to teach.

The major burden of making history the kind of subject that is needed in order for it to fulfill its function as the core and unifying agent for the social studies rests on those who teach history in the schools. They are the ultimate makers of the curriculum, and ultimately the responsibility for accelerating the evolution of the new history in the schools is theirs.

Let me close by repeating part of what I said some seven years ago at the Natural Bridge Conference on the Social Studies conducted by the Virginia Education Association:

> School history should not be a meaningless assemblage of the names of persons, states, and civilizations; dates and events; routes of travel and

military campaigns. These items are necessary for instruction in history, but the real content of history has to do with *people* who "lived and felt and had their being." It must treat of how they met and solved, or failed to solve, their many problems. How did they overcome, adjust to, or become overwhelmed by the physical characteristics of the regions in which they lived? How did they force nature to yield its riches, exploit those riches while yet conserving them, or lose the material basis of their society through failure to conserve? How, in modern times, has the dizzying pace of the acceleration of material progress become one of mankind's greatest problems, and what sub-problems does that acceleration pose? What ways have men tried for organizing their economic activity, and how well have they succeeded? Under what conditions has human liberty thriven or succumbed? How have men learned to work together peaceably to their mutual advantage? What causes have led them to conflict, and what means have they employed to eliminate conflict or the causes? How have civilizations developed? What institutions have civilizations found necessary to their existence and strengthening? What form have these institutions taken, and what successes or failures have they had? What personal and societal values have people developed as guides to their activities? What means have people taken to bring up their young so as to improve and enlarge their heritage? Such questions as these and the search for their answers are the stuff of school history. And in the course of their consideration our students should learn, to some degree at least, how the historian works to find out the answers.

NUMISMATICS IN THE CLASSROOM

by

Paul W. Kane

Robert W. Marvin

Why not make your history classes more interesting by giving your students the opportunity to touch something tangible from the past? How can this be done? One way is to bring coins and tokens that were used in years gone by into the classroom. Let the pupils handle and study these items and watch their interest increase; and, by all means, encourage students to bring in coin collections of their own. (For information as to where teachers may obtain coins, tokens, and slides of coinage, contact The American Numismatic Society, Broadway between 155th and 156th Street, New York, New York 10032.)

As an example, let us see how numismatics (the study or collection of coins, tokens, paper currency, and similar objects) can make a United States history class come alive.

During the study of the Colonial period, a teacher can bring in an "eight real" which was also known as a "piece of eight." These coins were minted in Mexico to be used by the Spanish in the western hemisphere. Any story about pirates makes reference to the "piece of eight." The fact that such Spanish coins existed in the English colonies can be used by the instructor to show how the mercantile system drained currency from the colonies and created the demand for Spanish coins.

The Jacksonian period witnessed the emergence of "hard time" tokens. These tokens were politically-oriented and were used as merchant advertisements. The importance of the Bank and the states' rights problems of the period become more meaningful to today's students when they examine the tokens and read such slogans as: "Bank Must Perish," and "The Union Must and Shall Be Preserved."

Tokens were also used during the Civil War period. Two types, patriotic tokens and store cards, flourished in the North. The patriotic tokens had likenesses of the *Monitor*, Lincoln, McClellan, and the American flag on one side, and slogans such as "Union Forever," and "Peace, Army and Navy" on the reverse. The store cards were used by local businessmen for advertising and change. As students

From *Social Education*, April 1971. Reprinted with permission of the National Council for the Social Studies and Paul W. Kane.

handle and examine these tokens, a direct bond with the past is established (some particular token might have been carried in battle by a Union soldier!). The monetary problems of the North become clearer to students when they realize that merchants had to issue their own tokens in order to have sufficient change with which to carry on business.

Other periods in the history of the United States witnessed the emergence of tokens minted to meet the needs of the era. In the early 1900's, tokens were frequently used in company towns and in the coal and silver mining areas of this country. Workers received them as wages, and the tokens were redeemable in company stores. Many denominations existed then which are no longer part of our currency system. The predominant ones were 1/2¢, 2 1/2¢, 6 1/4¢, and 12 1/2¢. The 6 1/4¢ and 12 1/2¢ date back to the "piece of eight." The 6 1/4¢ token was valued at one-half bit and the 12 1/2¢ token was valued at one-bit.

In the Depression years of the 1930's, many cities used what was known as depression script. This script was often used to stimulate trade. Sales tax tokens were also put into use during this period.

As is shown, the use of numismatic materials in the classroom can make an earlier historical period come alive, increase student interest, and help bridge the gap between past and present. Use coins and tokens in your classroom soon. You will be pleasantly surprised at the results.

III. Geography

THE PROBLEMS APPROACH
TO GEOGRAPHY

by

Marilee Jean Bradbury

"No girl is going to leave a comfortable home to go off into the hinterlands and marry some lumberjack she's never even met," said Judy.

"Some women would, particularly if they've given up hope of finding a husband at home," Donald argued.

"How about conducting courtships by mail?" Charlene asked.

"Not very practical when it took weeks for a letter to go from the coast to, say, Illinois," Judy replied.

"Just offer them money," said Frank. "Lots of women will do anything for money."

"But that's not the kind of wife you want when you're founding a city," said Charlene.

"Those men didn't know they were founding Seattle when they set up that lumber camp, and how—"

"Let's stop quibbling," said Donald. "We've got only 15 minutes more to figure out a practical plan for attracting women to a new and isolated settlement."

This student search for an answer to a problem which actually existed typifies some of the activities in classes participating in the High School Geography Project, an exciting program now being developed and tried out in 70 schools throughout the country. In 1961, the Project began the arduous task of reevaluating the objectives and content of present high school geography programs. The goal is to update and emphasize the important role geography should be playing in today's social studies curriculum.

The HSGP course centers around the *settlement theme*—where people decided to locate and why. The focus is on the interaction of man in his physical environment, the association of one settlement to another, and man's association with the world. The project has forged the tools for the course from multimedia materials and drawn up guidelines that take the student from his local environment into the world. With the materials, some guidelines, and plenty of time for creativity, the students become geographers.

From *NEA* Journal: April 1967. Used by permission of the *NEA* Journal and Marilee Jean Bradbury.

To determine the functions and patterns of settlements, students begin by studying their local area. They evaluate the interrelationships of sites; goods and services offered; interdependency; and accessibility of hamlets, villages, towns, and cities. Since my students live in a rural area in the foothills of the Rocky Mountains, they concentrate on analyzing the importance of tourism to many of Colorado's ghost towns. Students even predict which hamlets will fade into history and which will prosper by adding more antique shops, restoring gold mines, or building ski resorts.

Next, students expand their vista to the major cities of the United States. Within the *Network of Cities* unit they analyze the dominant role some cities play. They map and graph population densities, urban growth, highway links, and airline connections and then study them to determine the spacing and functions of urban settlements in a region, the accessibility of one city to another and of areas within a city, and the market area. As the program progresses, the settlement theme extends into the study of regions of the world.

The *Inside the City* unit offers an excellent example of the new and different materials available in the HSGP program. One of the activities centers upon the growth and development of a major American city called Portsville but actually based on Seattle. The materials consist of a 3' X 4' board map depicting an area of highlands, forest, and water. The map has slots on which small plastic blocks can be interlocked. The blocks are colored to represent land use—red for stores, blue for manufacturing, black for railroads, white for residential buildings, and gray for warehouses.

The class reads a brief narrative on the settlement of the region from 1851 to 1880, each student receives a designated number of blocks, and the fun begins. A small blue block represents the first permanent site, a lumbering camp. This symbol of a wilderness frontier settlement leads students into a frontier of their own where they face the challenge of developing the hamlet into a city.

In the process, one may see a ninth grader clutching a handful of blocks as he argues against the destruction of his multiunit homes to make way for a new railroad. Students grow heated in discussing the expansion of new fishing industries into residential areas along the scenic bay.

The continual growth of the city fosters new problems. As each 10-year period of development goes on the map, students discuss the growth, criticize others' opinions of land use, and prepare the way for the next 10-year period, for which they will receive additional blocks. In 1889, a fire swept through 120 acres of land, destroying the central business district. Realizing that such a catastrophe presented an opportunity to build an even better business district, the students attacked the problem with enthusiasm.

This nine-day exercise does not attempt to tell the students how citizens actually built Seattle; each student decides on land use and tries to justify his decisions to the class.

With the aid of teaching materials students can see change take place on a map during a class period. They can manipulate and direct the development and growth of a settlement. When the students eventually study a map showing the land use in Seattle today, they can compare the reality to their creation and evaluate both. Students who have wondered why it should be so hard to build a perfect city soon come to appreciate the problems of urban renewal, traffic, air and water pollution, and conflicts of land use.

The Project correlates geography with other parts of the curriculum, because geography—the study of man in a location, why he is there, and where he is going—cannot be separated from history, political science, sociology, and economics. In the *Political Process* unit, for example, students gain an understanding of geographical problems that arise with the drawing of a political boundary. Students may create and enact a hypothetical Canadian-U.S. boundary dispute similar to that between India and Pakistan.

Supposedly, the dilemma of two nations' claiming the same territory arises when gold is found in Maine. The teacher gives each student a role profile explaining whom he represents and his interest in the conflict. Students then form international arbitration committees and citizen interest groups.

The class analyzes treaties that once determined the boundaries, examines maps showing the disputed area, and reevaluates the need for gold in both countries. Each student assumes his historical role, and the play begins. With tape recordings, newspaper interviews, maps, opinion polls, and assorted readings as background, the committees hold hearings on the interests of the farmers and of gold company owners and the attitude of other countries' officials. Students then begin negotiating solutions to the problem.

If the objectives of the lesson are met, students understand the justification of a state's claim to a territory, how a dispute is settled through negotiation, and that boundaries limit the movement of people. When trying to reach a peaceful settlement of their hypothetical boundary dispute, students face the same problems and frustrations that professional politicians do.

Project activities range from reading aerial photos to choosing sites for a manufacturing company in the United States and in foreign countries. Students meet problems that require such skills as reading small- and large-scale maps in order to graph distributions or being able to measure time, distance, and population density in order to locate the point most accessible. The HSGP has abandoned the fact-memorizing, country-by-country approach to ninth and tenth grade geography.

Because of the nature of the materials, a teacher can divide the class into small groups to allow bright students to tackle sophisticated readings while the teacher can be working with slower students on less difficult materials.

In this inductive approach to geography, the individual becomes an investigator who asks questions of fellow students, justifies his own assumptions, and attempts to find situations that are similar to the problem he is studying. The teacher's job changes from leading to listening, from standing in front of the class to observing from the back of the room.

GEOGRAPHY: SIGHTED
SUBJECT-SANK SAME

by

Gary C. Fox

Geography as a distinct discipline has been sighted and sunk; presently it is foundering in the flotsam and jetsam, aimless in its course. Soon to become a vestige of yesterday, unless we arouse educators to its rightful importance, is geography—the scientific pursuit of the terrain on which man exists.

My recognition of this situation has not been sudden, but based on a gradual accumulation of experiences and observations. One such observation was made with a group of beginning seventh graders in a social studies class. When they were asked individually to go to the map and locate the Soviet Union, 22 in a class of 28 failed to do so. A similar observation was made in a World History class where only 7 of 31 were able to locate Iraq. The majority of the students failed even to locate the correct continent. Yet, many of the students were familiar with the Bagdad Pact and its members.

Also, I have encountered many servicemen lacking in knowledge about where they are stationed; be it state-side or overseas. And how many relatives of servicemen know anything about the military locations of their boys, except that they are far away. With troops presently stationed in Japan, Korea, Philippines, Canal Zone, Viet Nam, Turkey, England, Thailand, Iceland and Greenland, to mention but a few, it appears that we must be truly concerned with peoples and places beyond our immediate sectional interests.

Geography has suffered with its inclusion into various other courses such as social studies, history, current events, and government to the extent that many times it has been sacrificed, or even excluded from the curriculum. This has been brought about partly by some teachers making geography a static and sterile subject, giving only an arrangement of facts, without including a clear presentation of the ideas which produced the arrangement. Furthermore, too many

From *The Clearing House*, September 1969. Used by permission of The Clearing House.
Editor's Note: Is the study of geography as a distinct discipline doomed for extinction? The author looks at this real possibility with considerable alarm in view of the fact that the shrinking word places a greater emphasis on geography than ever before. He is an assistant professor of education at the University of Missouri in Columbia.

times the instructor is limited in geographical background and, needless to say, steers clear of the unknown.

Few teachers take advantage of the motivational value of maps and globes as a teaching aid. There is too little actual student participation in going to the map or globe in the classroom; this is often replaced by the typical "I point—you look" teacher approach. In many schools janitors appropriately call maps and globes "dust catchers," which indicates they are used infrequently. Many of the maps and globes are out-dated and need to be brought up-to-date regularly in this changing world.

While we have generated and regenerated a tremendous enthusiasm for the so-called "purer" sciences, is it not possible that we have relegated to obscurity this science which is one major vehicle mankind needs to combine all science and understanding in a compatible society? It is basic that the "how-to-do" must be accompanied by the "where-and-why-to-do" or accomplishment must be necessarily impeded or encouraged into regression.

The Soviet Union has a crash program in science and engineering; but American educators returning from Russia emphasized the importance that geography also has assumed in the Russian schools. They realize its necessity in the future and have stressed geography and foreign languages considerably more than we have in the United States.

In many higher educational institutions geography is offered as a separate subject. But many times I've heard college students, when asked if they were interested in taking a course in geography, reply in a helpless voice, "But I've never had a geography course before." We have missed the boat by not having formed patterns of thought and problem-solving along these lines in the elementary and secondary schools.

Geography must merit wider attention in the formulation of the school curriculum as a prerequisite for better citizens. Some administrators are hesitant to enlarge our ever-increasing curriculum with the addition of geography. However, the importance of geography in the future has been educationally forecasted by J. Hartt Walsh,[1] who lists geography as including place, space, economic and terrestrial geography, geopolitics, and the geography of man. It is thought that this will be one of the most useful, if not the most useful subject, in the curriculum of 2000 A.D.

1. J. Hartt Walsh, "Education in 2000 A.D.," *Nations Schools*, April, 1956, p. 47.

All teachers should be made aware that geography is not limited to any one class, but is an integral part of every class where place locations are mentioned. It should allow people to interpret problems on an international scope. It must be imparted with a realistic picture of the exact location, the mores and customs of the people, the human and natural resources.

The geography program in the elementary and secondary schools should be more concerned than it is now with the child's immediate local community. Experience should be provided at every grade level for pupils to explore, investigate, and discover ways of living within their local environments. And children should be led to understand how their ties with larger communities are evidenced within their immediate localities.

We must orient our teachers and parents in this shrinking world; isolation is impossible, so we must understand all of the regional differences at this time as they exist. Geography can be the basic foundation upon which world understanding is built.

MAPS, GLOBES AND CHILDREN

by

Marlow Ediger

In a world "shrinking in size" on account of constantly increasing speed in transportation and communication, elementary school children have a greater need than ever before for understanding information that can be obtained from maps and globes.

Pupils in the elementary school should be able to locate on maps and globes the places where "crucial happenings" occur. Skills that will help children gather information from maps and globes have to be developed along with favorable attitudes so that they will want to further their learning. The following activities for using maps and globes have been worked out to meet the pupils' interests and capacities.

Meaningful background learnings are important if children are to understand content read from maps. In the primary grades the children can take an excursion near the school for the sole purpose of noticing buildings and streets. These buildings and streets can then be represented by pictures drawn by the children on a large sheet of paper placed on the floor. (The paper should be big enough to take up at least one-eighth the area of the classroom floor.) Directions on the map located on the floor should harmonize with true directions. In moving from the concrete to what is more abstract, squares and rectangles can take the place of pictures representing buildings. The size of the map on the floor can then be reduced so that pupils develop the understanding that "reality" can be placed on a map in a small area. This provides the basis for later use of the scale of miles on a map.

Using county maps or city maps, pupils can trace the routes they take while walking or being transported by bus from home to school. What the pupils learn will be related to their own experiences. They can notice how a large area—the actual routes taken—can be represented on something small—the map. Children at the proper stage of readiness can note the distance scale that is used on the map. Computations can then be performed concerning the actual distances they travel by using the scale. The pupils can also trace their vacation

Marlow Ediger is professor of education at Northeast Missouri State College.

routes on state and national maps. Routes can be traced to the homes of relatives or friends who live far away.

Early in the primary grades children should have a variety of experiences pertaining to geographical concepts such as mountains, lakes, rivers, plains, and plateaus. Some of these geographical features can be observed directly in the environment close to the elementary school. Pictures, films, filmstrips and models can further expand these geographical concepts. Pupils can then make mountains and other geographical features by utilizing the sand table or clay. An accurate mental image of geographical features needs to exist before abstract symbols are used to take their places on maps and globes.

Children can keep a record of the local rainfall and temperature, recording this information on a bar or line graph. They can study other areas of the world that have similar temperature readings and amounts of rainfall, noting the locations of these places on maps and globes. Conclusions can be drawn about the reasons for similar temperature readings and amounts of rainfall by using a variety of reference sources. Pupils can also be encouraged to contrast areas that differ in temperature and rainfall, using maps and globes in developing major generalizations.

Pictures of farming activities, city life and manufacturing in different nations can be related to their locations on maps and globes. Many good questions about the scenes can be raised such as why certain crops are grown in a particular area or why an area has much snow in winter compared to a different area which has little or no snow.

To have pupils inductively discover the need for reference lines such as meridians and parallels, the teacher can use a classroom situation. The teacher can ask the children to describe where a certain child sits. If they state that the child sits toward the front of the room, point out that several children sit toward the front of the room. The children will then realize that, for an accurate description of where a particular child sits, they must mention the vertical row and the horizontal. The pupils can then transfer these learnings to a map or a globe by using meridians and parallels to describe the location of important places. As pupils progress in their understandings, the concepts of latitude and longitude and their purpose become meaningful.

For practice, the children can be asked to find the location of an important city or country previously studied in a social studies unit. For a change of pace, pupils with adequate background knowledge can try to find a place on a map, knowing only its latitude and longitude.

ORIENTING THE CHILD
TO HIS WORLD

by

Rose E. Sabaroff

The Importance of "Entering Behavior"

As psychologists become more interested in education and concerned with individual differences in learning, a new term has appeared, "entering behavior." What do children already know, or what is lacking, as they enter into a new learning experience? Programmed instruction is based on knowing this beginning point. The concern with children's previous knowledge is not a new one, however. Already in 1891 G. Stanley Hall conducted such an inquiry and published an article entitled, "The Content of Children's Minds on Entering School."[1] Nevertheless, the question today is a pressing one as we face a diversity of children, from those who have already interacted broadly with the world at a very early age to those who are growing up in very limited or deprived surroundings. The term "entering behavior" is a valuable one because it focuses attention so clearly on where the base line for teaching must be placed.

Three Investigations that Sample the Child's "Entering Behavior"

What kind of geographic world are various children living in? Recent studies of nursery and kindergarten children offer interesting insights.

Fostering Intellectual Development in Young Children (1962)[2] is a report of systematic observation in five preschool centers in the

Used by permission of the National Council for Geographic Education.

Rose E. Sabaroff is Head of Elementary Education at Virginia Polytechnic Institute and State University, Blacksburg, Virginia 24061. She has written many articles on geographic concepts for young children. Six articles published in the *Journal of Geography* won the 1960 award for the best articles published over a two-year period. Dr. Sabaroff is co-author of *Geography in the Teaching of Social Studies*, Houghton Mifflin.

1. G. Stanley Hall, "The Contents of Children's Minds on Entering School," *Pedagogical Seminary*, I (1891), 139-173.

2. Kenneth Wann, Miriam Selchen Dorn, and Elizabeth Ann Liddle, *Fostering Intellectual Development in Young Children* (New York: Teachers College Press, 1962). Reprinted with the permission of the publisher.

New York City area. I quote some of the conversations recorded while children were engaged in dramatic play:

Three-year-old Chris and Ashton were playing at going away on a plane. After a few minutes Ashton announced, "I'm getting off." Chris said, "No, you can't get off yet. We are going to California and that takes a long time."[3]

In one four-year-old group the children had been playing train for two days. One day they took a trip to California. They wanted a sleeping car and a dining car for this trip. The next day Eddie called, "All aboard to New Jersey." Later he called, "All aboard to California."
"Is that nearer or farther than New Jersey?" queried the teacher.
"Farther, of course!" replied Eddie.[4]

Another four-year-old group played at traveling by train. They arranged chairs for the train and found some old tickets to use. With a punch supplied by the teacher they were ready to begin. The teacher was the first customer. She bought a ticket to Detroit. Kenneth said, "I know that place. My Daddy is there." One child bought a ticket for Coney Island and another for Virginia. A third child said she wanted to go to France. "That's a *long* way, teacher. We won't get there till five," exclaimed Denise.[5]

A five-year-old group of girls were playing in the housekeeping area. They discovered a box of clothing and costumes and proceeded to dress up. The teacher recorded their conversation:

Ruth: Let's be different people! Let's be from different countries! I'm from France. That's a faraway country. It's the center of the world.
Alicia: I'm from Florida where the weather is always warm and you can swim all the time.
Patty: I'm from Africa. It's far away on the west and there are plenty of animals.
Emily: I'm from New York. There are plenty of cars and all different kinds of people.
Shirley: I'm from Mexico and that's far away over the river.
Debbie: I'm Dutch and that's fifty total miles away.
Rita: I'm from Puerto Rico. That's a very long way.
Renee: I'm from Jamaica where they dance and sing. (She started to dance and all the girls joined her saying they were dancing like their country.)[6]

Mattie, who is five years old, was playing with clay. She stuck pipe cleaners in the clay and placed green paper on top of them to make palm trees. "It looks like an island," said Mattie. "I made an island like where my mommy and daddy were." The teacher offered her blue paper for a sea. She tore some off and put it around the island, stuck in the clay, halfway

3. *Ibid.*, p. 40.
4. *Ibid.*, p. 42.
5. *Ibid.*
6. *Ibid.*, p. 26.

up the mound. (Note that Mattie has indicated by her action that she has an understanding of the relation of the land of the island to its surrounding water. The land goes beneath the water and the water comes up on its shores.)[7]

Here are three-, four-, and five-year-olds at play, using with some understanding, names of faraway places like California, Florida, Puerto Rico. True, they made errors. Someone seemed to think he could get to France by train, but the children knew it existed and knew it was a long way, "that we won't get there until five."

Another five-year-old in the same study did talk about a boat to Florida and another boat to Paris. Are educators all wrong when the say young children can best understand the Here and Now? Is it an error to say that the minds of young children feed on the concrete and observable world? Can children, indeed, learn with as great ease about the faraway as they might the near at hand?

It is worthwhile to probe a little deeper into some of the advanced concepts of space, distance, and land-water relations expressed by these modern three-, four-, and five-year-olds. Where are they getting their information? From reading books in school? From having their teacher give them this information? Probably not. The guidance the teacher gives the children in their play, the ideas she supplements in her reading to them helps, but the reason these children are at ease in some distant space relations is that for some children this has become their Here and Now.

The New York children who talk today about California, Florida, Paris, Detroit, Mexico, Puerto Rico, Jamaica may well have been there. They have already lived some of the experiences they are re-enacting in their play. And with a background based on travel, they are able to gain more from the vicarious experience offered them by television, movies, pictures, and stories. They have the concrete background to make the abstract more real.

Not only have children's experiences been broadened, but they have interacted with adults as they traveled, looked, and talked. What G. Stanley Hall said more than half a century ago still holds true, that ". . . we really see not what is near or impresses the retina, but what the attention is called and held to and what interests are awakened and words found for."[8]

Hall stresses the need for four factors to occur concurrently: to see, to have attention held to have interests awakened, and to be

7. *Ibid.*, p. 41.
8. G. Stanley Hall, *op. cit.*, p. 153.

provided the appropriate words. It would seem that these conditions may well have been present in the lives of the children described above.

Teachers working with children from lower socio-economic homes and from the slums do not find their children talking so glibly about California, Florida, or Jamaica. Many of these poorer children have not been exposed to such experiences nor have they had interested adults call their attention to important details and give them the words with which to express them.

The Institute of Developmental Studies in New York has been studying and working with pre-schoolers from the lower socio-economic groups.[9] Many of these children come to school not knowing the names of common fruits and vegetables, not knowing attributes like size or color for the objects with which they come into daily contact. In fact, some of these children do not even respond to their own names. Either these children have not seen the objects in question or they have had no opportunity to interact with a guiding adult in relation to these objects.

How do we help these children relate to the world?

The traveled children quoted earlier demonstrate the kinds of capabilities that develop when given a broad background of experiences and interested adults to interact with—interested and intelligent adults who can direct attention to important details and who correct inaccurate perceptions, adults who can and do take the time to give children the words for what they are seeing. We must start with what children can see and help them see more clearly.

Many inner city children have never "seen" in this guided, interactive way many of the things in their immediate environment—in their homes, neighborhood, shopping center, let alone the important features of their city at large. These children have to be taken to see their environment. They must be taken to the market and talked to—talked to repeatedly about what they are seeing. They must be taken to see where meat comes from; where milk comes from, how it is pasteurized and bottled. Attention must be called to the seasons. They must see a woods, a beach with the water rising and receding, a river, an island. They must see where the sun rises, where the sun sets, that they have a noonday shadow and where it falls.

The importance of verbal interaction with adults during this learning process is strongly emphasized by the researchers from the Institute of Developmental Studies.

9. Institute for Developmental Studies, Department of Psychiatry, New York Medical College.

This fitting process (fitting label to object or place), which consists of selecting the specific connection between word and referent (be it thing or place), occurs more easily when there is a verbal interaction with adults. The middle-class child learns by feedback; by being heard, corrected, and modified—gaining "operant control" over his social environment by using words that he hears. The child learns by interacting with an adult teacher be it in school or out who plays an active role in simplifying the various components of word-referent relationships. [10]

An older study worth considering concerns this same age group. Probst (1931)[11] gave a general information test to children in the second half of kindergarten, where the age range was five years four months to six years. They all knew

How many legs has a horse?
What do we use to cut cloth?
What do you use to cut meat?
What do you use a saw for?

High scores were also made on the following:

How many hands on a clock?
What are the colors in the flag?
Where are the clouds?
What did Jack and Jill do?
What does a cat scratch with?
What do we drink that comes from cows?
What do apples grow on?
Who makes money by cutting hair?
Who brings letters to the house?
To whose office do we go to have a tooth pulled?

Children knew the things that were an intimate part of their lives and for which they had first-hand opportunities for observation and learning. Low scores were made on items like the following:

From what animal do we get bacon?
From what does leather come?
From what do we get cotton?
How are trees made into boards?
What makes a street car go?

These items are more remote and require interpretation. It would require more than casual observation of bacon, leather, cotton, or boards to know the answers.

10. Vera P. John and Leo S. Goldstein, "The Social Context of Language Acquisition," *Merrill Palmer Quarterly of Behavior and Development*, X, 3 (1964), 269.
11. Cathryn A. Probst, "A General Information Test for Kindergarten Children," *Child Development*, II (1931), 81-95.

There was a marked difference in range of information between upper and lower halves of the socio-economic groups. It would seem that items in the environment to which attention had not been specifically directed or that were not greatly valued for that child in his environment were less well known.

Even our traveled children might have difficulty with interpretive type questions. Would they all know where bacon comes from? or cotton? or wool? Do they know where water in the tap comes from? Do they understand the sewage system or how electric power is distributed? Can they describe accurately all they have passed as they walked or were driven to school? Can they find their own way to the shopping center or park eight blocks from home? Do they know directions? Can they estimate 15 feet?

Laying a Geographic Foundation

Now, if we are concerned with laying a foundation for geographic education, the "entering behavior" is certainly very different for different children because of the varying experiences and learning interactions they have had with their world. We must help fill the necessary gaps. Nevertheless, there are many types of learning needed in common. Observation and interaction with the environment is basic to all geographic education, from nursery school through college.

There are five basic skills needed for the interpretation of maps and globes:

First, we must be concerned with location, including orientation and direction. The second basic map skill is a knowledge of symbols, both physical and cultural. The third requisite is some understanding of scale. Fourth, pupils need to develop an awareness of relative location. Fifth, the globe should be recognized as a model of the earth.[12]

An extended discussion of each of these skills is given in Sabaroff "Improving the Use of Maps in the Elementary School." Only three will be discussed here.

For all these map skills, interaction with the environment is essential. Children must take trips to observe thoughtfully the geographic features of the immediate environment. Attention must be called to both natural and cultural phenomena.

---

12. Rose Sabaroff, "Improving the Use of Maps in the Elementary School," *Journal of Geography*, LX, 4 (April 1961), 184.

Natural phenomena that influence human activities should be noted: apparent movement of the sun across the sky; changing seasons as they affect plants, animals, human activities; influences of daily weather changes.

To truly appreciate what they have seen, children must be guided to observe beyond surface manifestations—to find out not only what a thing is, but to try to understand how it works, why it is where it is, and to consider whether it could be otherwise. When exploration is purposeful, attention is "called and held to" relationships that might otherwise be overlooked.

Children must often probe beneath the surface to find answers to their questions. Why is the copper mine here? Where does the water in the lake behind the dam come from?

If children are looking with the intention of reproducing, of locating what they see on a map, they must be more precise in observing size, relative position of objects, and relative distance between them, or in noting the relation of an object or a phenomenon to its surroundings.[13]

Guided observation is being stressed because it is the foundation on which all other map skills are built. What we are able to see in the environment (and this must eventually include television, films, and pictures) provides the basis for understanding relationships and provides the basis for interpreting symbols on maps. Following are a few basic activities in which children may easily engage.

We can encourage children to orient themselves to familiar landmarks: "near the park," "beyond the store," "by the river."

Very early we want to develop the use of *up* as meaning away from the center of the earth; *down* as meaning toward the center of the earth. We climb up a hill and down a hill. We look up at a mountain peak and dig a hole down into the earth. We can look down at a river in the bottom of a canyon. Perhaps if we establish the correct meaning of up and down early enough, children will not have difficulty picturing a river flowing north. (And even very able youngsters described earlier often have difficulty with this.)

Eventually children must develop some understanding of sun behavior and some facility with cardinal directions. Through a series of outdoor lessons, we can call children's attention to the different position in which we see the sun at different times of day.

Where is the sun in the early morning?
Where is the sun at noon?
Where is it late in the afternoon?

13. *Ibid.*, "Map Interpretation in the Primary Grades," *The Elementary School Journal*, LXIV, 2 (1963), 61.

When answers to these questions are well established, children's attention may be directed to their noonday shadows. We want children to understand that shadows help them know cardinal directions. Once they have established their noon shadows as falling toward the north, we may have them face north at noon and label the direction behind them as south, to the right of them as east, to the left of them as west. All this must precede any labeling of cardinal directions on a map. And when maps are used, they should be viewed on a horizontal surface and be properly oriented with outdoor space. Orientation must be constantly checked and reinforced. Classroom walls (or corners) can be properly labeled as to cardinal directions. Learning direction labels is not so different from learning names for places or objects encountered in the environment. Children should be encouraged to use cardinal directions in their speech, and the teacher should help children orient themselves each time they enter a room or start on a trip together.

Scale is really another form of symbol, but more abstract than symbols of features that can be seen and interacted with more directly. However, if children are encouraged to observe with the intention of mapping what they have seen, they are faced with problems of scale, relative position, and relative distance between features to be represented. With guidance by a teacher, children can be helped to play out what they have seen, encouraged to ask questions about relations and find ways of putting this information in visible form. The first "map" representations usually use three dimensional objects like the play trains in the sequences discussed earlier. Almost always a reduction in scale is involved. A chair may represent a mountain, and a plank over a blue oilcloth strip may be a bridge over a river. Gradually children replace the three-dimensional objects with pictorial representations and eventually with semi-pictorial symbols. But understanding starts with life and real experiences and proceeds to the increasingly abstract. With proper understanding of children's entering behavior, teachers can systematically provide the experiences necessary to build word meaning as well as map meaning. We can be important guides in orienting the child to his world.

GEOGRAPHY AND THE CONTEMPORARY URBAN SCENE

by

Michael E. Eliot Hurst

ABSTRACT. This paper summarizes the objectives and content of a course entitled "Geography in an Urban World," given at Simon Fraser University. It outlines the manner in which this course is offered; teachers may be interested in this particular way toward a more relevant and meaningful geography.

A constant cry of students today is for meaning and relevance in terms of contemporary problems and the human condition. Geography is well equipped to deal with the present-day human *milieu*, and one hears from various geographic centers about courses dealing with poverty, the *third world*, urban transportation, and ecological problems.

In an effort to directly relate the contemporary surroundings of the undergraduate to geography, an introductory course was recently tried at Simon Fraser University with the theme "Geography in an Urban World." The theme was chosen since the "city" is something with which most undergraduates and high school students are very familiar and with which they can identify. The course utilized as many contemporary teaching techniques as possible, not just as gimmicks, but as integrated components of a total course presentation—movies, soundslide sequence, rap sessions, an "urban game." It is equally presentable at College or High School levels, and in the latter could draw on some of the materials of the High School Geography Project.[1]

Through such methods of presentation it was hoped to make the student more aware of his urban environment, its realities, its impact, its feelings, and its imageries; to make him more aware of the background to racial tension, urban poverty, urban affluence, and the urban power game. The city in its contemporary setting should be more than just bricks and concrete—by using geographical techniques and viewpoints the student should be able to see the city as an entity, a social and cultural place, an economic place, a political

Used by permission of the National Council for Geographic Education.

1. High School Geography Project, notably the segment, "Geography in an urban age" which includes a simulation game, "Parksville;" now published by the Macmillan Co., New York.

place, a place with particular networks of communication and movement, a place subject to the pollution and ravages of man. As such the city, through geography, can be seen to reflect all qualities of man—good as well as bad.

Space does not permit a very detailed synopsis of the course; in particular the wide range of reading material and movies utilized have been omitted.[2] A number of recent publications by Leinwand, McNee, Mayer, Perloff, Saarineen, and Rose should, however, be mentioned.[3]

Rationale and Introduction

A. The course is concerned with the city because the twentieth century world is an urban-dominated world. Virtually all countries are experiencing rapid urbanization, and in the next 40 years the population growth in the world's cities will probably be double the entire population growth that the world has experienced in the last 6000 years.

The city holds sway because it is the center of commerce, administration, politics, and most cultural activities; the mass media are urban-dominated—television, newspapers, radio, magazines are city-produced, city-conceived, and designed largely for urban and suburban audiences. Very few areas in Canada or the United States are not under the influence of an urban-dominated culture to some degree. As geographers we are concerned with an urban-dominated world, with cityscapes as economic and cultural mosaics, with cities as places of conflict; conflicts between ethnic groups, rich and poor, liberals and conservatives, automobiles and people, living and pollution; we are concerned with the mental images and feelings that men have of cities too, as they shape spatial behavior.

B. How do we conceive of cities? Are they all similar, is there

2. Complete references will be found in M.E. Eliot Hurst, *I came to the city . . . essays on the urban scene*, forthcoming, Houghton Mifflin, 1971/2.
3. G. Leinwand (general editor) *Problems of American Society* (New York: Washington Square Press, 1969 *et seq.*), especially the volumes on the negro, poverty, air and water pollution, traffic, the community, the slums, and the consumer; R.B. McNee, "A proposal for a new geography course for liberal education; introduction to geographic behavior," C.C.G. *General Series* No. 4, 1967, pp. 1-37; H.N. Meyer, "The spatial expression of urban growth," C.C.G. *Resource Paper* No. 7, 1969; H.S. Perloff (ed.) *The Quality of the Urban Environment* (Baltimore: Johns Hopkins, 1969); T. Saarineen "Perception of environment." C.C.G. *Resource Paper* No. 5, 1969; and H.M. Rose, "Social processes in the city: race and urban residential choice," C.C.G. *Resource Paper* No. 6, 1969.

some basic pattern or structure that can be identified as "urban"? If there is, do all cities look and feel the same—do we have the same feelings of "urbanness" about San Francisco that we have of Chicago, New Orleans, New York? If we set up certain generalities about cities, how does Los Angeles fit in? There are uniformities among Canadian and American cityscapes, but there are considerable diversities too. Each city has its *own* history, its *own* character, its *own* cultural setting, engenders its own particular feel of urbanness. There are trends to uniformity, but there are also factors which identify particular cities through the result of unique growth processes, political events, cultures, and institutuions, so that many cities are marked by a distinct individuality.

C. Current research in perception indicates that we respond to our own environmental surroundings only insofar as we feel and perceive them. Between our conception of the environment and the "objective" world lie cultural values, needs, goals, and expectations, which help us to build up *images, notions, feelings,* and *emotions* about our surroundings as they are selectively received by our ears, eyes, nose, and skin. These images and feelings are selectively patterned by our schemes of values, word usages, conscious memories, and subconsciously stored experiences. Thus the individual does not have a total picture of the "objective" world, but only perceives and feels what is within his range of assessment at that moment.

Among our findings, therefore, are the following:

(i) We already have a mental image of, and a feeling toward, the city.[4] This has been gained by living in an urban environment for 20 years or more, and by being subjected to urban-oriented information systems;

(ii) The kind of mental image and attitude we have about the city affects our behavior and the behavior of others. Obviously if we build an image of a city as a real swinging place, we will behave in a different way than if we view the city as a heartless, soulless, austere place, from which all we wish to do is to escape;

(iii) Our mental images and attitudes of the city differ. This can lead to conflict situations if the images and hopes for a city held by a business elite or middle class elite, which usually hold political control of a city via the City Council, differ from the hopes and images of some other subcultural group;

4. McNee, *op. cit.*, p. 21.

(iv) The mental images and feelings we have correspond only very roughly to the "real" or "objectively observable" world; thus we have some notions about cityscapes that are no more than illusions;

(v) This perception and attitude we have is "culture bound"; that is, our images are very much a reflection of the cultural groups to which we belong. In our case our "culturally bound" image of the city reflects contemporary North American cities, and it may well conflict with, and be at variance with, understanding cities of the past, cities of the present outside North America, and cities of the future;

(vi) This problem of developing a rationale for viewing the city is only a special case of a total geographic conception of earth-space.

The City in History

The city should be placed in perspective: urban origins, what have been the city's functions in the past, how has the city changed its dimensions, what were the pre-automobile characteristics of the city? This involves an evaluation of the impact of improved transportation and communication media, the concomitant change in space-time ratios, and the growth of the city as the central controller of an increasingly interdependent societal system. Following Mumford's broad technical classification which reflects (a) the increasing use of non-human sources of energy; (b) the increasing span of the networks in which man and machines are integrated; and (c) increased productivity, we can trace: (1) *Eotechnic* cities of ancient Egypt, Mesopotamia, Greece, Rome, medieval Europe (castle walls dominant), and Renaissance Europe (aesthetics of an elite group dominant). (2) *Palaeotechnic* cities, the rise of the industrial city of the nineteenth and early twentieth centuries (back-to-back housing, tenements, industrial squalor; individualism and brutalism). (3) *Neotechnic* cities, the twentieth century motorized city, with perhaps Los Angeles as the epitome (the development of the neon culture, slurbs, new means of disposing of space, the decline of space and the rise of the dispersed community relationships).

The City as a Cultural Place

The city is not undifferentiated, nor is it a meaningless agglomeration of people and services; rather it is a composite of many cultural and subcultural areas. In the mass society of the city residents rely to some extent in how they perceive and feel, on not just the whole city but on the many discrete areas and parts within a city; the images (and illusions) they hold help them to identify their own territorial area as well as other districts within the city. We all have points of reference within the city to which we may or may not ascribe some emotive meaning. In other words, there is no one "city type," there is no one "way of life" uniquely urban, but there are varities of urban experience which arise from the way different people perceive in the urban environment those particular systems in which they participate, identify with, and support. Physical space and social space in such relationships are not necessarily coterminous. Insofar as these differences are reflected in the cityscape they are of concern to the cultural geographer.

Although there have been challenges to this idea of spatially de-limited urban enclaves, the city does appear to consist of social seg-ments whose members are located in comparable positions in the social structure; the propinquity of the members means they share similar life chances, life styles, have access to similar opportunities, and are subject to comparable constraints. The consequences of this segregation on the political life of the city are dealt with below.

Italian, Swedish, Ukrainian, Chinese, Anglo-American, Afro-Amer-ican, French-Canadian, and Indian subcultures on the one hand, class life styles and ethnic ghettos on the other hand, are reflected in residence locations, house types, landscaping, consumption patterns. This dynamic culture-bound spatiality is reflected in patterns of land use, in the kinds and values of property, and in particular functions.

The City as an Economic Place

The city cannot exist only as a provider of the "good life." There must be an underlying economic process or economic base. Contem-porary cities are headquarters or subsidiary centers of a national economic system. Cities are increasingly dependent for their exist-ence upon their role as control centers in the large-scale market, institutional system, and governmental system. There are three broad levels of economic functioning:

(i) The first is the broad economic *raison d'etre* of the city; the urban concentration is possible only because the primary activities are or-ganized in such a way as to maintain a large population with little access to the earth; in return the cities function as economic places by selling products or services to the outside world. At this level we can study the inflows and outflows of goods and services to and from the city in the context of the rest of the national economy. Equally at this level, the city is the center of economic control over the rest of the economy.

(ii) If the first point is the *external* set of relationships, then this second level is concerned with the economic forces that differentiate the city internally. These internal forces are reflected in the value of land and transportation costs, which are manifest in the different uses to which various parts of the land area are allocated (subject to social and political control).

(iii) The third level concerns the micropattern of what has become a dominant urban economic activity—the pattern of tertiary activities: shops, movie theaters, ball parks, the corner store, the neighborhood center, community and regional shopping centers, downtown cores, automobile rows and strips.

The City as a Political Place

Culture and economics alone do not account for all interactions within the city; institutional arrangements, particularly political ones, complicate the urban pattern still further. We need to answer two broad sets of questions—(a) What is the political *milieu* and community power structure? Or, put simply, who rules? Is it some elite group of real estate developers, businessmen, or opportunists, or is policy-making dispersed among various groups or communities in a city? (b) How are the political controls manifest in urban development? Which public policies have, are, and will shape the city? Institutionally many of these policies are structured in the planning process and zoning ordinances.

Political factors are very apparent in North American cities; recently the accelerated separation of cultural groups has brought about the massive suburban movement of middle and upper income whites and the increasing isolation of lower income and mainly non-white residents of the ghetto in the urban core, which has been reflected on the one hand in the attempts to restructure political control in metropolitan areas by creating politically distinct suburban enclaves, and on the other in the increasing militance of ghetto residents.

The City and "Environment"

Considerable interest is currently focused on the conflict between uncontrolled urban living and the environmental setting of the city.

The key word is "control"; also of importance is the degree of toler-ance—how many people must die from a killer smog before steps are taken to control pollutants (*viz.* London). The "environment" is a wide concept and it covers the following categories:

(i) the "airshed," its relative purity or pollution;

(ii) the "watershed," the ease of water supply, as well as water pol-lution;

(iii) the "audio-shed," the relative degree and time exposure to per-ceived noise pollutants;

(iv) the "olfactory shed," the relative degree and time exposure to perceived unpleasant smells;

(v) the open space-recreation "shed," the ease and availability of short-distance recreation trips; and

(vi) any microclimatic factors.

The control of undesirable pollutants feeds back to the cultural, economic, and political factors noted above.

The Big Crunch: The City and Transportation

A combination of increased motorization and suburbanization has had a deleterious effect on one or more cherished urban goals, partic-ularly that of "accessibility." The city and the new mobility afforded by transport improvements have the potential to enlarge job oppor-tunities, economic opportunities, and social contacts. Many of these have not come to full fruition—the lowest income groups do not have access to the automobile; those who do find that there is a conflict between the space requirements of high car ownership and the con-strains of suburbanization, which result in congestion, time and mon-ey loss, and new kinds of transport problems. In reaching this situa-tion a number of unfortunate side effects have occurred—for instance the growth of car ownership and use has led to a decline in public transport with consequent effects on low income groups; the provi-sion of freeways and expanded surface streets has frequently oc-curred without regard to community or urban values. Most urban dwellers are caught daily in the big crunch.

How do we escape from these transport problems? By new urban design, by balancing transportation and land use, by utilizing both private and public transportation, by the use of new transport tech-nologies, and by community involvement in the whole planning process. These suggested solutions feed back to the cultural, economic, and political controls of the city, and lead on to the final section.

The City of the Future

This constitutes a brief trip into social-science fiction. There is no determined way of forecasting the future—there are too many unknown variables. However, we can indulge ourselves, and present a number of alternatives:

(i) Increased dispersal, mass suburbanization, reduced costs of communication, reliance on "information consoles" in each home, virtually a homogeneous dispersed city;

(ii) Reversal of this trend, back to concentrated form, face-to-face contacts, the rise of the "megastructure." The latter is a multi-purpose building or group of buildings, for example 100 stories high, housing up to 250,000 people;

(iii) Concentration and dispersion—greater dispersion at the fringe, greater concentration at the center, detailed separation of land use at the street level with high density nodes of linked activities;

(iv) The controlled environment: the old cities are replaced by new towns under geodesic domes, with controlled climates, no pollution, compact and ready access;

(v) An extension of (iv) to a closed system beyond this planet: "a new home among the stars," a hollow asteroid 20 miles long, 10 miles in diameter, cruising in space in a self-powered closed cycle world, housing up to one million people;

(vi) Annihilation by pollution or World War III;

(vii) External structures are of no consequence—of much more importance is the human condition, the radicalization of man.

Conclusion

We are going through a "revolutionary" age, when many students and many of the social sciences themselves are questioning the validity of old approaches and the relevance of the subject matter taught at school and college. Hopefully the course outlined here reflects a humanistic view of man's contemporary spatial behavior. If we are to understand the intricacies and diversities of the humanized landscapes and cityscapes we must look beyond the mere stockpiling of facts and the neat, elegant abstractness of the quantifier. This course is dedicated to the search for a relevant and meaningful geography.

FOURTH AND SIXTH GRADE STUDENTS' KNOWLEDGE OF TOPOGRAPHICAL TERMS

by

Arthur K. Ellis

Certainly a crucial factor in children's understanding of social studies material in the intermediate grades is their knowledge of commonly occurring topographical terms. These terms, for example, "bay," "river," "mountain," etc., are found repeatedly in social studies textbooks designed for fourth, fifth, and sixth grade children, and students are expected to be acquainted with them.

The purpose of a recent investigation carried out at the University of Oregon was to determine whether fourth and sixth grade children were indeed capable of identifying twenty-seven selected topographical terms through two different methods of presentation. As a means of presenting the terms to students, two tests, one written and the other pictorial, were devised.

The multiple-choice written test presented each term in written context followed by four possible definitions of the term in question from which the student was to choose the "best" answer. The pictorial test, also multiple-choice, was composed of projected color slides. The slides, oblique aerial photographs and photographs taken from viewpoints on the ground, were of common topographical features. For each term in question, four slides were presented from which the student was to choose the picture which "best" represented the term. It should be stressed that the two tests were parallel, item for item.

The tests were administered to 496 fourth and sixth grade students in twenty classrooms chosen by random selection from six Oregon school districts. Each child tested took both examinations.

It was found that, in general, those items which were relatively more difficult for the students on the written test were also more difficult on the pictorial test. Interestingly, the most difficult term for fourth and sixth graders on both tests was "cape." Most of the

Used by permission of the National Council for Geographic Education.

Arthur K. Ellis is an Assistant Professor of Elementary Education (social studies) at the University of Minnesota, Minneapolis 55455. He completed his doctoral work at the University of Oregon with a major in elementary social studies education. Dr. Ellis has had teaching and supervisory experience at the elementary, junior high, and university levels.

children tested did not know the meaning of the term despite the fact that capes abound along the Oregon coast and despite the fact that textbook authors apparently assume that children know the meaning of the term.

Rank Order of Item Difficulty for Written and Pictorial Tests at Fourth and Sixth Grade Levels

	4th Grade			6th Grade	
Term	W	P	Term	W	P
cape	1	1	cape	1	1
sand bar	2	2	channel	2	5
plateau	2	6	peninsula	3	8
cove	4	4	river	3	10
channel	5	3	cove	5	2
peninsula	5	5	tributary	5	3
tributary	7	9	sand bar	5	5
bay	8	8	plateau	8	9
rapids	9	20	coast	8	11
lake	10	14	plain	10	5
plain	11	7	bay	11	3
coast	12	11	lake	12	13
river	13	13	cliff	12	20
river mouth	13	16	river mouth	14	13
valley	15	15	valley	14	16
mountain	16	23	falls	16	27
cliff	16	25	mountain range	17	13
falls	16	27	sand dune	17	16
glacier	19	16	island	17	23
mountain peak	20	10	glacier	20	18
canyon	20	11	rapids	20	22
mountain range	20	18	mountain peak	22	20
sand dune	20	19	harbor	23	25
harbor	24	21	mountain	24	24
island	25	21	canyon	25	11
highland	26	23	highland	26	18
swamp	27	26	swamp	27	26

*Duplicate numbers indicate equal difficulty.

Fourth grade students also had considerable difficulty identifying such terms as "sand bar," "plateau," "cove," "channel," "peninsula," "tributary," and "bay." Sixth grade students had somewhat less difficulty in answering test questions than did fourth graders. However, in addition to "cape," they found "channel," "peninsula," "river," and "cove," moderately difficult to identify.

The table above summarizes the rank order of difficulty which students experienced with the twenty-seven topographical terms.

Conclusions

The data gathered in this investigation appear to warrant the following conclusions:*

1. Although a variety of textbooks are in use in the intermediate grades, the topographical terms included in the present study may be found repeatedly in most of them.

2. The written and pictorial tests of topographical terms devised for this study appear to be useful instruments in the examination of students' knowledge of the selected terms.

3. Both fourth and sixth grade students were better able to identify topographical terms when those terms were presented pictorially than when the terms were presented in a written setting. This would seem to indicate the desirability of using projected pictorial materials to represent topographical terms initially as they are introduced in social studies work.

4. At the fourth grade level, boys were better able to identify topographical terms than were girls. This was true in the case of both tests, written and pictorial. Since the large number of children tested and the impartial selection of examinees served to rule out chance factors to a great extent, it is assumed that possibly fourth grade boys' greater interest in topographical features was responsible for the higher achievement.

5. At the sixth grade level, where no significant differences in achievement by sex were noted, it is assumed that the two additional years of experience and recurrence of the terms served as sufficient reinforcement to the girls to enable them to attain comparable scores to those attained by the boys.

6. Sixth grade students achieved significantly higher scores on both tests than did fourth grade students. This would indicate that

*Data used to substantiate these conclusions are available from the author upon request.

considerable growth in the knowledge of these terms takes place as a result of the sixth graders' two years additional experience. It is, however, difficult to determine the exact source of sixth grade students' greater knowledge. Very likely it may be attributed to two additional years of classroom instruction, travel, films, television, and to other sources.

Recommendations

1. Teachers are not to assume that students know the meanings of topographical terms which appear in social studies textbooks. This investigator found that children often have wrong notions of the meanings of even the most commonly occurring terms. These terms must be learned by students through a variety of experiences if the words which represent the terms are to be truly meaningful.

2. The employment of projected pictorial materials which illustrate topographical terms would seem to be an effective means of introducing intermediate grade students to those terms which they face in their social studies textbooks.

3. It is recommended by the investigator that teachers encourage students to take pictures of the landscape as a means of promoting first-hand involvement and as a means of observing, recording, and communicating the natural surface features of the earth. Teachers, also, should attempt to assemble pictures representative of topographical features as a means of broadening children's concepts of the earth's surface features.

4. Universities and colleges concerned with teacher training in elementary school social studies could very well re-evaluate the courses which serve to prepare and improve teachers in the social studies. Courses of study might involve teachers in the techniques of exploring the environment, not only for its topography, but for its other resources as well.

The Earth as a Mirror

One of the most ingenious proofs of the rotundity of the earth was conducted by Professor Dufour of Morges, Switzerland, in 1881. He noted that only a flat mirror produced an image of the same dimensions as the object reflected. A concave mirror would produce an enlarged image, a convex mirror a smaller one. (The reader can check this by comparing the appearances of objects viewed in a concave magnifying mirror with those viewed in a convex wide-angle mirror.)

One day Dufour and a colleague, Prof. Forel, were fortunate to observe Lake Geneva in a state of unusual calmness. When they compared the reflection of the church tower of Montreaux, across the lake, with the unreflected image, the vertical shortening of the former was apparent. In fact, according to a paper read by Dufour to the Helvetic Society of Natural Science, after a while the roundness of the earth became as perceptible as that of a ball held in one's hand.

William M. McKinney
Wisconsin State University
at Stevens Point

IV. Economics

ECONOMIC EDUCATION IN THE
ELEMENTARY SCHOOL

by

Robert M. Bruker

The study of economic education is generally associated with high school and university curricula. However, the understanding of certain economic aspects at the primary and intermediate levels is often desirable and even essential. If tomorrow's citizens are to gain even a minimum understanding of economic principles, they must get it from the schools. For most of them college is too late, for others even high school may be too late. Something must be done at the elementary school level. Children at this age have a great interest and concern for the "how and where" of commodities and services with which they come into daily contact.[1]

One of the most noticeable facts about economic education in the elementary schools is the lack of information available on the subject. Relatively little has been written in the professional journals, and almost no attempt has been made to draw together the research which has been done on the various programs in operation in different parts of the country. It is my intention to present a general discussion of economic education and to mention examples of what has been done in recent years.

Most of the important problems of our nation today are internal rather than external. This can best be illustrated by a look at the executive branch of our government—the large majority of the departments in the President's cabinet are devoted almost exclusively to problems of a domestic nature. For example, witness the Departments of Post Office, Interior, Agriculture, Justice, Labor, Treasury, Commerce, Health, Education and Welfare, and the new Housing and Urban Development, and Transportation posts. Only the State and Defense departments have their primary concern in foreign affairs. Likewise, most of our internal problems are economic: inflation, recession, unemployment, automation, the farm problem, education, medical care for the aged, and many others. Furthermore, these issues arise at all levels of government—federal, state, and local.

Whether or not economic education is being practiced in an ele-

Reprinted from the *Peabody Journal of Education*, January 1970. © 1970 by the George Peabody College for Teachers. Used by permission.

mentary school classroom depends to a great extent upon our conception (or misconception) of the term "economic education." Lessons on money, banking, farming and transportation do not necessarily constitute economic education. Elementary school teachers have, in the past, shown a propensity for staying at the "thing" level in dealing with economics instead of developing principles and concepts.[2] Some common practices which have been reported will serve to illustrate this point. Suggestions for improvement are also mentioned.

1. *A general notion of who the "community helpers" are looks like a review of the civil service roster.* Some teachers spend their entire careers telling students about the mailman, the policeman, and the fireman without mentioning the dozens of other helpers in the community.

2. *Banking lessons always discuss the bank as a safe storehouse for our money.* Checkbook money is mentioned, as well as the profit aspects of interest paid for money in savings accounts. The real economic principles involved are often ignored. How can a bank afford to pay interest on savings accounts? Where do they get the money to do this? How can a bank, which keeps money for people, at the same time help stimulate the economy by putting money back into circulation?

3. *International trade.* This quite often becomes a study of imported items with omission of the economic facets such as the jobs created by international trade. This would be an excellent time to discuss the importance of a favorable balance between imports and exports.

4. *Transportation.* This can become an exercise in viewing trains, planes, trucks, and boats. It can also be a project involving the construction of these vehicles. It should be a unit which is concerned with transportation as a process of moving people and goods from one location to another.[3] A great deal of time could be devoted to the effect of transportation on land values, how plant locations depend upon the type of transportation available, job opportunities in the transportation industry, and community development.

5. *Savings is sometimes taught as only a moral virtue.* Often omitted is the fact that our very economy would collapse without the extensive use of credit. Also, at this time, the advantages and disadvantages of installment buying could be discussed.

Despite the fact that little has been written about economic education in the elementary school, there are a number of interesting and worthwhile programs in operation.

A lesson on "Bottle-cap economics," attributed to J. Robert Hendricks, was reported in the January, 1968, issue of *The Instructor*. Bottle caps were the medium of exchange for Mr. Hendricks' fifth grade project on our monetary system. Every child participated in the project and each began with ten bottle caps. Two youngsters were chosen to be bankers, two others comprised the Bureau of Fair Trade. The entire activity was scheduled to last for one-and-a-half hours, during which time the children could develop any device or type of "business" venture, or perform any service, which might help them increase their capital.

During the activity "money" could be deposited in, or borrowed from, the bank. Interest was paid at the rate of one bottle cap, per hour, for each three caps deposited. Loans were to be repaid at a rate of two bottle caps for every five borrowed. Contracts were issued which indicated the terms of each transaction. Collateral, such as head bands, combs, ball-point pens, and so forth, were required for loans.

In addition to the relative security of savings accounts and small loans, a number of "glamour" business ventures appeared. These included guessing games, puzzles, art work, and offers of assistance with homework; all designed to turn a fast bottle cap.

The Bureau of Fair Trade had its hands full, also. One boy was observed charging his classmates one bottle cap each time they wanted to leave the room. Two others, who lost their assets early in the activity, were intercepted planning a hold-up. In both instances, however, the Bureau was able to suggest more appropriate ways to make money.

This is a project which permits maximum involvement of the class members, and allows them freedom to use their various abilities in a positive fashion. In his evaluation of the activity, Mr. Hendricks states: "The group had a better understanding of the use and need for a medium of exchange. They were better informed about the purpose and value of interest rates, loans, deposits, economic competition, and profit and loss. They had drawn on mathematical, oral, and written communication skills in their economic project."

Bernice Sommers, a fourth grade teacher at the Charlton Heights Elementary School, in Ballston Lake, New York, turned a school need into a valuable lesson in economics and practical mathematics. Her class was trying to find a way to earn money for a field trip to

New York City to visit the American Museum of Natural History. At that time Charlton Heights School had no convenient place for the children to purchase school supplies. To satisfy this need, as well as to earn money for the field trip, the fourth graders organized a store.

Again, participation was the keyword in the project as every child had a task to perform. Some served as class officers, some drew up order forms and profit-loss graphs, while others did the necessary art work. Two students were needed to serve as bookkeepers in order to keep track of the shares of stock in the store, which were sold for twenty-five cents each.

The store activity was a rousing success, and when the shares were finally redeemed, they were worth $1.52 each, more than enough for the field trip. As Mrs. Sommers points out, the store was more than a way to make money for an outing. It provided practical experiences in arithmetic and economics, as well as in English and art. The children learned to understand interest, discount, and sales tax. Equally important, they learned the value of working together.[4]

It would not be difficult to modify these and other successful practices to suit a particular teaching situation or locality. Any primary grade teacher, for example, could set up an assembly line in her own classroom to demonstrate the division of labor and interdependence of workers. The concept to be gleaned from such an experience would be the realization that specialization enables goods to be produced faster, better, and at the same time, more efficiently.

The method used to develop this understanding must involve, as the other successful projects have, maximum participation by the children. The activity selected can be one of many, such as making candy, cookies, or applesauce. It could even be something as complicated as baking bread. After the activity has been chosen, and depending upon the size of the class, the children can be divided into several teams, each with a particular job related to the finished product. These jobs could take the form of mixing batter, rolling dough, cutting cookies, or whatever else is pertinent to the activity. When the entire process has been completed, and the children are enjoying the rewards of their labors, the teacher should repeat the experiment, but with one alteration. This time she should select only two teams and assign the remaining members of the class as "observers." Team "A" will continue to divide the labor, each child performing a separate function. On Team "B," however, each child will complete the entire process by himself. At the end of a pre-arranged time period, the observers, as well as the participants, will see first-hand the advantages of cooperation and interdependence of workers. The unit could be enriched by a visit to a local business or industry where division of labor is practiced on a much wider scale.

It is not my intention to disparage elementary school teachers. I firmly believe that there is no group of educators, or professionals anywhere, more important than those who practice at the primary and intermediate levels. I also believe these are our most creative and dedicated teachers, and that they should be our best qualified. In nearly every example of a worthwhile and successful program of economic education at the elementary level, the impetus has come from the classroom teacher who groped and felt her way through motivating and culminating activities designed to make economics more meaningful to her students. Most of the blame for her lack of training can be placed squarely on the shoulders of colleges of teacher education. There are offered courses in economics and courses in education, but "never the twain shall meet."

In recent years, more and more workshops in economic education have been conducted on the campuses of various colleges and universities. These have come about largely as a result of the labors of the Joint Council on Economic Education, which has served as a motivating agent to public schools and higher education institutions throughout the country. The Joint Council has worked diligently to sponsor national workshops and regional councils, and to encourage the revision of economic content of public school curricula. The next step is an in-service program conducted by trained personnel, offered in the school district, financed by the local school board, and for which college credit is granted.

1. Josephine F. Delva. "Integrating Economics in the Elementary Social Studies Program," *Social Studies*, Vol. XLVII, No. 8, December 1955, p. 294.

2. Harold J. Bienvenu. "Economic Education: Problems and Programs," *The Elementary School Journal*, Vol. LIX, No. 2, November 1958, p. 100.

3. *Ibid.*, p. 99.

4. Bernice Sommers. "Minding A Store Teaches Math In A Hurry," *Grade Teacher*, Vol. 84, January 1967, p. 138.

J. Robert Hendricks. "Bottle-cap economics," *The Instructor*, Vol. LXXVII, No. 5, January 1968.

Lawrence Senesh. "The Pattern of the Economic Curriculum," *Social Education*, Vol. XXXII, No. 1, January 1968.

ECONOMIC EDUCATION IN AN AGE
OF GREAT EXPECTATIONS AND
INSTANT SOLUTIONS

by
Albert Alexander
Edward C. Prehn

A candid examination of "Problems of the 'Seventies," "Students of the 'Seventies," and "Approaches of Professional Economists" provides the background for the authors' selection of criteria for a one-semester, twelfth-grade economics course. ALBERT ALEXANDER *is Executive Director of the New York City Council on Economic Education and Adjunct Associate Professor of American History and Economics at Long Island University;* EDWARD C. PREHN *is Chairman of Social Studies at Susan E. Wagner High School in Staten Island, New York.*

Economic education was the earliest, and perhaps the most persistent, most aggressive, and most successful, of all the movements to effect change in the teaching of the social studies. Spearheaded by the Joint Council on Economic Education and its network of affiliated local councils and university centers, the movement during the past twenty years has labored doggedly to develop new curricula, to provide better instructional materials, and to upgrade the scholarly background of teachers. Like so many other institutions moving into a second generation, it must now pause and reflect (does it have any other choice today?) on whether or not a "gap" is showing.

Foremost among the questions economic education must ask itself is the leading cliche of the day: "Is it relevant?". Of course the *question* is truly relevant. It always is; only its rude insistence jars us today, particularly because it is directed from without, coupled with the usual manner in which it is delivered.

Yet if there is one thing which the economic education movement has been striving for, it is relevancy. Commencing with a drive to reform and service the high schools, it next moved on to the lower grades, including kindergarten. Now it is devoting major attention to the introductory economics course on the college level.

What role is the economic education movement really playing today? What role should it be playing in the "revolutionary" 'seventies?

From *Social Education*, March 1971. Reprinted with permission of the National Council for the Social Studies, Albert Alexander and Edward C. Prehn.

Leo Cherne, Executive Director of the Research Institute of America, has pointed out[1] that we live in an age both of far-reaching industrial and scientific achievement and of "massive expectations and demands for instant solutions." Can a dynamic economy that generates a trillion dollars worth of goods and services, Cherne asks, plead poverty and helplessness in response to social needs? It is the inability of a nation which put a man on the moon within a single decade to make massive inroads in the perennial problems of poverty, racial injustice, and war, that lies at the heart of the malaise of American society today.

Problems of the 'Seventies

The problems of the 'seventies are a combination both of persistent economic and social problems of the recent past linked with serious emerging new problems, most of which are the consequences of our amazing economic and scientific advances. These problems range in the economic sphere from the economics of space exploration, inflation, unemployment, the amelioration of the lot of the disadvantaged, to the return to a full peacetime economy. But while our economic problem areas remain the same, the emphasis is very different. For example, in the coming decade, the challenge of unemployment will have to be studied more in terms of *who* is out of work rather than *how many* Americans are without jobs. A changing social atmosphere is bound to reflect itself in a reevaluation of goals and in an economy reflecting a greater social-mindedness.

Among the "new" economic problems is the impact of the military-industrial complex on the lives, present and future, of the American people. The military-industrial complex is not a conspiracy of "merchants of death" and lusty generals. Rather, it is a product of the times. During the course of the Cold War, the American defense industry burgeoned, and with the war in Southeast Asia, it became the nation's biggest industry. Directly it employs 8.5 million people— 3.4 million in the armed forces, 1.3 million Defense Department civilians, and 3.8 million industrial workers. It involves more than 120,000 industrial suppliers and hundreds of universities whose scientists do everything from basic research to the design and manufacture of nuclear warheads. Pentagon spending reaches into all fifty states. The military-industrial complex supplies one out of every nine

1. Leo Cherne, "The Trillion-Dollar Frustration," *Saturday Review*, November 23, 1968, p. 26.

jobs in the United States; accounts for one-third of all research activity; and devours 43¢ of every federal tax dollar. It is "an $80 billion-a-year juggernaut" consuming a tenth of the nation's gross national product.

Naturally, the ungainly growth of the military-industrial complex has raised serious questions. To what extent is it a direct threat to American democracy? How has it contributed to the misallocation of natural resources, the aggravation of ecological problems, and the growth of monopoly? And, can we afford to go on throwing billions of dollars into missiles and into Southeast Asia at a time when violence and crime are increasing, schools are in turmoil, pockets of poverty all too visible, roads and airports congested, and rivers and air polluted?

The second "new" economic concern is "the ecological problem." Many ecologists believe that the literal poisoning of our total environment is our most complex and most urgent problem. Can we have both a safe environment and a rising standard of living? Scientific and technological progress, which is now being excoriated in some quarters for polluting the environment, has also been responsible for the long life expectancy, low disease rates, and abundance that our nation enjoys. If we sacrifice the economy to ecology, will not our high standard of living, which is a part of our quality of life, slowly begin to deteriorate? Are we willing to pay the costs for a better environment?

The third "new" economic problem of the 'seventies is that "totally new economic ailment," the conglomerate corporation—the latest development in the combination movement in American industry. The antimonopoly legislation of the last 75 years was designed to deter vertical and horizontal combinations largely of the market-extension type. Old-fashioned mergers absorbed suppliers, customers, and competitors of giant corporations. By and large, antimonopoly legislation succeeded in coping with egregious combinations in the economic arena for which it was designed.

The conglomerate corporation, however, is a different species. Its component parts are unrelated in the conventional, "anti-competitive" ways that were taboo in the past. While promoters claim that conglomerates make possible the cross-fertilization of the knowledge and talents of the people involved, there are numerous special reasons why business managers of firms engaged in retail distribution, insurance, broadcasting, banking and so on, prefer to grow through merger rather than internal growth. Aside from a variety of tax, financial, and personal advantages for the individuals and the business enterprise involved, the acquisition of leading competitors enables the acquiring firm to become dominant in the industry. Product-related mergers (all chemical products or all food and kindred products, for example) have resulted in multimarket firms which have successfully eliminated potential competitors. Firms that hold commanding positions in one or more highly concentrated industries can enjoy high, non-competitive profits in some markets.[2] To what extent does the conglomerate corporation pose a threat to our free enterprise system, which relies upon market forces to keep competitors from becoming too powerful?

Students in the 'Seventies

Such, in rough, broad strokes is our socio-economic stage. In the center stands the student of the 'seventies. He is confidently looking forward to the recoding of genes, interplanetary space travel, and instantaneous communication with any spot on earth. Should we be surprised, then, if the "Now Generation" is unwilling to let his economic system be guided by Adam Smith's leisurely "invisible hand"? Unlike his depression-reared elders, he is undaunted by fears of depression and is impatient, discouraged, and disheartened by the slow process by which "the establishment" is dealing with the malaise of society—poverty, race, and war. In an age of "instant solutions" (real or imaginary), he is frustrated—and often just plain bored—by an educational system that deals all too heavily in "values" and too lightly in "discipline" during an era in which society is reevaluating both social change and personal expectations.

Indeed, impatience seems to be an understatement. Alienated youth is increasingly developing its own subculture, its own language, and its own set of values and interests that differ in many respects from the goals and pursuits of the rest of society. Today's activists demand courses that are interesting, motivating, and relevant. With words, expletives, and explosives, college dissidents, the Black Panthers and the Young Lords are denouncing capitalism and spouting the "higher virtues of a strange amalgam of Marxism and Maoism." (Lately, they have been joined by the so-called "radical economists" in the universities who contend that orthodox economics cannot deal with the important problems of modern society since it is based on the acceptance of the *status quo* in social relations.)

2. Staff Report on the Federal Trade Commission, *Economic Report on Corporate Mergers*, Washington, D.C.: Government Printing Office, 1969, pp. 71-72.

In the long run, the current revolution in American education will probably be the gravest and most dangerous threat that we face in the 'seventies. Turbulence and tension are so pervasive as to make any exercise in rational discussion almost impossible. Indeed, many radical students assume that "the revolution" is not far off, and hence consider activism more important than their studies under the circumstances.

The cult of "doing your own thing" has many worshippers. In a sense, this modern phenomenon actually demonstrates tremendous faith in the existing economic system. Living in and confronting an obviously successful economy, many activists take the American economic system for granted. (Indeed, many have known no other experience than that of relative prosperity.) Unfortunately, there are few rituals, little mysticism, and apparently little mystique in the prosaic worship of the market economy which seemingly pours out endless goodies.

The mentality displayed by today's romantic youth toward economic problems—we refer to the heartfelt approach to problems rather than to the mind-probing one—betrays a greater need than ever before for economic education. A Harvard College dropout describes this type of approach vividly:

> I learned more about economics in Paris coffee houses than I learned at Harvard, or have since. But before that, at the end of the freshman year, I went to New York: I still haven't gotten over that. I saw people sleeping in the gutter. I decided that I was a Communist.[3]

The academic-minded Communist of the Great Depression years would be somewhat startled at the spontaneous generation of "instant communism" in the affluent 'seventies!

Students fail to see, for example, how economics, encrusted in the symbols, numbers, and curves of explanation, ultimately acts for reform "to enhance the services of man." Students certainly are more aware of the demands on the economy than the state of the economy and its capabilities. They have all heard much about the new concerns centering on "the quality of life," urban blight, environmental pollution, poverty, the economics of race, increased consumer protection, and the reordering of national priorities. Yet economic growth is basic to bringing about improvement in our physical and social surroundings. Economics teaches, if nothing else, the prin-

---

3. Richard Todd, "Voices of Harvard '70," *New York Times Magazine*, June 7, 1970, p. 62.

ciple of opportunity costs: that the satisfaction of a particular need is at the expense of other needs. And, the decrying of a growing Gross National Product, in view of the *extra* demands being made on the economic system, logically is Kafkaesque!

Up to now, academe has borne the brunt of the "New Left" attacks. Will the battlelines shift to the business arena next? Already annual shareholders' meetings of corporations are frequent targets for disruption by youthful protesters. On another level, the Young Lords oppose "capitalists and alliances with traitors," while eschew-ing violence. When they affirm their opposition to violence, however, it is interpreted to mean "the violence of poverty and profits."[4] To many students ignorant in economics, profits is a dirty word. Grant-ed that there is only a small fraction of students who can be classi-fied as militants and revolutionaries eager to abolish the established economic and political systems, there can nevertheless be little doubt that the support of vigorous dissent against the economic system is manifestly large among college students.

"The Quality of Life"

Throughout the ages, and before there were economists or ecolo-gists, religious leaders and philosophers frequently examined "the quality of life," deploring its material aspects. Among the classic economists, John Stuart Mill and Karl Marx suffused their writings with comments on the need for an improved quality of life. Even conservative Alfred Marshall suggests that economics be used to pro-duce citizens "with cool heads and warm hearts" who would then proceed "to open up to all the material means of a refined and noble life."[5]

In recent years, as we know too well from the media, life's quality in our affluent society has been repeatedly questioned. Not surpris-ingly for the scientific-romantic age in which we live, this has led to "the enduring quest for a happiness index." Indeed, Professor Gar-rett Hardin of the University of California has suggested a new eco-nomic measure: Net National Amenities. Unlike the "given" or neu-tral measurements of economists, this one investigates items "that contribute positively to human well-being"—such as food, shelter, entertainment, and favorable surroundings.

4. José Yglesias, "Right On with the Young Lords," *New York Times Magazine*, June 7, 1970, p. 86.
5. Quoted in Laurence E. Leamer, *The Economist as Teacher*, Cincinnati: South-western Publishing Co., 1965, p. 2.

All this is by way of saying that economics, in spite of the balanced, objective, analytical atmosphere it seeks to create, is being strongly buffeted by the winds of subjective value judgments. At the very moment that students are clamoring for relevance, if not radicalism, the professional economist is devoted to his sharpening of his tools. Economists consider themselves practitioners of an applied science—the applications are concentrated on the science aspects—a concept of questionable status.

Furthermore, "most economic research," admitted the highly respected Brookings Institution, "moves slowly; it is rarely devoted to current developments. And it is usually more abstract than the analysis of current conditions requires." Compounding this problem is the additional one of communication when economists attempt to pass from graphics and equations to verbal interpretations.

Economists in the age of mathematics have carefully avoided value judgments. They seem to have lost sight of the role of values in their subject. Few economists have troubled to ask themselves the purpose of economics, or their obligation to shed light on what ultimately are the "awesome choices" which must be made. In fact, most economists boast that their credo demands concentration on the realities of *what is*, and not *what ought to be*. Paul Samuelson, the pace-setting author of college textbooks, in discussing his recent eighth edition, seems to indicate that an important change in the thinking of economists is being wrought. "The big change this time is that I'm trying to get the smugness, complacency and Establishment economics out of it. I have scrutinized every line and permitted myself more value judgments . . . now people are interested in the problem of inequality of income and race."[6]

The Economic Education Movement

The economic education movement brought the university professor of economics out of his ivory tower to peek into the high school classroom. The American Economic Association was the first professional association to initiate a movement for the reform of the social studies curriculum in the 1960's.[7] It was responsible for a series of reports, beginning with *Economic Education in the Schools* (1961), the report of the National Task Force, which provided the professional economist's view on the economic concepts we should attempt

6. *New York Times,* February 5, 1970.
7. Edwin Fenton, *Teaching the New Social Studies in Secondary Schools: An Inductive Approach,* New York: Holt, Rinehart and Winston, 1966, p. 331.

to teach in our schools; it supported annotated materials evaluation reports; it sponsored a valuable high-school textbook study; and it strongly backed an effective television course entitled "The American Economy," and a Standardized Test of Economic Understanding.

Economists, or at least a devoted and distinguished section of the profession, continue to hold a commanding lead over other social scientists in their involvement with the schools. A session on economic education, conducted by a standing Committee on Economic Education, is held yearly at the annual meetings of the AEA. The meetings are on an "analytical plane," and serve as "a forum for the exchange of information on carefully conducted experiments and measurement problems." In general, the papers are devoted to experiments in the teaching of the introductory undergraduate course in economics.

In addition, the Committee on Economic Education, under the distinguished chairmanship of G.L. Bach, has worked closely with the Joint Council on Economic Education, to stimulate the development of a standardized Test of Understanding in College Economics; the Committee is conducting a national survey on the effectiveness of programmed learning in teaching economics at the college level; it is testing the effectiveness of small-group teaching compared to larger section sizes, and is pursuing a study on the lasting effects of college elementary courses. The Committee also is attempting to stimulate the development of a few basic courses which can be evaluated and made available to junior colleges and other institutions lacking "enough trained economists to do the developmental work themselves."

Recently, with "the advice and counsel" of the Committee, the JCEE launched *The Journal of Economic Education*, a magazine devoted to improving "the information flow on experiments and alternative approaches to the teaching of economics prevailing at the college level."

Among the greatest successes of the economic education movement we must surely consider materials and evaluation of materials; in particular, the improvement and substantial upgrading of high school textbooks in economics. A prior look by a special committee of the AEA in 1963 labelled the previous crop "appalling."[8] A new

8. "Economics in the Schools. A Report by a Special Textbook Study Committee of the Committee on Economic Education of the American Economic Association," *American Economic Review*, Supplement, March 1963.

look at high school textbooks in 1969 revealed that five of the new texts—of the twelve texts on the market—now substantially meet the minimum criteria set forth by the previous committee report. So improved are the texts that there now exists an imbalance between the books and the abilities of the teachers who use them.

Speaking of the need to allocate more economic education resources to upgrade the economics preparation of high school teachers, the report continued: "It is questionable whether this task, like that of the texts, can be accomplished substantially within a decade."[9]

Unfortunately, the economic components of the United States history text and other senior high school social studies books still leave much to be desired. Regarding economics in history courses, an outstanding economist comments that "the quality of the non-professional economics is simply deplorable. . . . Nothing courteous could be said about such economic analysis."[10]

Approaches of Professional Economists

Having said all this, one must pause and examine the type of service offered by the professional economists. How do they contribute toward preparing students to think intelligently about major economic problems in modern society? There can be little doubt about the high level of the consulting economists. However, one must question their expertise in economic education programs in the schools.

Today's trained economist is preoccupied with the analytical tools of the trade and its mathematical supports—differential calculus and advanced statistics—for research ends. Understanding plays a secondary role to skills—a reversal of the training of social studies teachers. Emphasis on quantitative analysis and theory gives many undergraduate courses the appearance of applied mathematics courses.

In the next ten to twenty years, college students will be trained in the methodology of model building, with "dimensional analysis, the theory of measurement and numerical taxonomy," together with the theory of forces and a digital computer simulation. Unfortunately, the shorthand of mathematics does not provide verbal arguments for drawing conclusions or offering policy prescriptions.

9. Norman Townsend-Zellner, *A New Look at High School Economics Texts*, Center for Economic Education, California State College at Fullerton, 1970, pp. 28, 54.

10. George J. Stigler, "The Case, If Any, for Economic Literacy," *The Journal of Economic Education*, Spring 1970, p. 82. Also see Albert Alexander, "Does the American History Textbook Still Wear a Gray Flannel Cover?", *Social Education* March, 1969.

What most economists seem to forget—as one economist admitted "with the arrogance that characterizes our profession"—is that few high school students excel at abstract studies. No more than five percent, for example, study high school physics. College graduates reared on a diet of economic mathematical analysis will hardly, if they choose a teaching career, be fit teachers for economic education programs for the schools. Price theory, already unnecessarily complicated and unnecessarily abstract, will become even more so.

So intense is the appeal of models and figures (mathematical, of course) that many professors would, if they could, squeeze out the social matrix as early as the elementary course. When informed that students might be coming to college with better preparation in economics, one professor was delighted. "This may enable us to abbreviate the institutional background material in the elementary course and get more quickly into the meat of the subject." The "meat" in this case meant "exploring analytical tools and applying these tools to descriptive policy questions . . . We need to teach a narrower range of concepts, but really to teach them, almost in drillmaster fashion. And we should remember that using economic tools to interpret events in the economy and to analyze policy issues helps to clarify the meaning of tools."[11]

Increasingly, economists seek a grounding in differential calculus and abstract statistics. Specialization abounds—the AEA lists a full page of specialties. Economics, it would seem, is rapidly putting itself into the position of the modern physicist whose studies transformed the simple model of the nineteenth-century atom into a veritable scientific jungle.

Graduate education is increasingly elevating itself to teaching tools: analytical tools in general and mathematical tools in particular. Obviously, new graduates for whom tools are the whole of economics will determine the content of future introductory courses. Again, this will leave "most liberal arts students in general and potential teachers in particular thoroughly convinced that economics is indeed a dismal science."[12] Devoting "a significant portion of the introductory course explicitly to applications of analysis and solutions of poverty problems might well make both economics and economists more self-reliant—and so make economics significantly less dis-

11. Lloyd G. Reynolds, "Discussion," *Papers and Proceedings, American Economic Review*, May 1969.
12. Henry H. Villard, "Discussion," *Papers and Proceedings, American Economic Review*, May 1968.

mal."[13] There is a great need to make abstractions meaningful, to involve students, and to discuss relevant problems.

It may seem strange to some that one should have to pose the question of relevance in economics. What subject could be closer to earning one's daily bread? the sociosphere? human relations? Unfortunately, as economics is now "structured," it is of more interest to the economist than to the general public. In its obsession with mathematics, economics seems to have severed its links with the vast new learning in the field of social relations. Certainly, the use of economics as a tool for fashioning a better society is not uppermost in the minds of economists who freely state that they are not concerned with values. Moreover, questions of interest to economists are not always relevant to society. Problems related to collective decision-making, group and community life, group identity, public goods, and the grants economy—to cite a few examples—have been generally neglected by economists who boast that what the student has learned in college has been "not only institution-free, but value-free as well." However, economic behavior, it must be remembered, always takes place in a society patterned with political institutions. And, an understanding of economics by all is ultimately necessary for the functioning of a self-governing society increasingly marked by collective economic decision-making. For effective citizenship, students need a good reading knowledge of economics within a liberal arts format. This makes a good high school course in economics essential.

Criteria for a Twelfth-Grade Course

What would be the criteria for a one-semester twelfth-grade economics course, geared to the demands of the 'seventies?

First, it should be a realistic, relevant, down-to-earth course which attempts to create a lifelong interest in "real world" economic problems. It would foster economic understanding for citizenship in the sense in which the National Task Force uses the term, that is, it would provide an introduction to the economic process: to concepts, facts, and principles. It would aim to develop the kind of economic understanding needed to function responsibly as a citizen and a decision-maker in a democratic, basically private enterprise economy. In short, it should be politically-oriented (political economy, if you will).

Second, a good twelfth-grade course would present an overview of

13. *Ibid.,* p. 49.

our economic system, its institutions, and its problems. The course would start with the economic problem; what, how, how much, for whom; the scheme and process of economizing, opportunity costs, and the meaning of the term: economic system. While the basic structure of the discipline would be emphasized throughout the course, it would of necessity also describe economic institutions because before a person can think analytically about, let us say, the farm problem as it exists in the United States and in the Soviet Union today, he must know in each instance what the facts really are. And, in the process, he must unlearn a great deal of economic folklore too.

Third, the course would develop a disciplined way of thinking intelligently about society's major economic problems. This goal can best be met by teaching a few basic principles—the fundamental tools of economics—and then applying them to a number of vital problems involving an understanding of private and public policy issues. Student reaction and understanding ultimately must go beyond the mathematical obstacle course that the professional economist has designed. Since a choice in public policy becomes more and more compelling, the necessity for understanding the lessons of logic and choice becomes more necessary.

How we phrase an economic problem is important. If we are dealing with the problem of poverty, we should concern ourselves with the realities of the situation: What should be done? How should we do it? What are the alternatives and costs involved?

Fourth, it would provide a preview of the scope and methods of economics against which subsequent courses either in high school or college should take on added meaning. In short, it would develop a few simple models which would serve as tools for continuing economic analysis, but it would stress understanding more than mathematic skills. During the 1950's, concern for economic growth was the great obsession. During the 1960's the stress was on the amelioration of poverty. During the 'seventies, ecological matters loom as major problems. But, with a basic kit of economic tools in his possession, the high school student of the 'seventies will be better equipped to understand the new *cause célébre* of the 1980's and 1990's.

Fifth, the economics of the 'seventies would not shy away from current controversial issues. It would try to capture "some of the excitement that is economics," that is, "a sense of unresolved issues, of free men grappling with choices that involve trade-offs—a little more success in achieving full employment coming perhaps at the expense of a little less success in maintaining stable prices."[14] It would nurture in high school students, within their capacities, skill in the use of their basic tool kit of economic analysis to explore the issues surrounding medicare, collective bargaining, farm price policy, ecological problems, the military-industrial complex, and public spending which makes economics so perplexing, so fascinating, and so infuriating to many people.

In short, economics should weave together the worlds of "what is" and "what ought to be." Admittedly, discussing values in class carries controversy with it, but an antiseptic approach is both dull and unreal in high school.

Sixth, the economics course of the 'seventies would be a selective course. It would present evidence of the "courage to exclude" as well as the "imagination to include." Elementary textbooks, seeking to incorporate new developments and to keep up with graduate instruction, tend to become abridged economic dictionaries. While John R. Coleman discovered no single way to be most effective in teaching economics, he set up certain direction signs: Teach less, but teach in greater depth. Emphasize the ties between economics and the various social studies. Stress critical thinking with the use of raw data and sources which provide "evidence." And develop and use new materials in greater abundance.[15]

It would be a boon for all students—but especially for the underprivileged and the non-academic child—if we would "recapture the simplicity and grasp the essentials which distinguished the early works of political economy."[16] Failure to deal with the economic world as students live it may alienate them, encourage imitation, or induce an escapist attitude. We must "teach how to research," "teach how to learn," and "teach how to innovate." In economics, as in other subject areas, we have failed to come to grips with real needs of students, and particularly those of the non-academic-minded student.

Christine P. Ingraham, in *Education for the Slow-Learning Child*, says that the non-academic type of student constitutes 15-18 percent of the school population. And, for a variety of reasons, he now stays in school longer, so that he will continue to be a problem for economics teachers. For these students, appropriate and varied teaching

14. John R. Coleman, "Second Thoughts on Economics in the Schools," *Social Education*, February, 1965, p. 77.
15. Joint Council on Economic Education, *Newsletter*, May, 1964, p. 8.
16. Jean Coussy, "Adjusting Economics Curricula to African Needs," *International Social Science Journal*, Vol. XXI, No. 3, 1969. p. 394.

techniques are necessary. Teachers must often prepare their own classroom learning materials, designed to meet their needs and abilities. *Reach* before you *teach* is the order of the day. Responsibilities are incumbent upon the teacher beyond the subject matter—which must be kept simple—and these include the teaching of reading comprehension and study habits. The teacher must always appeal to such students as consumers, producers, union members, and taxpayers. The role of the teenager in the economy—his importance, contributions, and problems—serves as intrinsic motivation.

Preparation of Teachers

Few advocates can be found who are willing to suggest replacements of the teacher by electronic and other mechanical equipment. Students need teachers, if only to decry them! Hence, when we understand that only about half of the nation's 60,000 social studies teachers have ever undertaken formal study of economics, the major problem in economic education confronts us.[17] No more than 50 percent of all prospective social studies teachers take a course in economics for their preparation—in most cases only one.[18] A 1968 survey of the Joint Council on the state requirements for certification reveals that 22 states require no economics courses for high school teachers of economics. Even more states have no requirements in economics for teachers of social studies in high school (36), junior high (38), and elementary schools (17).

G.L. Bach and P. Saunders, in a now famous survey, concluded that there is little lasting effect from study in fewer than five courses.[19] Acting upon this conclusion, an Advisory Seminar to the California State Department of Education drew up a Report and Recommendations delineating *College Preparation for Teaching Economics* (1966). A minor in economics with 21 semester hours was recommended for teachers of grade-twelve semester courses in economics. For all social studies teachers, grades 7-11, a three-course sequence in economics would be mandated, while all teachers K-12 would be responsible for a basic course of three semester hours stressing economic reasoning, basic concepts and models, and applications to problems and policy situations.

17. G.G. Dawson, *Nationwide Survey on Economic Education of Teacher-Trainers*, New York: Joint Council on Economic Education, 1967.
18. M.L. Frankel, *Proceedings of a Symposium on Public Policy and Economic Understanding*, N.Y.: American Bankers Association, 1970, p. 50.
19. G.L. Bach and P. Saunders, "Lasting Effects of Economics Courses at Different Institutions," *American Economic Review*, June, 1966.

It would be difficult to quarrel with these suggested requirements for teacher certification. Realistically, of course, we are confronted with the present mathematical orientation of the profession, a matter we already have discussed. No doubt the Advisory Seminar was aware of this when it cautioned: "Guidelines are of little avail if economists in the departments of economics do not seriously consider their adoption and implementation." (p. 11)

"Quality of life" is the great concern of the revolutionary 'seventies. In essence the critics of the Establishment are voicing their frustrations against an economic world too slow to meet the challenges of providing the qualitative and quantitative changes necessary for new life styles. The need for economic education is indeed more relevant today than a generation ago because of these demands. Although gratifying progress has been made in this area, the professional economist too often appears unconvinced that his discipline is for the layman. If real progress is to be made toward economic literacy the economist must abandon his never-never land, which unfortunately becomes more and more remote from the economic perplexities of the ordinary citizen.

AN ECONOMICS UNIT THAT
REALLY WORKS!

by

James Powell

The idea for the following project came on the spur of the moment one morning in an 8th grade United States Government class. Since our 15 minute homeroom or advisory period is a part of the 1st hour, I had been searching for subjects and materials to use as media for a continuous guidance project.

We were beginning the study of a chapter on Money, Banking, and Consumer Buying. A well motivated discussion of student savings accounts proceeded. This was the springboard for the basic idea of our project.

I asked the class to determine how much a student could save this year if only one cent per day could be set aside. Tommy figured very quickly that one cent saved for 180 school days would be $1.80. This did not seem to strike a real spark with the class until Marilyn asked, "What would the amount be if the entire class saved one cent per day?" A few moments later Janet reported that the class could save $63. The group expressed great amazement that only one cent per day saved by each of our 36 members could build such a large amount of money in such an elementary way.

David, who was overly endowed with energy and enthusiasm remarked, "Let's do it!" Without any thought on my part, I answered, "Ok, it's a deal!" Hands with pennies in them ready to contribute to this activity were raised before another word was said.

With much interest created in only a few moments, I realized that the idea held all kinds of possibilities. I began to jot down ideas about how the activity could be organized. One thought led to another until two pages were filled with questions and ideas.

First, I knew there must be a good reason for saving the money. Would these funds need to go through the financial office of our school, and would this meet school policy? What accounting system would be necessary? When the amount grew to ten or 15 dollars, what would we do with it? Would all students in the class contribute each day? Could more than one cent per day be deposited by stu-

From the *Oklahoma Teacher*, January 1971. Used by permission of the Oklahoma Education Association.

dents? Would parents critize such an activity? Would the class interest die in a few weeks? How much time would this project consume
each day? What would the end result be with the money collected?
Just how much educational value is in such an activity? After thinking over each question in greater depth, I began to find answers and
solutions, at least in my mind.

I had heard of other schools, both junior and senior high, having
project studies about banking, money, stock markets and budgeting.
I had in past years touched on these subjects briefly myself, but in
no detail. In some cases I had heard of projects where the teacher
had allotted each student in class a certain amount of money to buy
stock and in this way he could watch his stock in the paper each day.
But the whole activity takes place only on paper in a classroom,
play-acting type situation. This is fine, but the students are not exposed to reality, and I am fairly sure that interest falls by the way-
side quickly.

Young students desire immediate action. Detailed theory of money, banking, stockmarket, budgeting, and interest earned on money,
they would not tolerate. We would organize a bank both in practice
and theory at the same time.

Each student expressed interest and willingness to participate in
this activity in a written commitment. After discussing the duties of
the officials of a bank, we agreed we would need only a president,
vice president, secretary, and treasurer. Although we would deviate
from actual banking procedures, we would pattern our bank as nearly as possible after the mechanics of a real bank.

Since all students would be future stockholders, everyone would
be eligible to hold an office if elected. We wrote the four offices on
the board and those who were interested in the positions listed their
names under the position wanted. Almost half the class volunteered
as candidates. We voted by secret ballot and elected four officers.

The secretary and treasurer were given the task of making a roster
of all students so that deposits could begin the following day. This
ledger method for use in collecting and accounting for individual
deposits must be kept very simple. This roster was marked off in
columns for the remainder of the year. Each monthly column was
divided into four sections representing the weeks in a month. Our
secretary suggested marking an X for each one cent deposited.

During a previous discussion, the class decided that any amount of
money could be deposited at any one time. This of course, would
make it possible for some students to deposit money ahead for weeks
or months. The secretary and treasurer worked as a team of tellers

when deposits were taken. They moved to the back of the room at the beginning of each day.

The treasurer supplied an idea that proved to be a real time saver. Envelopes were given to all those who wished to make a deposit that morning. They wrote their names on the envelopes and the amount they wished to deposit. These were given to the secretary to be recorded. This procedure eliminates unnecessary movement and noise in class and there needed to be no line waiting to do business. The names were marked off and envelopes were ready for use again the next day.

To keep a record balance of money deposited, a ledger book with the following columns: date, deposits, withdrawals, and balance, was used. In this way we could audit the accounts each day.

Since everyone in the class was participating, the next discussion concerned the subject of stock. How would we determine the value of the stock and distribute shares of stock in our organization? We kept our discussion pointed toward how corporations organize by means of selling stocks. We decided to issue one stock certificate which would equal one share of stock for each one cent deposited.

An interesting experience occurred when a name for our organization was needed. All students were invited to submit one or more names on pieces of paper. Quite a variety of names were offered and at this time the officers worked as a committee to select the best five names to be voted upon later by the entire class. When voting was completed, our organization was called, "THE KIDS OF E104 SAVINGS AND LOAN."

Now our organization had a name, officers, and stock holders. Deposits were coming in daily. We were taking no longer than the fifteen minute advisory period each morning to conduct this business. Occasionally at the very beginning of organization more time was needed, but this was kept at a minimum.

The next step was to elect a board of directors to make policy for the corporation. All stockholders agreed that the four officers would automatically become board members. It was agreed by the membership that six more members would be selected, making a total of ten on the board of directors. This was accomplished by having those who were interested volunteer and then elected by vote of the entire group in the same manner we used for the election of officers.

After three weeks the treasurer reported that deposits amounted to $7.02. Now came a most important decision. What were we going to do with the money at the end of the school year?

We used the chalk board to list ideas so that all could see. Again by voting, we eliminated all choices but two. One was to purchase a school banner with our school name and emblem on it to be used by our marching band. The other idea was to have our emblem and name painted on the base drum which had never been done at our school before. All students seemed quite happy with the two ideas for which the money would be spent. A few days later we found that the banner would cost $117.50. Linda was the first to ask the question which most were thinking. It would cost about $170.00 for both banner and drum. How could we accomplish this if our yearly deposits amount to only $63.00?

This introduced a new subject in our continuous study of the banking business. We spent the next few days discussing the various methods used by savings and loan associations and banks to make money, other than charging interest on loans. After all this is a business and banks operate to do a service for the public, but most of all they operate to make a profit for their stockholders.

What could we do in our organization to increase our capital? We knew that we were not paying out interest on savings like real banks do, but why not loan money and charge interest? This would make some extra money.

The board of directors met to formulate policies and methods for loaning the money we had on hand.

Loans would be made to our homeroom group only. No loan would be for more than 50 cents. All loans must be paid back in seven days. Rate of interest would be ten per cent. A promissory note must be signed by the borrower and collateral put up to secure the loan. The item of collateral must have a value worth more than the amount borrowed. The note could also be secured by having a co-signer who must have the necessary collateral.

It was an easy task to bring to the attention of the class a discussion on realistic interest rates used by real banks. They understood we were really charging a very high rate of interest—ten per cent for only seven days. Several loan forms obtained from a local bank were explained as used in actual banking procedures. After giving a short quiz I found that most students understood such terms as default, foreclosure, bankruptcy, garnishee, credit rating, security, mortgage, and assets. These were the terms we were using in our own transactions.

The secretary and treasurer again took the job of designing a promissory note form and making a master ditto so it could be reproduced and on hand for our customers. The loan business began to thrive, especially when lunch money was forgotten, or an afternoon assembly was scheduled by the music or drama department which usually cost 50c to attend. Also, basketball games and wrestling matches after school offered good prospects for making loans. Loans were always made during the first hour in the morning because students at this time knew of the activity and their need for money to attend. If they had forgotten their money then we made the loan.

A few mornings later Darla seemed disturbed and finally admitted that she could not see how it would be possible for our organization to have the necessary $170.00 to meet our obligations by the time school closed in May. At the rate we were progressing at this time she figured we would do well to have a total of $75.00.

Banks, we agreed, make most of their profit by loaning out money at a higher rate of interest than they pay in interest to their depositors. We also found that a real bank invests its surplus money in various stocks, bonds, or governmental securities. We reasoned that it would be proper for our organization to raise assets by accepting other activities. So we began to deviate from actual banking procedures in an effort to make money.

Students agreed to make and donate chocolate fudge to be brought to school the following Friday. This would be sold after school near the front entrance where most of the students leave our building. On Friday morning 14 boxes of fudge were brought to my desk. Selling seemed to be more fun for them than the idea of making money for the bank. In fifteen minutes we had increased our bank capital by $14.15.

A few weeks later students who did not furnish fudge decided to bring homemade cookies and brownies. On that Friday we earned $2.73 and found that candy sold much better to our student body than cookies.

Some time later we discovered a type of cinnamon sucker we would purchase wholesale and when sold for 5c each, we would make $25.00 profit on each carton we sold. The carton cost $12.00 which we paid for from our funds on hand, and after a few sales after school, we had increased our assets another $25.00.

It was time now, I thought, to enter into another phase of economics by way of the stock market. The students had become familiar from normal classroom conversation with the terms stocks, bonds, and similar words. Our library furnished copies of the daily newspaper to each student, so we devoted a couple of days to looking over the stocks listed on the New York and American Stock Exchanges. I also scheduled a local stock broker to come and explain the market in some detail for us. On this day we used the entire class period instead of the usual 15 minutes. I was familiar with one stock found in the over the counter group of stocks, and with a recommendation from the broker, the stockholders of our organization decided to buy ten shares. This amounted to $38.75 which was paid for out of our cash assets. What a joy it was for me to find these 8th grade students checking the market each morning before they came to school to see how their stock was listed the day before!

The class had been in their banking business for six months when Linda wanted to know if there were any possibilities of ordering the banner and charging it until we had the money available to pay for it. The board of directors met and made plans to draw up a request to the principal to see if funds were available for such a loan. The letter was drafted in the form of a request, contract, and promissory note all in one. Since our organization's assets are tied up until May 15th when we will liquidate all assets, our request was for a loan from the general fund in the amount of $117.50. This would completely pay for the banner. The loan was approved by the principal and the board of education. The banner was purchased and presented to the band for use the remainder of the school year.

Our savings and loan association had been in operation for seven months now, had assets in the amount of $139.40 with about three more operating weeks to go. Our second project, painting the bass drum was later completed.

It is with a great deal of pleasure that we share our experiences with others so that those interested may have as much fun as we did.

A "BLUE CHIP" TEACHING UNIT

by

Robert M. Bruker

It may well be that we are indebted to the Soviet Union for the launching of one of the most massive educational aid programs this country has ever known. Shortly after the first Sputnik was placed in orbit around the earth, Congress passed the National Defense Education Act and in the decade since its enactment, this piece of legislation has enabled many schools to improve the science training of our youth.

Though the NDEA constituted a "crash program" for the sciences and mathematics it did produce some ancillary results for other academic disciplines. The group most aware of the rapid dislocations which come in the wake of scientific advances is the social scientists. Of all the social sciences, Economics is the most underdeveloped area of the high school curriculum. While I would not be radical enough to propose that every high school offer course work in economics, I would certainly urge that every high school include a meaningful unit on economic education in their social studies classes and that the focal point of this unit be the stock market.

For sometime I have been concerned over the American high school student's apparent lack of understanding of the stock market and the world of investing. Even the simplest terms in the investment jargon are usually confusing to many high school students. Our economic system is often defended with such trite expressions as, "we have the highest standard of living in the world," or "our freedom of enterprise gives us the right to work at any job we choose." High school students who can merely present well-worn cliches (often of doubtful validity), which are the product of memorization rather than of reflective thinking, will not fare well in defending our capitalistic system against other economic systems.

One of the most important things we can teach students who intend to terminate their education with attainment of age sixteen or the completion of high school, is an understanding of our economic system. Traditional social studies instruction is evolutionary and be-

Reprinted from the *Peabody Journal of Education*, May 1968 © George Peabody College for Teachers. Used by permission of the author and the publisher.

gins with the home. From here it gradually spreads to the community, the city, county and state, and finally the nation, with the major emphasis always on growth. High school students should become more involved in the economic life of America; this can best be accomplished by having them purchase a share of stock and becoming a "capitalist."

This certainly isn't an unique idea, it is being practiced in several schools throughout the country. The New York Stock Exchange is keenly interested in the project and employs a full-time educational consultant to assist teachers whenever possible. In addition, they publish a series of booklets, *You And The Investment World*, which is an excellent supplement to textbook material.

A project of this sort must begin with the teacher and an adviser. Nearly every community has a broker or a securities dealer who is associated with a brokerage firm in a larger city. These men and the firms they represent are always willing to help the schools with personal visits and audio-visual presentations. With a few hours of preparation the teacher and adviser can lay the foundation for an extremely exciting and worthwhile teaching unit.

At this time it would seem prudent to set forth several guidelines which should be adhered to:

1. The main objective of a stock-purchase project should be educational. No promise of profit should be made to the students.

2. Conversely, there is an element of risk inherent in any investment and a loss is not impossible. As a matter of fact, considering the cost involved in buying and disposing of small amounts of stock, and the fact that it will be held for such a short time, a loss might be expected. This possibility could be used as a valuable lesson.

3. Monetary participation in the project should be on a voluntary basis. Whether a subject contributes money to the stock purchase or not, he will profit from the experience and be able to participate in other phases of the project.

4. The amount of money to be invested should be determined by the students. Judging from past experience, I would suggest placing a limit on the amount each student could invest. If one student gets too much control of the stock the educational objectives of the unit could be seriously impaired.

5. Competition between the classes should be kept to a minimum as this also could overshadow the objectives of the unit.

6. Near the close of the school year the stock should be sold and the money received pro-rated among the participating members of the class.

Newspapers play a vital role in this unit and the class should never be at a loss for financial news. Most school libraries subscribe to several newspapers and every student has access to a paper in his own or a friend's home. Obviously, in order to be of value, the newspaper must contain financial news and the stock market quotations. Some classes may elect to take a special six-month subscription to *The Wall Street Journal.* I have found that once the stock is actually purchased students will by-pass even the sports section and comic pages to see what the market is doing.

The actual classroom phase of the unit begins with a discussion of capital as a tool used to produce goods. Capital is not necessarily money, it may take the form of a factory, a truck, or even a farm. Money is a medium which may be used to purchase these tools. The sources of capital and the methods used by corporations to obtain capital should be fully covered in this discussion.

Following the discussion of capital, the teacher and adviser introduce the financial pages of the newspaper and explain how to read stock market quotations. This lesson should evolve around these questions:

1. Who can purchase stock?
2. What determines the price of stock?
3. How does a stock exchange function?
4. Why do corporations offer stock for sale to the public?
5. How are those events described on page one of the newspaper reflected in the financial pages?

As soon as the students possess the vocabulary of the investment world and understand its basic concepts, they should elect "student brokers." These brokers will hold a series of meetings with the teacher and the adviser to discuss the salient features of various stocks. After narrowing their possibilities to seven or eight stocks, which they consider good investments, the student brokers report to their class on the progress which has been made. After questioning the brokers and making known their arguments for and against the various stocks the class members vote for their preference. Certificates of ownership can be drawn-up and presented to those students who participate in the project.

As social studies teachers we should be concerned with teaching about economic as well as political democracy and pointing up the opportunities which exist under our system of free enterprise. A project of this type can be utilized in most high school social studies classes and perhaps with certain junior high groups as well. Teachers can perform an invaluable service to students by introducing them to the remote and often mysterious world of the stock market and providing a philosophical and operational understanding of our country's economic system.

V. Political Science

POLITICAL STUDIES IN THE SCHOOLS[1]

by
Robert E. Cleary
Donald H. Riddle

A basic controversy exists in the United States as well as abroad over the primary purpose of the study of politics in the elementary and secondary school. Most political scientists feel that politics should be studied for the same reason other areas of knowledge should be studied: to acquaint an individual with information, to allow him to expand his ability to reason, to give him every opportunity to be a thinking, functioning individual—in short, to allow him to become an educated man. Within this framework, a second-order goal of political studies in the United States is to acquaint students with the nature of government and politics, especially American government and politics.

A number of educators have argued that the immediate objective of political studies in the schools is carefully oriented toward a related but somewhat different goal. Good citizenship is so important to our nation and is so difficult to develop, it is declared, that the making of good citizens must be the immediate objective. Good citizenship is extremely important in a democracy. Americans are far from agreement, however, on what it involves. Who is to define good citizenship? One man's good citizen is another man's criminal. What about civil rights demonstrations, sit-ins, and the whole role of peaceful protest in American society, for example? Even if good citizenship were to be defined, how can it be attained? Not only is the concept a nebulous one, but it involves attitudes and values that are extremely difficult to form. It may even be self-defeating in many situations to attempt to structure them.[2] Moreover, good citizenship is likely to be influenced more by developments outside the school

Reprinted from *The Educational Forum*, May 1968. Used by permission of Kappa Delta Pi, an Honor Society in Education.

Robert E. Cleary is Associate Dean in the School of Government at the American University. He is specializing, as a political scientist, in problems of civic education in the schools. Donald H. Riddle is Dean of the Faculty at John Jay College of Criminal Justice, City University of New York.

1. This article is adapted from Chapter I of *Political Science in the Social Studies*, the 36th Yearbook of the National Council for the Social Studies, and appears with the permission of the National Council.

2. For an excellent discussion of the complexity of desirable civic attitudes, see Gabriel Almond and Sidney Verba, *The Civic Culture: Political Attitudes and Democracy in Five Nations* (Boston: Little, Brown, 1963).

than by those in the classroom, for academic instruction plays only a small role in the formation of the attitudes and habits of citizenship.

To the extent that the values of citizenship can be developed in the classroom, an honest inquiry into the nature of government and political interaction is more likely to result in good citizenship than a controlled attempt to develop particular attitudes and ideas. Good citizenship is a goal of political study, but the way to achieve this goal is through an effort to enlarge student horizons. In this sense there is nothing unique about the study of politics as compared with other social sciences, and no need to orient instruction to conform to a particular mold.

What, then, is the place of political science as a discipline in the elementary or the secondary school classroom? A number of educators and political scientists have argued in recent years that pre-college students should become familiar with the nature of political science as a discipline. For example, Jerome Bruner develops the thesis that the structures of the various intellectual disciplines should form the framework for the elementary and secondary school curriculum.[3]

Evron M. and Jeane J. Kirkpatrick argue that "One of the most important responsibilities of the secondary school teacher is to inform students about the existence of a field of inquiry into government and politics and to give them some indication of the complexity and difficulty of many public problems. . . . [While it is not] possible to make political scientists out of secondary school students . . . it is possible to teach secondary school students something about political science: what it is, what it does, the complexity and the difficulty of the problems it deals with."[4]

Norton Long declares that education in the social studies has a threefold objective: acquainting students with factual knowledge and a means of ordering it, imparting an understanding of the methods of inquiry and verification, and imparting an appreciation of the basic values of our society.[5]

Bruner feels, then, that the disciplines should provide the framework for social studies education, the Kirkpatricks believe pupils should know what political science is, and Long feels that the student should be acquainted with the broad outline of political science

3. Jerome Bruner, *The Process of Education* (Cambridge, Mass.: Harvard University Press, 1960).

4. Evron M. Kirkpatrick and Jeane J. Kirkpatrick, "Political Science," in *High School Studies Perspectives* (Boston: Houghton Mifflin, 1962), p. 122.

5. Norton E. Long, "Political Science," in *The Social Studies and the Social Sciences* (New York: Harcourt, Brace & World, 1962), pp. 88-89.

as a discipline along with its methods of inquiry. Students should know what political science is and they should be acquainted with its scope and methodology. They should also know what it is not.

One thing it is not is a unified science with an agreed-upon structure. Political science *may* provide a useful framework for political studies in the elementary and the secondary school. There are a number of approaches and concepts which *can* provide unity and give order to political studies. The focus of study, however, should not be on political science as a discipline. The main ideas of the discipline might form the framework for study, but the overall purpose of social studies education is not to acquaint young people with the existence of various disciplines such as political science. Rather, within the framework of a cultivation of the intellect, the purpose of political studies is to provide young people with an understanding of the nature of government and its methods of operation.

As Long points out, the social studies educator is attempting to acquaint students with various means of pursuing knowledge, ordering it, and evaluating it. It is not information about political science *per se*, however, which is central to the elementary and secondary school student. With rare exceptions, he is not a scholar attempting to expand the boundaries of knowledge. Instead, he is attempting to expand *his* knowledge about and understanding of government and politics. In this endeavor political science is a tool to be used by the teacher according to the capabilities of the students concerned. Knowledge and understanding are best imparted in a framework, rather than in bits and pieces. Political science can offer a framework that students might employ to organize their study of government. (Actually, it presents a choice of frameworks for such a purpose.)

As students expand their horizons and develop their understandings of the political world, it is likely that they will gradually become acquainted with the existence of the discipline of political science, as well as with some of the leading methods of inquiry used by political scientists. This is desirable, for students should know that the discipline exists and should have an idea of how political scientists are attempting to expand their understanding of government. This is not a goal in itself at the pre-college level, but a means to an end—the improvement of the political understanding of the average student. In doing this, social studies teachers might well utilize much of the information and many of the techniques of political science. A primary result of such an emphasis is quite likely to be the development of better citizens who are knowledgeable about their rights, their duties, and the limitations of reasonable choice in their society and their world.

TEACHING LAW IN THE
ELEMENTARY SCHOOL

by
Joseph C. Johnson, II
Henry L. Sublett, Jr.

It is surprising that the democratic society in which we live, funda-
mentally respectful of the law and dedicated to life governed by it,
has given so little attention to the specific study of legal principles as
a part of the general education of girls and boys. Any concentrated
study of law has been reserved for college students preparing for
careers in it, though students in other fields may take such courses as
business law, tax law, or school law. On the pre-college level, however, little is offered in this field other than the usual civics courses
and indirect approaches to it through other courses in the social
studies curriculum. And, we should remind ourselves, high school is
terminal formal education for many of our citizens.

Some work has been done recently on the matter of acquainting
young people with the law. John Paul Hanna has pioneered in this
field with his book, *Teenagers and the Law.*[2] Ratcliffe and Lee report an interesting Title I project in law instruction for Chicago
inner-city teachers and children at various grade levels.[1] Most of the
general concern, however, seems to call for the study of law at the
secondary school level. The present writers support such study. It
should be part of general education and it is long overdue. Children
everywhere in the United States are bombarded by a network of
laws: laws on the international, national, state, county, city, and
parental levels. Our laws today are proliferated at a much more rapid
rate than they were twenty-five years ago. And, in many cases, new
laws are added with no provision for the repeal of anachronistic ones.
If we wish to help youth grow in real understanding of laws and basic
legal principles, however, the present writers believe that high school
study of the matter should be preceded by a special social studies
unit on law in the upper grades of the elementary school—perhaps at
the fifth or sixth grade level. The following curriculum planning
procedure is suggested as one possible point of departure. Its primary
objective would be to determine the practical feasibility of teaching

Reprinted from the *Peabody Journal of Education*, September 1969. © George
Peabody College for Teachers. Used by permission of the author and the publisher.

certain basic principles of historical and contemporary comparative law by stressing those law bases which have real-life meaning for pre-adolescents.

The initial step could be taken by providing an opportunity at the local level for the involvement of attorneys, elementary school teachers, supervisors, administrators, and curriculum specialists in the planning of an experimental six to eight week curriculum unit. Planning at the local level is important. Without it, specific local educational needs may well be only partially served or negated entirely. It is also believed that local planning will foster development of personalized, meaningful insights and understandings of a particular educational situation at several different levels. At one level, teachers, supervisors, administrators, and curriculum specialists would gain a knowledge and appreciation of certain law principles and their significance for the elementary school child. At another level, attorneys working with these educational personnel would attain a more comprehensive perspective with regard to the educative process. Finally, elementary school pupils would gain a greater knowledge and appreciation of law as it pertains to them individually. Thus, the proposed procedure would make a multi-leveled approach to law through its concomitant individual meanings to the elementary school child, his educational leaders, and society's interpreters of the law.

It is suggested that the planning group engage in a series of intensive sessions, probably on a weekly basis over a period of several months. Planning would include a consideration of teaching procedures and the selection or development of certain reading, evaluation, and discussion materials, grounded in the following major law themes: (1) history and evolution of law, (2) the child and his contractual agreements as they pertain to his monetary responsibilities and peer commitments, (3) certain local laws, and (4) specified comparative state and national laws. In considering the themes, primary attention should be given to materials and experiences which stress the elementary school child and personal meaning these themes can have for him.

After the completion of the planning phase, the unit would be given a trial in the classrooms of the teachers who had taken part in the planning. The unit would be continuously evaluated and modified. Evaluation of the learning of certain aspects of the law themes could take the form of a series of observations utilizing check lists of those points emphasized. Other evaluational procedures might include an appraisal of attitude modification as derived from the results of inventories developed during the planning phase. Educational and legal consultants from the local and regional community could be invited to evaluate the materials and appraisal instruments developed for the unit.

Granted, this curriculum proposal makes provision for the initial accommodation of only a small number of elementary school children. However, the present writers are of the opinion that the theoretical structuring, the involvement of local individuals with differing educational orientations, and the anticipated resultant emphasis on the child and his relationship with the law should adequately compensate for the limitation. We believe that the emergent unit will have significant educational merit. It could provide a basis for generalizing to all upper elementary school children with respect to their knowledge of, and their relationship to the foundation of our civilized society, our laws.

REFERENCES

1. Cahn, Lenore L. (ed.) *Confronting Injustice: The Edmond Cahn Reader.* Boston: Little, Brown and Company, 1966.

2. Hanna, John Paul. *Teenagers and the Law.* Boston: Ginn and Company, 1967.

3. Ratcliffe, Robert H. and John R. Lee. "Law in American Society," *Social Education,* XXXII (April, 1968), 341-344.

4. Starr, Isidore. "Law and the Social Studies," *Social Education,* XXXII (April, 1968), 335-340, 344.

VI. Anthropology

THE ROLE OF ANTHROPOLOGY
IN ELEMENTARY SOCIAL STUDIES

by

Richard L. Warren

The past several decades have seen an accelerated interest in the relationship of anthropology to education and to the social studies curriculum in particular. What began as exploratory questions and speculations, primarily by anthropologists, about the uses to which anthropological theory and data might be put has progressed at this date to ambitious projects in curriculum development involving individuals with a variety of interests and scholarly backgrounds. Furthermore, the social studies teacher who wishes to inform himself of such developments will find available a growing bibliography in which theoretical formulations, the nature and progress of experimental units, and rationales for curriculum revision are treated.[1]

Prior to the initiation of curriculum projects the contribution of anthropology to the social studies was largely the product of the interest and labor of individual teachers and in some instances of particular school systems. Such efforts can in retrospect be subsumed in three categories: (1) courses in anthropology at the high school level, sometimes required, sometimes elective, developed to a considerable degree in private schools; (2) units of study in the elementary schools, generally with a cross-cultural emphasis; (3) the application of certain anthropological concepts to the organization and analysis of traditional social studies material, this primarily at the secondary level but also to a limited degree at the elementary level.

In recent years three projects have been initiated that propose to make contributions to the social studies program at both the elementary and secondary levels in terms of both content and organization. The projects do not encompass the full range of specific activities in which anthropology is being related to the social studies. Nevertheless, in their scope and distinctive emphases they present models that

From *Social Education*, March 1968. Reprinted with permission of the National Council for the Social Studies and Richard L. Warren.

1. See, for example, "Bibliography on Anthropology and Education." Anthropology Curriculum Study Project. Chicago, 1964; Raymond H. Muessig and Vincent R. Rogers. "Suggested Methods for Teachers," in Pertti J. Pelto. *The Study of Anthropology.* Columbus, Ohio: Charles E. Merrill Books, Inc., 1965. pp. 81-116; Robert G. Hanvey. "Anthropology in the Schools." *Educational Leadership* 22:313-316; February 1965.

teachers will find useful to examine. It is therefore appropriate to identify and briefly describe the projects.

The Anthropology Curriculum Study Project[2] sponsored by the American Anthropological Association is preparing and testing three units designed for secondary school world history programs. The units are described as follows:

> One has to do with the very long early career of our species, with man the hunter-gatherer. Another focuses on the major cultural transformation triggered by the beginnings of agriculture: the growth of peasant and urban societies. The third provides a model for analyzing historical societies in anthropological terms and applies the model to the analysis of classical Greece.[3]

In their totality the units are planned to cover a period of twelve to fifteen weeks. The units do not presume a background for the teacher in anthropology; each provides a series of detailed lesson plans, a wealth of supportive teaching aids, and selected essays by anthropologists on subjects appropriate to the units. While these units are prepared for secondary schools, they are, in the opinion of this writer, in their form, content and emphasis germane to a consideration of anthropology in the elementary social studies curriculum.

A second major project is the Anthropology Curriculum Project at the University of Georgia that is engaged in preparing units for "A Sequential Curriculum in Anthropology for Grades One—Seven." The first units, to be used with grades one and four, now in various stages of preparation, testing, and revision, have focused on the concept of culture. The units include relevant background essays by anthropologists, extensive background material for teachers, texts and study guides for pupils, and illustrated booklets on several primitive cultures. Throughout the material there is considerable emphasis on the need to master the vocabulary of anthropological theory and research:

> Anthropological material is frequently used in the public school, but, in the absence of emphasis on anthropological concepts and terminology, the contribution that anthropology has to make to an understanding of man and of different cultures is frequently obscured. The material deliberately introduces anthropological terminology which may at first be somewhat difficult for the student. As his familiarity with these terms increases,

---

2. Anthropology Curriculum Study Project, 5632 South Kimbark Avenue, Chicago, Illinois 60637.

3. *Newsletter.* No. 4. Anthropology Curriculum Study Project. Chicago. Fall 1965. p. 1.

however, it is expected that they will help him to organize and interpret in a more meaningful manner the world in which he lives.[4]

Each unit is arranged so that the teacher is encouraged to use the pupil's experience in his own culture as a point of departure for understanding the way other people live.

The third project is the Social Studies Curriculum Program of Educational Services, Incorporated,[5] the focus of which is the development under the leadership of Jerome Bruner of a course in elementary social studies. The course is a study of man, his nature and evolution, and five "great humanizing forces" are selected as worthy of explanation, "Tool making, language, social organization, the management of man's prolonged childhood, and man's urge to explain."[6] With this project anthropology is not the single organizing discipline; the approach is interdisciplinary. Because, however, the first units being evolved and tested draw primarily on studies and methods characteristic of anthropology, the project is immediately relevant to this discussion. For example, one of several pedagogical techniques to be utilized with students is contrast. Bruner states:

> We hope to use four principal sources of contrast: man *versus* higher primates, man *versus* prehistoric man, contemporary technological man *versus* "primitive" man, and man *versus* child.[7]

There is an impelling reason for calling this project to the attention of teachers. The rationale for the organization of this course, the kind of materials pupils are to work with, and the supplementary materials for teachers reflect an emphasis on involving pupils in the discovery of structure in human behavior and history—of discovering generalizations that describe and explain man's persistent behavior across time and divergent cultures. What effect this emphasis might ultimately have on the organization and content of the social studies curriculum is obviously a matter of conjecture, but it presents an issue that must be confronted in any consideration of a revision of the social studies curriculum. Professor Krug's recent article in *Social*

4. "Teachers Guide, Grade 1, Concept of Culture," Anthropology Curriculum Project, Publication No. 2. University of Georgia, Athens, March 1965. p. 2. (Mimeo.)
5. Educational Services, Incorporated, 15 Mifflin Place, Cambridge, Massachusetts 02138.
6. Jerome S. Bruner. *Man: A Course of Study*, Occasional Paper No. 3. The Social Studies Curriculum Program. Cambridge, Massachusetts: Educational Services, Incorporated, 1965. p. 4.
7. *Ibid.*, p. 20.

Education is a provocative example of such a confrontation. A statement from it follows:

> While there is no question that in the search for structure, Bruner's discovery approach is valuable and should have a place in the social studies curriculum and in the lively, dramatic study of history and the social sciences, to build the entire social studies curriculum on the structure theory is fraught with grave dangers. Much in history and in the study of human personality and group interrelationship which cannot and should not be fitted into a structure or even related to something else, is eminently worthy of teaching to our children.[8]

These projects are generating specific materials that can be tested by a teacher. In a more general sense they represent useful models for teachers to use in thinking about and in beginning to explore possible applications of anthropology to the social studies. The projects have also been described in order to identify some unresolved questions including fundamental assumptions about the capabilities of elementary school pupils, the appropriate way of organizing the records of human behavior so that children can make sense of them, the extent to which children can make productive use of the vocabulary of cultural analysis, the appropriateness of particular units of study to grade levels and traditional social studies topics, and the kind of preparation teachers need to teach such units.

Such questions can, of course, be ignored. It is not unheard of for a teacher or a faculty, especially in this day and time, to accept counsel that a particular curriculum innovation is a "good thing" and simply proceed to make use of it. In this respect many of the units being prepared are persuasive; in their comprehensive attention to teacher needs they offer assurance that no special training is prerequisite to making use of the units. If, then, a teacher wishes to incorporate some aspect of anthropology into the social studies program, he need not feel intimidated either by a lack of specific preparation or by the difficulty of anthropological materials with which he may already have at least a passing acquaintance. The transition, it is asserted, can be not only painless but a vigorous, satisfying learning experience as well.

These developments seem to suggest that the concern to make the social studies curriculum as contemporary to our era as are curricula in the natural sciences will result ultimately in a revision in which anthropology has an important ordering role. Whether or not it will

8. Mark M. Krug. "Bruner's New Social Studies: A Critique." *Social Education* 30:401; October 1966.

is conjecture; whether or not it should is also conjecture but a question that any teacher who proposes to make use of anthropological materials should see as integral to the experience. However, skillfully prepared prepackaged units in anthropology are and however committed a teacher is to make meaningful use of them, there is a need for teachers to maintain a detached, critical point of view. The teacher's orientation ought to be exploration rather than adoption.

In an introductory chapter to this book, *Education and Culture*, George D. Spindler observes, "Anthropology goes in a number of directions and utilizes a number of approaches. It is a sprawling and diversified field. The anthropology of education, though it is only one area of application, exhibits the same characteristics. It is therefore unrealistic to describe one anthropological approach that will also characterize an anthropology of education."[9] He goes on to describe what he considers to be the "character structure" of anthropology. The discipline is eclectic, drawing in varying degrees both concepts and research techniques from other fields such as psychology and sociology. At the same time the anthropologist is basically committed to direct observation as the primary instrument of data-gathering—and direct observation of whatever range of behavior is manifest in a community of individuals. As Spindler expresses it, "No person is too lowly in status or too uninformed to be worthy of attention . . . and anybody, anywhere can be an informant." Another important aspect of the anthropological approach is the assumption that there may not be a "direct correspondence" between behavior and belief and that certainly few members of any culture can articulate all the complexities of the belief system to which they are committed. The search by the anthropologist for the reality of any culture, including the relationship between behavior and belief, makes the case study, holistic approach basic to anthropology. Here there is "a commitment to analyze the interdependent function of apparently separate aspects of behavior" between, for example, the socializing role of the parent in the home and of the teachers in the classroom. The perspective of the anthropologist is cross-cultural, too; each culture "is seen as one variety of human behavior among many possibilities." Finally, Spindler suggests there is manifest in anthropological research a humanistic inclination—that is, a meaningful concern for the improvement of the human condition.

9. George D. Spindler. "The Character Structure of Anthropology." In George D. Spindler, editor. *Education and Culture.* New York: Holt, Rinehart & Winston, 1963. p. 5.

At first glance the "character structure" of anthropology might seem irrelevant to an elementary teacher's beginning experience with anthropology in the social studies. The materials the teacher uses will draw directly on the results of anthropological research and will certainly reflect basic assumptions and methodologies of the research. Nevertheless, there is for the teacher the need to establish empathetic contact with the anthropological approach. The study of man is at least the implicit focus of the social studies curriculum. If anthropology is relevant to making this focus more explicit, both the substance *and* the process of anthropological research have much to offer the social studies teacher.

FIELD ANTHROPOLOGISTS AND
CLASSROOM TEACHERS

by

Paul J. Bohannan

There are three major areas in which anthropology is relevant in primary and secondary schools. First, of course, it is important as a subject matter. A great deal of anthropology is already taught in the schools. Often it is not called by its name, but Eskimos and Bushmen and Pygmies are standard fare in the primary grades. L.S.B. Leakey is a national hero in our junior high schools, and non-Western and world history courses are laced with anthropology. Much of this anthropology seriously needs upgrading to meet professional standards of relevance and accuracy and (ironically enough) to remove from it inaccuracies and romanticism such as those that have been introduced into American Indian studies by the Boy Scouts. But, on the other hand, some of it is already of pretty good quality—particularly the anthropology of early man and evolution.

Second, anthropology, better than any of the other social sciences, provides a method of investigation that is suitable for the study and evaluation of classroom procedures and cultures. Anthropologists, over the decades, have evolved a way of analyzing and presenting small communities that can almost without alteration be switched to the study of schools and the cultural associations among classroom, community cultures, and the educational systems of our nation. It is, at the moment, becoming stylish for anthropologists to study schools. People from other disciplines are also studying classrooms and schools in the community, and are borrowing extensively from anthropological techniques when they do it. It is becoming obvious—and heartening—that we shall within the next few years see the efflorescence of a large body of data and no inconsiderable insight about the educational process in our own society, with a good bit of interesting comparative material. The school is, after all, one of the main "institutions of cultural transmission" in modern societies; education is one of the most vital activities that any society must carry out. Finally we are getting around to investigating it directly.

From *Social Education*, February 1969. Reprinted with permission of the National Council for the Social Studies and Paul J. Bohannan.

Paul Bohannan is Professor of Anthropology and of Education at Northwestern University. He is also a member of the American Anthropological Association's Advisory Committee to the Anthropology Curriculum Study Project.

The third point, however, is the one to which this article is devoted: the technique of anthropological field work offers great insight into some of the problems of teachers, both during their training and in their classrooms. I have found, to my great astonishment and delight, that teachers take to these ideas and techniques with almost no adaptation at all. It is very soon possible to develop in the teacher an awareness of social and cultural dynamics, as well as a mode of action which enables him to participate fully and vitally and at the same time to stand back far enough to see what is going on. It offers a proven device to control his emotions and his actions so that he stays in touch with the real world—with what is going on out there in the classroom.

I shall first give a brief description of what an anthropologist does in the field. I shall then review the seminar at Northwestern's School of Education in which eighteen M.A.T. candidates and I first investigated these ideas, and will then make some overt comparisons with the classroom teacher and a few concrete suggestions about how the teacher can use these techniques and ideas.

The Cultural Anthropologist in the Field

Like the teacher, the field anthropologist does his job with his entire personality. His acceptance into the community, and his ultimate success or failure, depends almost as much on what he is as a person as on what he does as a trained professional. It is well to keep this idea in mind as we explore the job of the anthropologist.

The anthropologist, as ethnographer, is faced with the task of going into another culture and adjusting to it as he learns it. This learning is no mere question mongering—it means getting the other culture into his mind and his muscles, learning to speak its language as well as he can, and participating in the life of "his community" to whatever degree his people and his own personality will allow. Then, even more difficult, he must return to his own culture and must devise ways of communicating in English, what he has learned in a foreign tongue and alien culture. And he must do it so that there is as little warping as possible of the values and ideas current in the culture he has studied—no mean task when all of the technical terms in English have themselves been developed to explain and adjust American and British cultures.

The first task for the field anthropologist is to learn the language. In the process, of course, he must learn new facts about his own language—about the strange ways in which he is accustomed to put-

ting things to himself, and about the particular limitations and elas-
ticities of English. Even more important than learning the words, he
must learn to "hear," in the sense of understand in *their* terms, what
it is that his informants are trying to tell him. If they do not answer
his questions straight, it's three to one that the difficulty lies in the
question and the way the ethnographer is asking it. In the course of
learning the language, he must also learn new sets of gestures (and
hence the literal "feel" of that language may be much different) and
new ways of evasions and new ways of hiding things from one's self.
In short, he must learn new aspects and new deep meanings of his
own "body English" as well as of his own spoken English.

In this process, the anthropologist is constantly discovering himself as he investigates and records the data concerning the people he
studies. It is no easy matter to get over *assuming* you know what is
being said out there in the "real world." But you cannot really look
at the real world of a foreign culture until you can see it in its own
terms the very while you look at yourself looking at it.

Thus, both teachers and field anthropologists are in unparalleled
situations for getting their own cultures straight in their own minds.
They will discover, in the course of doing their work, that much of
what had seemed common sense—ordinary background of ordinary
social life, about which it had never before been necessary to think—
is suddenly thrust into prominence and awareness.

In short, the teacher (like the anthropologist) must be made aware
of his own values, his own unstated assumptions, his very bodily
movements, if he is to learn the culture of his students. And the
greater the difference between his own background and that of his
students, the more aware of it he becomes—and hence, ironically, the
clearer his job will be.

In short, if you are going to use your personality as the primary
tool in your work, you have to learn something about your own
personality and the cultural idiom in which it is accustomed to express itself. Only then are you in a position to modify or utilize your
own techniques of learning and hence of teaching so that they do
indeed serve the ends that you intend them to serve.

An anthropologist selects a people he is to study on the basis of
two major considerations: his own capacity to live the kind of life
these people live, and the problems which are currently paramount in
his discipline. In this way, he will know that such-and-such a people
or institution or situation is "ready" to be studied, and that he can
likely make a significant contribution to the knowledge in the field.
Both these considerations are important.

It is necessary first to have an overt and intellectual goal in mind—
that is, for the field anthropologist to learn something about the way
a specific human group, whatever it may be, faces some of the fundamental problems of human living. It may be a problem in law and the
way in which conflict is either settled or handled in the absence of
settlement. It may be a problem in economy, and the way in which
provisioning is taken care of in the absence of familiar institutions
such as markets. It may, indeed, be a problem in cultural transmission, and the way in which present-day schools drive a wedge between generations and turn some of the children into near schizo-
phrenics because of the double messages that they receive at home
and at school. The consideration is always that the discipline has the
conceptual equipment to confront a problem, but needs more facts
and ideas to solve it, and that the individual practitioner has the
requisite imagination and nerve to turn new ideas and new data to
the benefit of the discipline.

However, there is another matter here: every individual field worker goes to the field with a developed and entire personality and mode
of life. He obviously cannot make himself entirely over. Therefore,
he must select a people whose temperament and mode of life he
finds bearable. Not admirable, necessarily; not even pleasant. But
bearable. After all, a field worker is going to be living with these
people for a period of from one to three years, and if he did not find
them at least minimally congenial, it would be absolutely impossible
for him to do his job. Yet, if the anthropologist works among his
own people, he is not going to have to alter the frame of reference of
his very life—and it is this very alteration that leads to anthropological insight.

Therefore, the first requirement for an anthropologist is to find a
place to work in which he is not grossly uncomfortable, but with
which he is not overly familiar either. Now, this seems to me to be
precisely the situation of any neophyte teacher—particularly those
who have chosen to work among the various ethnic groups in our
country that are different from the one in which they have grown
up. It is especially true of American middle-class teachers who, in
line with the commitment to middle-class values of helping others,
have chosen to face the ethnic groups of the inner cities.

An anthropologist cannot use interpreters as a short cut for learning the language. If he does, he is not going to get to the heart of the
meaning that these people attach to their institutions for living. He
cannot both understand what they are about and allow himself the
luxury of somebody else's doing his analysis and telling him how to

behave (although if other people have been there before him, some of their hints may be useful—but they may be also worse than useless).

Again, I think the parallel is evident: the teacher cannot depend on somebody else, either his own teachers, or his principal, or anybody else, to tell him how to do this job. He must himself learn to communicate with his charges. The problem of communication may stem from no more than a difference in age. (I was acutely aware when I first faced a ninth grade of middle-class Americans that I, a middle-class American, had not dealt with 14-year olds since I was 14, and that the world had changed a lot since then.) However, in the present day in which we are trying to upgrade the schools of our inner cities and to educate a greater range of Americans to ever more demanding social roles, I venture that a large proportion of teachers find themselves face to face with people whose language they do not understand—in some cases because it may not be English, in others because it may not be the standard dialect of English, in still others because there may be secret languages or other secret modes of communication among students who zealously keep the teacher from understanding their private means of communicating.

The anthropologist—and the teacher—must also discover the degree to which he or she can be taken into the community that is the subject of study. In some African communities every anthropologist is required to live as a chief because the people will not accept him on any other basis. In some American communities every teacher is required to present himself as a middle-class arbiter or morality because the students and the community will not accept him on any other basis. You must learn to work within an ascribed status, perhaps trying to change it a little, but more importantly, understanding the constrictions that it puts on your activities and your opportunity to learn.

In some African communities, the people are delighted when an anthropologist wants to live among them, in superficial ways at least, as they themselves live. In the same way, in some American communities some teachers will be welcomed into strange ethnic groups, but this experience, I judge, is exceptional. I think it is unlikely that most teachers will find themselves allowed to speak the local dialect, even if they learn to understand it. Middle-class teachers in lower-class Negro schools are faced with having to learn to understand a kind of English which they are never allowed, by their students, to use. They have to be circumspect enough to discover the limitations (either from self or from community) in living with and utilizing the culture of the people they teach or study.

Learning a language can be a tricky matter because no two languages structure the sense world in precisely the same way. When, as children, our five senses are culturally educated, we also learn that language in terms of which we shall for the rest of our lives cut up our perceptions in order to communicate about them. When we learn only one language, the result is necessarily a monoglot's view of culture and the whole world.

Therefore, in the process of learning a new language, an anthropologist begins to know overtly what he has formerly perceived only covertly: a specific organization to his cultural and social world, a palette of color, as it were, with which life in his particular latitudes is always presented and perceived. This kind of self-knowledge is the essence of field anthropology—and, I suggest, of successful teaching.

Something else happens too: we discover not just the way we see the world, but we also discover some of our feelings about it—about morality, about cleanliness and godliness, about money, and about ambition. We may thereupon become indignant, angry, frightened. The "way out" of these feelings is, for the untrained, to blame the other guy, and belittle his culture and his values. This is one way—but a naive way—of saving your own value system, making it unnecessary for you to question your own assumptions and your own feelings.

This set of threats to the individual is usually called "culture shock," especially in its more acute form. Culture shock may occur to anyone when he finds his feelings threatened by matters he does not understand, and his actions made insecure by social situations in which he cannot make accurate predictions. Culture shock is a result of having to face situations in which you do not know what you are expected to do next, and hence any action you take may lead to misfortune or disaster. It is a kind of psychic deprivation, and can lead to serious consequences if you do not know how to deal with it, and yet cannot run away.

Let me give two examples of culture shock—both from my own life. One of these occurred in the Ivory Coast, long after I knew about culture shock—and indeed, only a few days after I gave a series of lectures on it. I proceeded immediately from an Eastern university in the United States, where I had been giving my lectures to a group of students who were proceeding overseas, to a conference in Abidjan. Everything went swimmingly until the weekend. I had accepted an invitation from an African colleague in the conference for Sunday, an invitation that I thought I ought for my own edification to accept, but which I was quite unenthusiastic about. A few hours later

I felt I had to turn down another invitation from a group of French participants to spend Sunday with them at the beach swimming and picnicking. Then, on Sunday, I was stood up by the African. Now, I know perfectly well that such behavior on the part of the African was not, by his standards, anywhere nearly as rude—indeed, insufferable—as it was by mine. Something else had come up, and it would have been extremely awkward for him to have notified me. However, when I realized what had happened, I went to my hotel room, pulled the blinds, and went to bed. I was emancipated enough not to blame him—I blamed his "lousy culture."

Within a few minutes, fortunately for me, I realized what I was doing—and recalled that I had only a few days before told my audience that if you are lonely or angry or home-sick or feel ill-used, you had better ask yourself, "Buddy, what's biting you? What are you trying to get by with?" I had, to cover my own disappointment and to keep from being annoyed at my own "virtue" in keeping the standards of my own culture about invitations, labeled *his* culture inferior. I dressed again, pulled up the shades, went out and found some people, and had a good day.

The other example is not so trivial. When I had been among the Tiv of Nigeria for about ten months, I hired a young man Tiv as my servant—what was called a "steward" in Nigerian English. He was not a good steward. However, he could read and write in Tiv, and he took an immense interest in my work. I subsequently learned that the interest arose because he had been brought up by white missionaries and needed, like me, to learn his own culture intellectually and as an adult rather than as a by-product of being a child. He began to write text for me in the Tiv language and to help me with my ethnographic investigations in many other ways. I soon realized that I had a very important assistant here. I turned him into my "scribe" and hired another steward. He and I became good friends, and we worked together several hours almost every day.

One evening, he came back from the river where he had been bathing and swimming. I asked him casually if anything was going on, and in a casual way he replied that a man had drowned in the river. I discovered through questioning that the man was a stranger who could not swim, and had stepped off a drop-off a few feet from the bank. Nobody had tried to save him. I knew my scribe to be a strong swimmer. "Didn't *you* go after him?" I demanded. "He wasn't mine," was the laconic answer.

This incident upset me. I found that one of my most basic values had been flouted: the worth of individual human life. It took me several days to realize that this was not one of *his* basic values, and that in fact I had shocked *him* a few weeks before when he had learned that I had not seen my parents for four years, or my brother for seven, which to him showed absolutely appalling neglect. It took me several days to learn to like him again.

It is out of just such events that culture shock is made, and it is out of just such experiences that one comes upon the "cure" for it: learning what one's own values are, then either abandoning them or else making an intellectual commitment as well as an emotional commitment to them, so that they need never turn up again merely as raw feelings. I do not mean that you cease to feel strongly about such things. I only suggest that you know which things you feel strongly about and then govern yourself sensibly when you are in some other ethnic group.

Thus, it is out of culture shock that the anthropologist gets the most important part of his understanding of his data, and learns to do his job better.

In fact, the anthropologist becomes the medium in which the two sets of cultural values, those of his mother culture and those of the subject culture, are brought into focus. The next few years of his life are to be spent in trying to translate into English, for communication to his colleagues the very values that he learned in order to get along with and to understand the culture and the communications of his informants.

It seems to me that many middle-class American teachers are in a "field situation."

A Seminar for Teachers in
Anthropological Method

In the spring of 1967, I ran a seminar at Northwestern for 18 M.A.T. candidates, all of whom were teaching in ethnic groups other than their own. One of the candidates was a young man from middle-class small-town New England who had chosen to go into lower-class Negro schools of Chicago, another was a Wisconsin Lutheran girl who was teaching in a school made up almost entirely of second- and third-generation Eastern European Jews. Some of the other candidates were teaching Puerto Ricans, others were teaching new arrivals from southern Europe. Some were teaching in Chicago communities made up of a combination of Appalachian whites and American Indians; still others in schools that were operated especially for delinquent rejects from the public schools; two were teaching in the psychiatric ward of a city hospital. All of them had in common that they could not merely call upon the culture of their youth and of their college days to see them through their present situations.

After a short introduction to the basic concepts of cultural anthropology—the way in which social relationships structure themselves, and the way in which any people in communication need, and daily re-create, a culture for their interaction—we began a series of reports about the kind of problems that they faced in their daily work. Some rather astonishing results were soon apparent.

Whereas they had formerly been asking such remote and philosophical questions as whether their task was to change the culture of the groups they were teaching to some sort of middle-class WASP amalgam, they began to realize that this was not the immediate point. Except for the new arrivals, almost all of the various ethnic groups in the United States already knew middle-class WASP culture. They learn it on television, in magazine ads and comic books, on the city streets. Some of them actively—hostilely—reject it. Some of them are uncomfortable because they do not know what unimagined doom their trying to emulate it might bring about. The point is not whether you are going to teach them middle-class culture—obviously, you are. It is one of the cultures—and the dominant one—that is here to be dealt with.

The question is not whether you are going to teach it to them, but rather how you understand what their difficulties with it are, and the fact that two cultures are seldom an either/or proposition. When you discover this, you and they can decide in concert whether you are actively engaged in teaching it to them or whether they are going to reject it. You know where you stand—and you have not only communicated across a cultural barrier, you have gone a long way toward explaining that cultural barrier to them.

The seminar considered ways and means that mathematics can be taught to youngsters who do not see its function in their daily lives; we talked about how to teach literature in such a way that cultural differences become the essential point rather than the block to understanding. We talked about problems in teaching history and science and social studies—and in every case we discovered that the secret was an additive element: the inclusion of cultural differences in understanding and using such subjects. We even began doing a comparative study of roadblocks that different ethnic groups put up against good study habits. There are vast pressures in some lower-class groups against studying, and if a child studies, he may have to do it on the sly. In upper-middle-class third generation European-

Jewish children, the problem was how to make them behave in study hall—until it was discovered that they refused to study in study hall for good reason: if they did not do their studying at home, their parents called the teachers demanding larger homework assignments.

What we really accomplished in this seminar was that, for these teachers at least, there came to be an awareness that communication is affected by culture, and that *it is the teacher* (just as it is the field anthropologist) *who must make the major adjustment.* Only in that way can any real appreciation of the overt situation be learned. And only then can any real program of change and upgrading be instituted: on the basis of knowledge not only of facts but of the internal attitudes of the students. And, most important of all, of the teacher.

We also discussed the attitude of middle-class Americans to the problem of power. We discovered that most of the neophyte teachers had never before in their lives been in a position of power, and as a consequence they were not only worried about the way in which their exercise of authority would be received in their student's ethnic groups, but they had never adjusted to an image of themselves as powerful people in terms of their own values. They began to realize that the power of every authority figure must be limited. We began to ask, "What is worth enforcing in this particular situation?" Discipline? This problem turned out not to be especially difficult for most of these student teachers. Their problems of discipline were reduced vastly when they understood that listening behavior and attention are shown in different ways in our different sub-cultural groups. Quiet in the classroom? In most cases, it was necessary in the teaching process. Picking up scrap paper off the floor? Except for one young lady who decided she would demand it as an eccentricity of her own, we decided that we would not spend any of our authority on *that.*

In short, what matters? What is worth making a fuss about if you are to do the teaching job? I know that many school administrators take quite a different view of this—but I ask them, too, to get in the act. What is worrying *you* about this situation? What is really worth taking a stand on? Is it important in the educational process, or is it just your middle-class background showing?

Teachers in the Class Room

I decided as a result of this seminar that such training is almost essential to the training of teachers who will be working "cross-culturally." I have no doubt that it will allow them more profitably to work in and live in the communities of their students. Such teachers can, I trust and hope, avoid in large measure that greatest of personal and social tragedies in our schools—the teacher who, under constant threat of cultural strangeness, either becomes so authoritarian that education is impossible, or so apathetic that education seems scarcely desirable, or so angry that education seems "too good for them." It is teachers in this situation who have, quite understandably, let educational critics and civil rights leaders to believe that lower-class schools are the worst staffed (when, in fact, many people in them began as hand-picked experts and even volunteers). Apathy and anger are the great protectors of the self. When all else fails, they still protect.

There are a few simple questions that must consciously and repeatedly be asked: Why am I angry? Why am I homesick? Why am I discouraged? Why am I hostile. Why am I afraid?

The answers to these questions can almost always be found in the fact that your expectations have not been fulfilled, that you are left high and dry, not knowing where to turn or how to behave, that you have "failed."

And, of necessity, that leads to the next set of questions: What are these people doing and saying *in their terms?* What are their purposes, their underlying and unstated value positions? What do they want? And finally: Why are *they* angry and afraid?

From the answers to these questions can come, in many cases at least, and by some teachers, a firm basis for achieving the cross-cultural communication whose absence is one of the primary plagues in our schools today.

Teachers are, to repeat, in some ways like field anthropologists: since they work with their entire personalities, and since their fundamental problem is one of cross-cultural communication, and since their feelings are as important a cue as their intellects to discovery of hidden cultural differences, some training is necessary if they are to avoid the destructive emotions which make impossible the very job they set out to do. Field anthropologists have faced these problems; some have found solutions to some of them from which, it is apparent, teachers can profit.

INTRODUCING ANTHROPOLOGICAL CONCEPTS
IN THE PRIMARY GRADES

by

Frances Emmons

Jacqueline Cobia

The initial reaction of a primary grade teacher to the idea of teaching anthropological concepts is often negative. One obstacle is the teacher's lack of knowledge of anthropology. Another is the idea that anthropology is just too hard for primary children: it's a college subject.

However, once a teacher is willing to teach anthropology, he is likely to discover that children react enthusiastically. They do not find the subject matter too hard. The teacher is also likely to see that behind the concepts of anthropology are many facts and ideas that he has been transmitting all along. His fear of personal inadequacy will probably give way to interest in anthropology and self-confidence in teaching it. All of the teachers in Juliette Low School who have taught anthropology have been impressed with the high degree of pupil interest.

This article tells how a first and a second grade teacher introduced anthropological concepts in the primary grades.[1] An elementary teacher who reviews this account of their experiences will quickly realize two things. The activities these two teachers used to reinforce conceptual learning are similar to devices used in regular elementary teaching, adapted to the content of anthropology. The language of anthropology, however, is more abstract than words that appear in much social studies teaching.

One of the main concepts in anthropology is the concept of culture. To make this concept meaningful, we first tried to build up the idea of what an anthropologist does. We focused on the role of the anthropologist as a participant observer and asked each child to report on something that his family did. For first grade children reporting on family activities is exciting.

We used part of our daily sharing time for reports of the partici-

From *Social Education*, March 1968. Reprinted with permission of the National Council for the Social Studies, Frances Emmons and Jacqueline Cobia.

1. The units prepared by the Anthropology Curriculum Project, University of Georgia, gave a common core for teaching that made it easier to introduce anthropological concepts.

pant observers, and we used some of our language arts time to write experience stories based on these reports. To emphasize the need for accuracy in reporting, we asked children to write one sentence statements about what they saw. This helped demonstrate to the children the variety of ways that ordinary activities are carried out and the need for exact reporting.

The participant-observer experience stimulated offshoots in many directions. Children began to ask questions about how the anthropologist would really understand what was going on if he were to study other people. We were able to establish the idea of people having different languages and the need of the anthropologist to speak the language of the people he is observing. Language differences automatically led to the idea of differences in groups in various parts of the world, and the globe was used to help children locate areas of the earth occupied by the people they were to study.

Use of the participant-observer technique in the context of the family can be more than the study of an anthropological method for data collection. It can help to develop the concept of the family in American culture and lay a basis for asking questions about families in other cultures.

For example, to ask and answer the question "What does your daddy do to make a living?" or "What kind of work is your daddy in?" sets the stage for asking a parallel question, "What kind of work does an Arunta daddy do?" The technique of participant observation related to a particular cultural trait leads very naturally to the method of cross-cultural comparison. This is the method by which the anthropologist looks at behavior in one culture in contrast to behavior in another culture. Primary grade children find such comparisons fascinating.

In the primary grades we are not concerned with the formal introduction of the concepts of trait variability, trait universals, and cultural patterning. What we try to communicate is the idea that people have common needs. Because they have learned to meet these needs in different ways, there are differences in the way people do things. Formal concepts may be introduced to the students later. The teacher, however, must know the concepts. Otherwise he is likely to present cultural patterns as so many discrete and bizarre ways of behaving rather than as understandable, functional variations in human behavior.

We do not merely talk about differences in behavior; we try to involve the children to such an extent that they identify with behavior in a culture. Role-playing, dramatization, and the stimulation of cross-cultural comparison appeals strongly to the primary grade child. "Let's pretend" is equally attractive to boys and girls, but it is strictly sex-typed, boys imitating males and girls imitating females.

To enact the role of a Paleo-Indian, Arunta hunter, Kazak herdsman, Mayan priest, or Hopi gardener is more than play. This requires the child to ask himself questions as to what he would do in a particular environment with the tools that a people have. He therefore has to know something about tools and how they are used. Knowledge of tools leads the child to ask questions about what people in another culture have to know about their environment in order to survive. The idea that people we think of as primitive have an organized knowledge system is a striking one to young children. How a group can go about applying this knowledge in the best way leads into the concept of social organization, a base for which is laid in the consideration of family activities.

"Let's pretend," when done honestly in terms of the behavior in a culture, helps transmit the idea that people we think of as being very primitive have many skills that advanced people do not have. In practicing cross-cultural comparison, children become aware of the need for specialized skills in technological cultures. Here is a base for the investigation of division of labor and interdependence in different cultures. Such investigations will give added meaning to a subsequent study of interdependence and cooperation in American culture.

Sometimes activities that fail technically turn out to be the most meaningful. We always try to engage in activities that duplicate those in a given culture. A favorite one for boys is tool making. They are often unsuccessful at this. Trying to attach a stone point to a spear or an ax head to a handle can be a difficult task. Therefore the activity conveys an idea of technical skill better than a picture or films could.

One day we attempted to make an Arunta house, not a small model but a large one that the children could enter. We went out to a nearby wooded area and collected a large supply of limbs and small branches. After we had managed to get it up, it fell down on the children. We thought at first that this activity was a failure, but then we heard the children saying the the Arunta must be smart to build their own houses. We then realized that they had learned something more important—that even the Arunta had skills that made it possible for them to survive in their own environment.

Many of our activities are selected to convey the idea that differences in human behavior are related to differences in the artifacts in a culture. One of the favorite activities was to have a Kazak meal. We sat on the floor and tried to eat in Kazak manner using only a few utensils. We found this very awkward, but when we asked ourselves "How could the Kazak follow their herds if they had to carry around tables and chairs?" we were able to understand better the idea of cultural patterning—that things in a culture have to fit together in a certain way in order for people to live.

One of the questions we asked was whether children could see any similarities in the way the Kazak lived and the way American cowboys lived. This simple question led us to ask more questions about the Kazak environment and the cattle and sheep country of the West. The children were able to see how similarities in environment led to similarities in using that environment, even when there is a great difference in the technology of the people.

In addition to role playing, another way that children enjoy learning anthropology is through art and craft activities. During the anthropology unit, the "art" time is devoted to anthroplogically related activities. Making houses from clay, sticks, straw, mud, paper maché, and grass sod is interesting for children, both inside and outside class. The Kazak winter house is one appropriate subject for this activity. Another art activity especially useful in the study of American culture is the construction of picture books. All kinds of flat pictures may be used to make both individual and class books.

The study of a group can also be enriched by playing its music. This activity helps children to learn differences in musical sounds and to perceive that all people do not have the same kind of music. It also seems to stimulate children to attempt to create art like that of the culture they are studying.

There are many opportunities during the school day to introduce anthropological concepts incidentally rather than as a lesson. For example, primary grade children find the subject of food very interesting. In talking about what they have for a meal at the school cafeteria, and why they eat certain things, the class can also discuss what children in other cultures eat. The fact that a Hopi child eats *piki*, or an Arunta child eats a *witchetty* grub can be related to the economic system of the culture. Such illustrations will give the concept of division of labor a dimension that is not merely definitional: food is an end product necessary for survival, and all people have different ways of dividing up the responsibility for obtaining it.

In studying about a culture, young children prefer topics that have some kind of concrete referent, such as tools, ways of making a living, or house types. Partly for his reason, archeology has great appeal. Primary grade children know only a little about religion and government and seem to find these more abstract subjects less interesting. It is usually difficult, within the short time allotted to the anthropology unit, to develop reference points for such topics.

The lack of interest in abstract ideas, however, needs to be qualified. Sometimes, depending on the way a unit develops and the interests of the children in the class, even the idea of social organization can be a very exciting one. One year there were a few boys in a second grade class who became very interested in the concept of Aztec military government. One of the boys had a father who was an army officer, and he just knew that the army didn't run the United States. This served as a point of departure from which looking at a headman in a tribe, a priest king, a military ruler, and a democratic government took on a different meaning.

Young children are fascinated with archeology. This has in part to do with the use of tools—our children love to bring in tools and make displays of tools used by archeologists. Another reason is that archeology tells about how man uncovers artifacts. For the children, excavating artifacts is like hunting for buried treasure. Just as there are clues to find treasure, there are clues to find a site. Before you excavate, you must make a map to show where the treasure is located. All of these things make finding out about archeological methods very appealing to children.

Another reason for its appeal is that in Savannah somebody is always digging up something old from a house or a road bed. One year a lot of old bottles were found when a roadway was cleared. Some of the parents of our children had gone out to hunt for these bottles that took on a nice color with age. We used this as a starting point. First we asked what people would think about our culture if they dug up things we have today. Then we raised questions about what kind of artifacts endure and how the archeologist goes about reconstructing the life of people from only a small part of the evidence they leave. The idea of the archeologist as a scientific detective of the past has strong appeal for children.

In Savannah there is a children's museum, which helps youngsters to visualize some of the work of archeologists. Our area also has a number of reconstructed fort sites that display principles of archeological methodology. Ocmulgee National Park at Macon gives an opportunity for an extended field trip to an impressive Indian site. Field trips to sites and museums help children understand the idea of archeology as a science because they can see excavations and the interpretations and reconstructions based on excavation.

But we believe that a teacher can find opportunities to make anthropology meaningful in many ordinary things. When we were talking about dendrochronology, or tree-ring dating, it was easy to ask a child to bring in a cut from a tree. When we were talking about stratigraphy, it was simple to dig a hole in the playground and see the various strata of earth. The sandy loam was easy to dig, and the earth, shaded off even at a shallow level from the thin black top soil into several different colored layers. A terrarium in the classroom, with objects placed at different depths, was a convenient way of illustrating the principle of stratigraphic dating.

In communicating the idea of how man entered the New World, we made use of map work: in fact, we found maps just as useful in anthropology as in geography. Children need to know where people and things are in space. We used the globe and wall maps as well as desk maps to help children get an idea of the location of people and things. Most of the time we drew the maps freely from a model; the idea was not to produce an accurate map but to give children an idea of relative location.

Pictures and three-dimensional models were useful ways to teach that the Indians in pre-Columbian America developed in different stages. We have not always been successful in teaching the idea that some Indians did not go beyond the archaic stage of hunting and gathering. However, the various activities—from cooking with heated stones dropped in water to building models of Mayan religious centers—helped children to understand that Indians had a more complicated way of life than just hunting.

In addition to class discussion and explanation, we try to engage the pupils in activities that add meaning to the concepts. Art work, modeling, role playing, listening to records of native music, seeing pictures and films, making scrapbooks, murals, and dioramas, putting on puppet shows, writing class plays and experience charts, making tools and artifacts, bringing in things from other countries and telling about them, learning songs and dances from other cultures, and reading stories about other people are all methods that primary grade teachers use to convey ideas to young children. These methods, adapted to the content of anthropology, give meaning to anthropological concepts.

The use of the language of anthropology is a challenge to the primary grade child. He loves to master new ideas and words and to learn something that even his parents do not know. His success in seeing the new conceptual world that anthropology opens up to him is self-motivational.

At the present time our children are asking, "When are we going to study anthropology?" Their eagerness to study a new subject and to master difficult material reflects the success we have had in introducing anthropology in the primary grades.

BUILDING ANTHROPOLOGICAL CONTENT
INTO ELEMENTARY SCHOOL SOCIAL STUDIES

by

Jack R. Fraenkel

A third grade class, in studying about desert nomads, is discussing the changes that might occur if suddenly the desert could have all the water it needed. After many examples of change in ways of earning a living, education, urban growth, and the like, have been offered, the teacher introduces the dimension of how people feel about change. The following discussion takes place:*

Teacher: With all these changes in the desert, what would happen to the old ways of life?

Deborah: They would be forgotten and they wouldn't use them any more.

Ronald: They probably would use them, because their ancestors—just like in Hong Kong. They don't quit doing what their ancestors done.

Donna: Well, there would be quite a lot of changes.

Teacher: What kind of changes?

Donna: Well, their jobs.

Teacher: What do you think the old nomads, the old people, would think of this new way of life?

Freddie: Well, they wouldn't like it too much, because they would probably want to stick to the way that their ancestors did it.

Brenda: It would probably be strange to them.

Teacher: Strange in what way?

Deborah: They would feel sort of funny—like they were just being born and all that.

Duke: I don't think the old people would like it too much, because they would think their way was better.

Teacher: Why?

Duke: Because they was taught it, and they would want their sons to do the same thing. Anyway, they would grouch.

Deborah: In a couple of years they would start changing and year by year, pretty soon, they would be modern.

Teacher: What do you think the children would think about this?

Mark: They would probably think that they had a new world.

Deborah: They wouldn't think it was so important. But their parents would think it was more important, because they have been that way more years than the children have.

From *Social Education*, March 1968. Reprinted with permission of the National Council for the Social Studies and Jack R. Fraenkel.

* All conversations in this article were taken from taped recordings in classrooms and are reported here in the language style used by the pupils.

The above sequence represents one example of a teacher discussing anthropological concepts from the curriculum developed by the Taba Curriculum Development Project at San Francisco State College. Under a grant from the U.S. Office of Education, social studies guides for Grades 1-6, as developed in Contra Costa County, California, are being reshaped and systematized.

A basic assumption of the project is that exposing pupils to key concepts and generalizations from a variety of social science disciplines will provide them with a greater awareness of what they and their society are all about. Such an awareness, it is hypothesized, will enable them to find sense and order in the world in which they live, and thus, hopefully, function more effectively in it.

As a result, the units that comprise each of the grade level guides are being structured accordingly. Each unit is organized around a generalization (henceforth referred to as a "main idea"), supported by a number of sub-generalizations (sub-ideas). In grade four, for instance, one main idea is that "people, influenced by their culture, may use the same natural environment in different ways"; in grade six, one main idea is that "civilizations change when they meet a new culture, but that often these changes are one of degree." These "main ideas" serve as the focus of a unit and provide a basis for the selection of several samples of factual content that assists pupils to make comparisons and contrasts. (Such content may then be extended or reduced in amount, depending on the particular backgrounds and interests of pupils involved.) A variety of learning activities are then sequentially arranged in each unit to help pupils acquire an understanding of the main idea around which the unit is organized.

Key anthropological concepts thread their way through all the grades. Selected for their power to organize and represent vast amounts of specific factual data, these concepts are introduced in the first grade and then developed and built on in the succeeding grades.

For example, the concept of change is dealt with at each grade level. The first grade deals with the changes that take place in family composition. The second grade is concerned with the changes occurring in the jobs people do in a community, how new and different services develop as needs change, and how specific methods change as new knowledge is acquired. The third grade then focuses on the varying ways people of selected cultures meet their needs, and how these ways change. Communities in the Near East and Asia are sampled to represent both underdeveloped and modern communities existing under a variety of geographic conditions, and then compared both with each other and the communities the children already know.

In the fourth grade the emphasis is on the differing ways that the same natural environment, represented by the state, is used by successive and different cultures. The fifth grade then concentrates on the continental United States, building on concepts developed in the fourth grade of changes and adjustments necessitated by an influx of new people from a different culture. The sixth grade concentrates on Latin America, changes within it brought about by events elsewhere in the world, and additional changes resulting from their earlier changes. Theoretically, at least, each grade level adds in complexity, generality, and abstractness to the ideas and concepts developed at earlier levels.

Throughout all of the units, comparing and contrasting of cultures is emphasized. This is illustrated in Figure I, using an example from the third grade. Several things should be noted about it. Two cultures have been selected to compare and contrast with our own. The solid arrows represent the main sequence and flow of content (i.e., what specific, factual content is dealt with); the dotted arrows represent the opportunities that exist for comparing, contrasting, and synthesizing. Pupils are encouraged at various points in the unit to make generalizations about each of the individual cultures under study, and then, in turn, to arrive at an even more synthetic generalization based on their earlier attempts. It is argued that such comparing and contrasting assists the pupil to arrive at an understanding of the main idea around which the unit is organized. Note, however, that a sample of two other cultures would meet the anthropological criteria and the criteria for teaching cognitive skills just as well as the two represented here.

Anthropological ideas and concepts seem especially important for a number of reasons. Not only can they help us decrease ethnocentrism but they can also help pupils to:

1. see the cultural factors at work in their environment, and what effect such factors have on people;
2. realize the differences in values and expectations that exist throughout and between societies;
3. observe not only the differences but also the similarities that exist between and among human beings;
4. realize how culture helps to assure conformity to the rules as well as perpetuation of the values and norms of a society, and;
5. realize how shifts in one part of society introduce changes in another part.

It should also be evident from Figure 1 that the organization of the curriculum involves more than just anthropological concepts. Each of the units in the curriculum attempts to develop and implement simultaneously several objectives:

*A generalization containing Main Idea I of Grade III: People of a hunting society are dependent upon their immediate environment and their own skills even though modern influences are changing their lives; people of an industrialized society use the skills of others and are much less directly dependent on their environment.

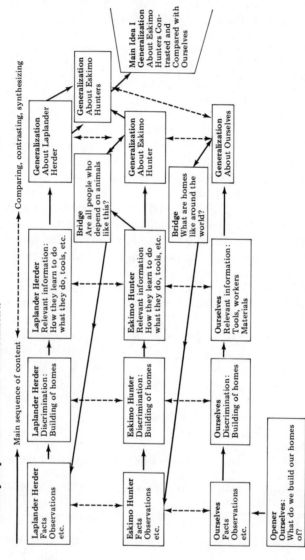

Main sequence of content ----→ ←----- Comparing, contrasting, synthesizing

Figure 1.

*This generalization is from the revised edition of the unit for Grade III: *A Study in Comparative Communities.*

We are indebted to Virginia Urrutia, one of the teachers in our June, 1967, Leadership Workshop, for preparing the idea of this chart.

128

1. *Basic Knowledge.* Each unit contains a number of important concepts and generalizations, as well as specific facts drawn from one or a variety of social science disciplines.
2. *Critical Thinking.* Opportunities are provided in order that pupils learn to conceptualize, interpret data, develop generalizations, and to apply known principles and facts to explain and understand new situations.
3. *Attitudes, Feelings, and Sensitivities.* The units offer a variety of learning experiences that attempt to modify feelings and attitudes, and to channel them in constructive directions. An especial emphasis is placed on extending sensitivity to cultural differences and on the dignity and worth of all people, no matter what their station or position in life may be.
4. *Skills.* Emphasis is placed on systematic practice of all important skills. These include both academic skills, such as gathering and evaluating information, as well as group skills, such as cooperating productively with others on a group project.

The organization of the curriculum can be represented schematically as shown in Figure 2.

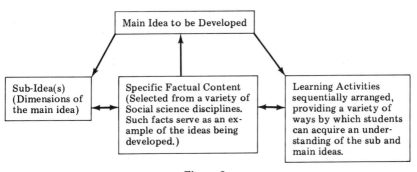

Figure 2.

Classroom Examples

What follows are two examples of classroom dialogue that illustrate how teachers trained in the process being developed by the Taba Project can assist pupils gain anthropological insights. The first sequence involved a third grade class that had been studying the Zulus as an example of a tribal society in Africa. The teacher's purpose was to help children realize that people generated ideas themselves.

Sequence I

Note: During approximately thirty minutes of discussion, the children had discussed changes and agents of change in a tribal society. The following listings had been put on the chalkboard.

Changes	People Who Brought Changes
Metal tools	Peace Corps
Metal pans	Missionaries
Medicine	Traders
Nurses	Travelers
Schools	World Health Organization
Books	
Bicycles	
Bigger buildings	

The teacher then moves out beyond the data and the following sequence takes place:

Teacher: Do you think these people would have discovered these things all by themselves someday without the help of all these other groups for teachers?

Chrystal: No

Teacher: What do you think—how would it be? If these people hadn't come to them?

Chrystal: Well, they'd still be living in their old ways—for instance their houses—until they just get so old, centuries and centuries. And maybe someday they'd find out about these ways and these things.

Carmel: Maybe they would find out about our ideas—like if one African moved to America and traveled around and then came back to his village and traveled all around and spread it and told them. Maybe some wouldn't believe it.

Teacher: How could he help them to believe what he saw?

Carmel: Tell them, or take a picture or something.

Chrystal: Or he could do it himself and start building that kind of buildings.

Teacher: Start building better buildings after what—after what he had seen?

Chrystal: If he wanted to, he could show them how they did it.

Gary S.: Some people wouldn't believe it unless they went over there, because almost all people believe that they already have everything. I mean, if the African came back and told the natives, they probably wouldn't believe it.

Brian: Yes, because they would finally learn. If they couldn't learn what we have here, how did they learn what they already are doing?

Teacher: Say that once more.

Brian: If they can't learn what we learn here, how could they learn what they already had learned there?

Sequence II involved a sixth grade class discussing the Mexican educational system.

Sequence II

Teacher: All right, how about education? You remember in Mexico we had what kind of an educational system?

John: Well, Mexico is improving its education and the children go to school and come home and teach their parents what they have learned, because when their parents were young they didn't have the chance to go to school.

Teacher: Why didn't they?

John: Because there weren't enough schools and teachers, and there weren't enough people that knew how to read and write.

Teacher: You mean there weren't enough teachers that could possibly have taught those people to read and write?

John: Yes.

Susan: Well, in Mexico they have a motto for education. "Each one teach one." So that when the children come home from school they teach their parents or maybe their sisters or brothers who can't go to school, and their relatives.

Teacher: Does this help the educational standard in that country?

Mark: Well, each person could teach another person and then the person that was taught could go on and teach someone else and it spreads the education. Some people have never even gone to school; they get educated by someone they know.

In all of these examples, children are endeavoring to analyze and to reason about the relationships that exist between people and their culture. Though the curriculum as a whole stresses an interdisciplinary approach, these examples may be viewed as attempts to make pupils aware of anthropological insights and to gain an understanding of some of the key concepts and ideas found within the discipline, even though they are not given the formal label "anthropology" for them.

MATERIALS FOR TEACHING ANTHROPOLOGY
IN THE ELEMENTARY SCHOOL

by

Marion J. Rice

A variety of printed, visual, and audio materials are available for the teaching of anthropology in the elementary school. A limited amount is explicitly anthropological in content. The bulk is social studies in content, drawing on concepts and generalizations from anthropology.

In this review, emphasis will be placed on materials that are explicitly anthropological. However, some attention will be given to four other types that are available: experimental or developmental nonprofit social studies projects explicitly incorporating anthropology concepts; social studies graded and supplementary series, commercially available through textbook publishers; and children's trade monographs or novels, either about a subject or a people based on anthropological scholarship. Some reference will also be made to sources of records, films, and filmstrips.

The comparative study of cultures. "A Sequential Curriculum in Anthropology, Grades 1-7" is being developed by the USOE funded Anthropology Curriculum Project at the University of Georgia.[1] Month-long units are being developed for each grade level. Primary grade units currently available are "Concept of Culture," Grade 1, and "Development of Man and His Culture: New World Prehistory," Grade 2. "Cultural Change," Grade 3, will be available in the Fall 1968.

"Concept of Culture" for Grade 1 is an ethnographic description of the Arunta, Kazak, and American cultures. Certain cultural traits are held constant for cultural contrast and comparison.

"New World Prehistory" for Grade 2 introduces archeological methodology as a scientific means of finding evidence of extinct cultures without written records, gives a survey of the five developmental stages of the pre-Columbian Indian, and presents the Hopi as a type study of an Indian group in the formative stage of development until recent years.

From *Social Education*, March 1968. Reprinted with permission of the National Council for the Social Studies and Marion J. Rice.

1. For additional information, write: Marion J. Rice, Project Coordinator, Anthropology Curriculum Project, University of Georgia, Athens, Georgia 30601.

ANTHROPOLOGY

133

"Cultural Change" for Grade 3 places a descriptive emphasis on special types of changes taking place in different areas, such as planned village change in India, urbanization and industrialization in Japan, and detribalization and nationalism in Africa.

The structure of each unit is designed to convey a scientific conception of the field and methods of anthropology. The scientific terminology of anthropology is emphasized, especially with respect to concepts of function and relationships. This concept emphasis reflects the view that communication of a discipline depends on its systematic treatment as a system of discourse. The key concepts in the language of anthropology are regarded as critical to the understanding of reality as perceived by the anthropologist.

Orginally, it was thought that an analysis of the concepts of anthropology would reveal an hierarchic structure of complexity that would serve as the basis for a graded "sequential curriculum." It was found, however, that complexity is a function of the level of explanation, rather than of the concept *per se*. The sequencing now reflects merely the logic of the curriculum builders, and no claim is made that grade unit arrangement is inherent in the concepts of anthropology. For example, the grade 7 unit "Life Cycle" might just as well serve as a point of entry to anthropology in Grade 1 instead of "The Concept of Culture," except that "culture" is a more significant organizing concept than is "life cycle." Learner maturity, however, would require modifications in the verbal input load at any grade level.

Each of the units developed thus far has five kinds of material: teacher essay, teacher guide, pupil text, pupil workbook, and achievement tests. As a teaching package, however, these materials are deficient in the lack of visual auditory, and simulation materials.

A teaching film "Archeological Methods" has been produced. The simple line-drawing picture books at Grade 1 are being replaced by ethnographically accurate illustrations. Future plans call for a photographic essay on "Cultural Change," using an American city as a type study of industrial-urban change.

An ethnographic study in depth. "Man: A Course of Study"[2] is a one-year, upper elementary social studies course, developed by the Educational Development Center. The structure of this course is still designed to answer three main questions outlined by Dr. Jerome

2. For additional information, write: Peter Dow, Director, Social Studies Program, Education Development Center, Cambridge, Massachusetts.

Bruner: "What is human about human beings? How did they get that way? How can they be made more so?"

While "Man: A Course of Study" is not designed for primary grades, the Netsilik films have been used in connection with the MATCH Boxes and Newton resource units discussed in this paper. Furthermore, the EDC method of the study of a culture in depth is an alternate method to the study of several different cultures used by the Georgia Project.[3] Some of the material can also be adapted to the primary level. Primary grade teachers, therefore, should be familiar with this development.

In its present form, the one-year course consists of two parts: an introduction and two units on the Netsilik Eskimo. The introduction gives a perspective of differences in innate and learned behavior. It analyzes uniformities and differences in the life cycle in man and in the salmon, sea gull, and baboon. The baboon material examines their environment, socialization, troop organization, and communication system as an analogue to the Netsilik. It also gives a vocabulary and frame of reference for thinking about human behavior. The original baboon film, made under the direction of Irven DeVere, highlights the baboon study.

Principal material for "Man: A Course of Study" consists of the Netsilik films, produced under the direction of Asen Balikci, professor of anthropology at the University of Montreal. The films are edited to reveal the yearly season migration cycle—summer stoneweir fishing, fall caribou hunting, mid-winter and spring sealing. The film, together with the written materials and teaching aids, is designed to show a human society in a microcosm and to make children more conscious of their assumptions concerning their own culture.

A teaching package. An intensive two-week treatment of an ethnic group or anthropological topic through a teaching package is offered by the MATCH Box Project of the Children's Museum, Boston.[4] This USOE project has developed four prototypic units for the primary grades that draw on anthropological or ethnographic data. These are "The City" (1-3), "Algonquins" (3,4), "Houses" (1-3), and "Netsilik Eskimos" (3,4).

The term *MATCH* stands for Materials and Activities for Teachers

---

3. A paper evaluating the comparative and in-depth approaches to the study of culture may be obtained from the Anthropology Curriculum Project, University of Georgia.

4. For further information, write: Fred H. Kresse, Director, *Match* Box Project, Children's Museum, 60 Burroughs Street, Boston, Massachusetts 02130.

and Children. A MATCH Box contains materials, equipment, supplies, and activities to foster the teaching and learning of specific subjects. The Boxes contain a high proportion of real objects and require little or no auxiliary equipment or supplies from the school. In every Box there is a Teacher's Guide that facilitates teacher use of the Box in working with the children.

A limited quantity of these materials may be available in late 1968. At the present time, the Boxes are confined to the pilot sets and are not available for general use.

Courses of study. The Social Science Program of the Educational Research Council of Greater Cleveland is one of the oldest and most successful of the developmental social studies programs. Concepts from anthropology are made explicit in teacher guides; pupil texts are scholarly correct and intellectually honest; anthropological units with different emphases are included at the second, fourth, and fifth grades; and the material is well packaged.

The second grade course "Communities at Home and Abroad"[5] includes a study of the Arunta of Australia as a type of slowly changing community and the Eskimos of Northern Alaska as a type of rapidly changing community. The Greater Cleveland Social Science Program, like that of the Georgia Project and the Educational Development Center, includes teacher background materials in addition to pupil resources.

Resource units. The most common type of material for teaching anthropology is the resource unit. Examples of very complete resource units are "The Australian Aborigines" and "Life in the Arctic: The Eskimo" developed for Grade 3 by the Elementary Social Studies Project Team of the Newton Public Schools.[6]

These units might be described as studies in cultural geography because of the emphasis placed on the physical environment and cultural adaptations. However, both units are rich in ethnographic data and include extensive treatments of attitudinal and belief systems, an aspect of culture not usually emphasized at this grade level. In the development of these units, the Newton staff has had the collaboration of anthropologists at Harvard. Preliminary Netsilik Eskimo material was made available by Educational Services, Inc.

Examples of resource units that are mainly teacher guides that

---

5. For additional information, write: Director, Social Science Program, Educational Research Council of Greater Cleveland, Cleveland, Ohio 43133.

6. For further information, write: Newton Public Schools, Division of Instruction, 88 Chestnut Street, West Newton, Massachusetts 02165.

include anthropology have been developed by the Taba Curriculum Development Project, San Francisco State College, and the Asian Studies Curriculum Project, University of California, Berkeley.

The Taba Curriculum Development Project,[7] in association with the Contra Costa County Schools, has developed a social studies series that sets forth anthropological concepts at several grade levels. The third grade course is "A Study in Comparative Communities." The communities examined are the Zulu, nomadic Arab, Boat People of Hong Kong, and the Swiss.

"Changing Japan" is a resource unit for upper elementary grades but may be adapted to the primary grades.[8] Like the Contra Costa units, it is multidisciplinary and takes the form of a teachers' guide, outlining content and learning experiences. No claim is made to introduce anthropological concepts, although Main Idea V focuses on Japanese culture.

Social studies graded series. Major textbook houses publish graded social studies series for the elementary grades. Content is mainly drawn from geography and history; behavioral content is not made explicit, and there is little attempt to identify anthropological concepts or data.

These basal series nevertheless include a great deal of data that might be described as anthropological, especially at the third grade level when application of the expanding environment approach permits an encounter with cultures and people outside of the United States, home, school, and community triad. The incidental inclusion of anthropological data results in part from the fact that archeology, a branch of anthropology, is the science that supplies the data for prehistory. It is largely immaterial whether the content is denominated historical or anthropological. Archeological data, however, do not usually appear in primary grade material because "history" is an intermediate rather than primary grade subject. Examples of chapters of units incorporating archeology are "When Man's Problems Began"[9] and "How Early Man Lived and Learned."[10]

Another reason social studies texts present a great deal of informal

7. For additional information, write: Director, Taba Curriculum Development Project, San Francisco State College, San Francisco, California 94132.
8. For additional information, write: John U. Michaelis, Director, Asian Studies Curriculum Project, University of California, Berkeley, California 94720.
9. Paul Nagel. *World Cultures: Past and Present.* New York: Harper and Row, 1965. pp. 19-33.
10. Prudence Cutright and John Jarolimek, general editors. *Living in the Old World.* New York: The Macmillan Company, 1966. pp. 26-43.

anthropology results from the fact that life and people in other lands have always been a part of school geography content, whether organization has followed culture world, climate, or type study models. The country format of data, presentation does not preclude superimposition of the analytic and synthesizing principles that form a common bond between anthropology and cultural geography.[11] However, the burden is placed on the teacher of first becoming familiar with the conceptual system of anthropology, which is not made explicit in the basal series.

Some of the more recent interdisciplinary social studies books claim inclusion of concepts from anthropology.[12] A difficulty lies in the fact that the term "concept" is used in as many different ways as there are authors and consists of whatever statement the author finds useful as a unifying principle.

Trade monographs. Many juvenile titles are published in archeology, ethnology, language, human origins, and related anthropological topics. There are a number of book lists that will assist teachers in identifying anthropology books suitable for young children. The most rigorous and selective list is the *AAAS Book List for Children,*[13] arranged according to the Dewey classification system. Headings include such topics as archeology, anthropology, and culture. The companion *Science Book List for Young Adults*[14] is perhaps one of the best ways for a teacher not trained in anthropology to obtain scientifically correct listings suitable for teacher use.

The most comprehensive list is the *Publishers Trade List Annual,*[15] which gives a very complete subject guide to books in print and suggested age-grade placement for juvenile books.

The Horn Book Magazine is one of the best sources to identify new children's books. Subject classification, however, is so limited that the entire list of annotations must be scanned.

Music. Major record companies such as Decca, Columbia, and RCA produce records and tapes of the music and language of people of

11. Delia Goetz. *At Home Around the World.* Boston: Ginn & Company, 1965; Mae Knight Clark, *Living in Our Country and Other Lands.* New York: The Macmillan Company, 1966.

12. Edna A. Anderson, *et. al. Silver Burdett Primary Social Studies Series.* New York: General Learning Corporation, 1967; Vincent Presno and Carol Presno. *Man in Action Series.* Englewood Cliffs, New Jersey: Prentice Hall, Inc., 1967.

13. Hilary J. Deason, compiler. Second Edition. American Association for the Advancement of Science, Washington, D.C., 1963.

14. *Ibid.,* 1964.

15. R.R. Bowker Co., 1180 Avenue of the Americas, New York 10036.

different cultures. Folkways Records has one of the most extensive lists.

Films and filmstrips. Anthropology films produced for elementary children are virtually non-existent. Anthropology films produced for mature audiences are best identified in the film catalogues published by universities.[16] Such films may be frequently used with children.

The best source to identify related social studies films is the new NICEM 16mm educational film index.[17] Multiple subjects need to be consulted—for example, anthropology is a subhead of "sociology"; archeology, of "earth science"; and Indians—U.S., of "social science." Most related films are classified by country under the general head "Geography—World."

As with other teaching material, both films and filmstrips need to be carefully reviewed prior to final selection for teaching use. On inspection, many films and filmstrips contain inaccurate or inappropriate material.

Pictures. Life and *National Geographic* remain two of the best sources for pictures. Some of the series published by Life-Time, such as the *Nature Library* and *World Library*, are also a valuable picture source.

Summary. Materials especially designed for teaching of anthropology in the primary grades remain limited. They reflect an eclectic rather than a discipline approach to content organization, and a focus on home, school, and community tied to an expanding environment theme. It is not until the third grade that most primary grade pupils get out of their own culture. Anthropologists have been aloof to social studies curriculum building. Contributions of anthropology to the social studies have been mediated by other disciplines: archeology by history, social anthropology by cultural geography, and human origins by biology.

There is, nevertheless, adequate material available for teaching anthropology in the elementary school, even though it may not be explicitly organized as anthropology. The major challenge is for elementary school teachers to become more familiar with the concepts of anthropology in order that they may give a greater emphasis to this important discipline.

16. For example, see the American Indian series of the University of California Extension Media Center, Berkeley, California 94720.

17. National Center for Educational Media, *Index to 16mm Educational Films,* New York: McGraw-Hill Book Company, Inc., 1967.

VII. Sociology

ETHNIC PRIDE BEGINS AT HOME

by

Marjorie G. Unger

February is Brotherhood Month, and Negro History Week begins on February 8. Here's how one teacher made the purpose behind these observances meaningful to her students.

Name a few black Americans that children look up to. Thurgood Marshall? Julian Bond? Diahann Carroll? Bob Gibson? Or how about Flip Wilson?

Fine. But ask the children in my school, and they'll probably rattle off a lot of names that will surprise you—for example, Captain Rudy Costa, who is community relations coordinator for our police department, or Dr. George I. Johnson, who is a dentist and former Norwalk Councilman, or Mrs. Corine Wright, who owns and operates a beauty salon on South Main Street.

They're all black Americans who have become leaders in our community. And the reason our youngsters know so much about them is that these adults, along with 34 other black community leaders, were written up in a book that received wide distribution in the Norwalk, Conn., schools last year.

An Appropriate Title

The title of the book is, appropriately enough, *Black People Making History in Norwalk*. The authors? None other than the seventh- and eighth-graders in my language arts classes.

Let me point out that this really *is* a book I'm talking about, not just a few copies run off on the school duplicating machine. It's 70 pages long, professionally printed and features an attractive semi-hard cover. You can find it on the shelves of all our city's libraries, and it's in constant demand for use, in language arts and social studies classes throughout our city.

I certainly hadn't planned on the project becoming as important as all that. I was simply looking for a suitable activity for Brotherhood Month and Negro History Week.

In the course of looking over materials produced by other teach-

Mrs. Unger teaches language arts in the Benjamin Franklin Middle School, Norwalk, Conn.

A 70-page booklet (right) giving biographies of important members of their black community was prepared by Norwalk, Conn. middle-graders with the aid of official form letters and the questionnaire shown below.

Dear ——————— :

    February has been designated as Brotherhood Month throughout the Norwalk School System as a pilot program month for special observances during the school year. There will be a variety of programs presented, including closed circuit television, assemblies and classroom activities.

    Mrs. Marjorie Unger, language arts teacher at Benjamin Franklin Middle School, has informed me that her students have selected as their project. "Black People Making History in Norwalk," as a means of highlighting Negro History Week. Their project will be a part of the Brotherhood Month Observances.

    Benjamin Franklin students have chosen you as one who has played a significant role in Norwalk. They would like to interview you (in person, letter, or telephone) in order to write your biography as one project of the Language Arts program.

    I would greatly appreciate it, if you would give them your assistance and encouragement, when you are contacted.

                              Sincerely yours,

                              Barbara Littlejohn
                              Director of Intergroup Programs
                              Board of Education

Dear ——————— :

    Enclosed is a questionnaire prepared by students at Benjamin Franklin Middle School. It is designed to enable them to write a brief biography of you. Please feel free to leave out any questions you consider personal, or add anything which you feel will help a teenager recognize the values by which you have attained your position as a productive citizen of our city.

    Your cooperation will help our young people, who may be confused and discouraged by the conflicts in our world, realize that success in one's life is related to concern for others; and that each individual, by the way he lives, makes history.

    This is our way of observing Brotherhood Month and Negro History Week in the Norwalk Schools.

                              Sincerely,

                              Marjorie Unger
                              Benjamin Franklin Middle School

---

QUESTIONNAIRE

Name ——————————————— Occupation ———————

Place of Business ——————————————————————

Where were you born? ———————

Briefly describe childhood in terms of living conditions, parental guidance, problems or obstacles, educational opportunities. . . .

How . . . Why . . . did you choose or get into the kind of work you are doing?

Hobbies . . . . . .

What was the most rewarding or exciting moment in your life?

What is the philosophy, belief or creed you followed in your life which helped you?

What advice would you give teenagers today?

Please add any information you consider might be helpful . . . . . .

Add any information which you would like included in your biography, such as organizations you belong to, offices you have held, honors you have received and institutions you have attended . . . . . .

Reprinted by permission of Marjorie G. Unger.

ers, I came across a number of biographies of black Americans. A fine idea, I thought. Why not do the same with *my* youngsters? But not the "usual" biographies—there were more than enough biographies of George Washington Carver already.

My first thought was to ask the children to write about living black Americans: well-known persons like Jackie Robinson and Sammy Davis Jr., whose lives would be sure to interest the children. Then it occurred to me that I could take it one step further and have the youngsters write about black Americans in our community: the doctors, dentists, teachers, ministers and others whose lives could easily serve as models for the children.

The more I thought about it, the better the idea seemed. The project would commemorate Brotherhood Month by helping black students gain a measure of ethnic pride and white students gain a measure of understanding. It would honor Negro History Week by showing *all* my students that black people are very much a part of America's history and that the way they live right now helps determine the future course of this nation. It would also show the children that many adults have overcome obstacles by education and hard work, and that adults really do care about what happens to the younger generation. And it would all be neatly packaged in an activity that stressed reading and writing skills.

Few Problems

If you're thinking of trying this project in your own classroom, you can expect a few problems. But they won't be serious ones. The few problems I faced were all "mechanical," easily spotted and easily solved. For example, I had originally intended having the children interview the community leaders face to face. It soon became obvious, though, that the scheduling involved was too complicated to be carried out, since the interviewers were on one schedule and the interviewees on another. We substituted duplicated questionnaires for face-to-face interviews.

The first step, then, was to familiarize the children with biographies and questionnaires. I brought in a number of biographies for the children to study. (I used books I knew the children would enjoy—for example, an easy-to-read biography of baseball star Sandy Koufax.) Then I assigned each child the task of interviewing someone. It could be anyone at all—a parent, a relative, a school crossing guard or the cop on the corner. The children wrote up their interviews and, without disclosing the names of the people interviewed, I read the youngsters' efforts in class.

The purpose of the discussion that followed was to show the

children what kind of questions should be included on the questionnaire. Obviously, they would have to be questions that brought out important or interesting facts. With the interviews that had just been read serving as examples of what or what not to do, the youngsters had no trouble deciding what should or should not be included in the questionnaire.

I added one item that is not usually included in biographical questionnaires: What advice did the interviewee have for teenagers? Not customary perhaps, but terribly important for young people in the first years of adolescence.

From the answers the children gave, I put together a questionnaire, typed it up and duplicated copies. We were ready for our next step—selecting the community leaders we wished to interview.

Community Service

The people we were looking for were successful black men and women—not successful in terms of money or social position, but in terms of usefulness and service to the community.

The director of our Intergroup Programs—which work for better ethnic relationships and coordinate instruction in integrated classes—supplied us with a number of names from people she knew in the community. The children added many more—policemen, teachers, ministers, relatives and so on. By the time we were finished, we had an imposing list of 65 community leaders.

The Intergroup Programs director sent off a letter (see page 142) to the 65 residents, explaining what we were trying to do and asking their cooperation in answering the questionnaires they were soon to receive. A short time later, I sent out the questionnaire (see page 142) to everyone on our list. A total of 37 people returned the filled-out questionnaires to us.

I tried to spread out the job of writing the biographies as evenly as possible, with each child having the opportunity to work on at least one biography. At first, I assigned the biographies as the questionnaires arrived one or two children to each. But later, as the mail got heavy, I put as many as five or six children on a single biography. (I found that an easy way to do this was to put the questionnaire on the overhead projector and let the children take it from there.)

Each finished biography represented the joint effort of all the children who had worked on it—a sentence from one child, a paragraph from another child, an important point from still another child. The youngsters were encouraged to edit and polish each other's contribution, so that when they signed their names to the finished product it really *did* mean they had participated.

For the most part, the biographies ran to a set pattern, although there were often flashes of wit and wisdom. The children noted the subject's place of birth, facts of childhood, educational opportunities, hobbies, present job and the various honors received.

Perhaps the most interesting of all the information included in the biographies was each community leader's advice to today's teenagers. The advice ran heavily in favor of continuing one's education, showing patience and tolerance for other people and exhibiting firmness in the face of social injustices.

Here, for example, is what one woman who is a neighborhood resource worker had to say to my student: "If you make a mistake (and life gives us many such opportunities) try to learn something from your mistake. As for the others you are going to meet in life, judge your fellow man as you would like to be judged, not by his color—not by his creed—and not by where he lives. There is an old saying, 'There, but for the grace of God, go I . . .' Because of generations of mistrust and misdeeds, the burden of the world's survival is placed on the shoulder's of today's teenagers. If the world is to survive, it is up to you!"

And this from the biography of a local football coach: "His advice to teenagers is to continue their education, pursue their ambitions, inquire about things that they don't understand. If there is a law they disagree with, fight to change it; but always have a solution to replace the law they wish to abolish."

There's nothing startlingly new about any of this advice, of course, but it shows that there are many people who are interested in bridging the generation gap.

Different Ideas

After the biographies were written, I typed them up and ran them off on our duplicating machine so that each child could have his own copy. That was the end of it, I thought . . . but other people had different ideas.

Some of our administrators were so impressed with what my youngsters had done that they had the biographies printed Multilith, with an eye-catching, semi-hard cover and plastic spiral binding. The superintendent of schools wrote a forward and our principal and the Intergroup Programs director both contributed introductory material. As I mentioned earlier, the book was circulated to city and school libraries and to many social studies and language arts classes, where I'm told it's still being used.

There was still one more high point in store for my middle-school authors. In May we had an open house at the school for the authors, the community leaders, parents, other teachers and board of education officials. The children got a chance to meet the men and women they had been writing about, and everyone present who had contributed to the success of the project got a copy of the book.

Good projects have good followups—and ours was no exception. In the classroom, we used the biographies as textbooks for discussion purposes. We didn't just limit ourselves to a study of writing effective biographies, but also talked about the qualities that made the community leaders so special.

We had one followup that was particularly enjoyed by the children. I had them fill out questionnaires about themselves and then write each other's biography. However, each child filled out his questionnaire as though he were an adult and the biographies were written accordingly, complete with envisioned professions and advice to "today's" teenagers.

The result was an encouraging—if imaginary—glance into the future: Many of my youngsters had graduated from Harvard and Yale, had established themselves as doctors, lawyers and teachers, were busily acquiring civic and professional honors and were seriously advising the younger generation to follow in their footsteps.

Positive Results

Over and above the reading and writing skills it developed, our project did a lot of things for a lot of people:

Black children and their parents were proud of their place in the community. Ethnic pride begins at home or black is beautiful—take your choice.

White children and their parents were impressed by the accomplishments and by the religious, educational and moral values emphasized by the black community leaders.

The community leaders were, by and large, brought closer to the younger generation. Many of them expressed a desire to continue some kind of relationship with the youngsters. For example, one dentist at the open house extended this blanket invitation to the children: "If any of you have any problems, stop in at my office at any time."

And the children themselves acquired a clearer insight as to their place in society. They recognized that they are responsible *today* for the way history will be written. To quote one student: "Someday kids at Benjamin Franklin will be writing *my* biography."

VIII. Skill Development

THE ROLE OF SKILLS
IN ELEMENTARY SOCIAL STUDIES

by

Helen McCracken Carpenter

The gentle groundswell of change that characterized social studies instruction for many decades has become in the last few years a volcanic eruption of colloquy, publication, experimentation, and reform. From all indications, the streams of educational lava can be expected to well forth at an even greater rate in the next few years. The extent to which this flow is likely to seep into the classrooms to benefit the social studies teaching and learning of the three Americans in every ten now enrolled in formal education cannot be assessed at this time. Herein lies the difficulty in attempting to take bearings on the current situation in any definite way. Analysis, of necessity at this time, involves factors that are fluid.

Skill development in elementary social studies is not at the forefront of attention in the current ferment. Of the forty projects within the national spotlight, less than a fourth deal in any way with the elementary grades and most of these focus on subject-matter content or materials. Only three touch the core of concern here, and the findings of these are not yet available. It is necessary then to look at implications of general developments in considering the function of skills in elementary social studies.

Points of Continuing Agreement

Skill development has always been recognized as an important responsibility of elementary education. In fact, the need to teach young citizens the three R's was advanced as a major justification whenever and wherever the drive to establish public schools was underway. Concern for competence in reading, written expression, and arithmetic, now dignified as "the new math," is still central to the goals and curriculum for six- to twelve-year-olds. Achievement in these basic skills is of vital concern to social studies instruction because reading with all its varied purposes and forms—parallels with increasing utility, as an avenue to learning in this field, the growing maturity of the child; mathematics supplies the foundation necessary

From *Social Education*, March 1967. Reprinted with permission of the National-al Council for the Social Studies and Helen McCracken Carpenter.

to progress in developing a sense of time and chronology; and the expression of ideas and understandings in writing is, next to behavior, the truest yardstick of comprehension. As horizons in education widened, other skills were added to the program. Examples include the cluster concerned with locating, organizing, evaluating, and applying information; communicating orally; participating in group undertakings; listening; and observing. The relevancy of all these to progress in social studies is admitted and responsibility for fostering competence is accepted. Concern today then does not involve lack of recognition, by either teachers or administrators, of the need for skill development in the social studies program.

There is common acknowledgment also of the reciprocal relation of factors involved in the instructional situation. One helpful result accruing from viewpoints of psychologists shaping current thinking has been to highlight the inextricable relationship existing among all elements in the educational process—objectives, subject matter, method, materials, pupils—that has been obscured at different times in the past as the spotlight swung, over-emphasizing one factor and then another. The same is true within the category of objectives. The close connection of the cognitive to the affective realms—of knowledge and intellectual skills and abilities to attitudes, appreciations, and values—is manifest. Knowledge supplies the substance for the development of skills and provides standards necessary to value formation. Intellectual skills function both in the gaining of knowledge and in the process of valuing. In turn, affective elements color interpretation of knowledge and the effectiveness of skill development.

Among the several classifications of goals to which social studies teaching is directed, agreement is general that the development of skills should receive major attention. The scales tip heavier to skills than to knowledge because of the rapid rate in the obsolescence of much information today and, therefore, of the diminished transfer value of knowledge. Skills, however, represent more generalized learnings and thus are likely to be applicable continually in all facets of an individual's life. With reference to value formation, skill development weighs somewhat heavier for different reasons. The heart of the matter here concerns substantive values—the qualities of mind and character constituting moral excellence in an individual as well as concepts of ideals, customs, and institutions necessary to the good society. In a pluralistic nation like ours, social studies instruction in public schools cannot approach this area head-on. It *can* teach the process of making value judgments. Because skills are generally considered to pertain to *process* rather than to *product* of learning, skill development provides children with basic tools for arriving at their own values.

Unanimity continues also on the identification of skills that should be developed. The new social studies incorporates no categories beyond those set forth in the 33rd Yearbook of the National Council for the Social Studies.[1] Hence, on need, relative importance, and scope of skills in elementary social studies, thinking has changed little in recent years. It is in the approach to skill development involving method and organization that challenging considerations arise from the current stirrings.

Focus on Inquiry Through Problem-Solving

Accelerated exploration of the nature of intellectual growth as a key to improvement of educational experiences has been a major trend in the ferment of the last decade. Perhaps the most seminal single stimulus to the movement was the appearance of Bruner's capsule-size *Process of Education*,[2] reporting findings of experimental programs in science and mathematics as well as the thinking of scholars from a variety of fields participating in the 1959 Woods Hold Conference. Renewed attention to inquiry, or discovery, as a method of learning to think is the facet of the total trend with the most pertinency in the consideration of skill development. Inquiry is considered to be the process by which a child, more or less independently, comes to perceive relationships among factors in his environment or between ideas that previously had no meaningful connection. The new understandings evolve through application and reorganization of past experiences. Insight and self-confidence grow as the child meets successfully situations of increasing abstractness and complexity; as he moves up the ladder from observation, classification, and application to generalization.

Thus the inquiry approach views the learner as an active thinker—seeking, probing, processing data from his environment toward a variety of destinations along paths best suited to his own mental characteristics. It rejects passiveness as an ingredient of effective learning and the concept of the mind as a reservoir for the storage of

1. Helen McCracken Carpenter, editor. *Skill Development in Social Studies.* Thirty-third Yearbook. Washington, D.C.: National Council for the Social Studies 1963.
2. Jerome S. Bruner. *The Process of Education.* Cambridge: Harvard University Press, 1960.

knowledge presented through expository instruction directed toward a predetermined, closed end. The inquiry method seeks to avoid the dangers of rote memorization and verbalization as well as the hazard of fostering dependency in citizens as learners and thinkers. Advantages of the inquiry approach are considered to be in self-direction as a motivating factor for learning and in development of a form of mental behavior essential in a democratic society. The measure of ultimate success in education through inquiry lies in the degree to which the teacher becomes unnecessary as a guide.

The parallelism of ideas such as these being examined today to John Dewey's concepts of long ago is evident. Dewey's belief in the development of reflective thinking by means of inquiry shaped the philosophy and functioning of the children's school founded at the University of Chicago in the mid-1890's.[3] In the years following, Dewey elaborated his ideas on reflective thinking and its relation to education in a democratic society[4] that Kilpatrick[5] as his disciple helped keep dominant into the Twenties and Thirties. Although the last three decades have witnessed many changes in American education, the desirability of developing citizens who are independent and skilled inquirers has been recognized in theory even though efforts to realize the goal languished. To Dewey and to leaders in the current movement, an important approach, or strategy, facilitating inquiry is problem-solving. Dewey's analysis of the mental state involved has become a classic,

> ... *reflective* thinking, in distinction from other operations to which we apply the name of thought, involves 1) a state of doubt, hesitation, perplexity, mental difficulty, in which thinking originates, and 2) an act of searching, hunting, inquiring, to find material that will resolve the doubt, settle and dispose of the perplexity.[6]

Although slight differences in classification of the elements involved in problem-solving exist, the pattern is essentially as follows but does not necessarily proceed neatly in the rank order given:

1. an awareness and identification stage
   Consisting of a feeling of disturbance, perception of factors involved, and clarification of the core of the obstacle

3. John Dewey. *University Record.* 1:417-422, No. 32; November 6, 1896.
4. ———. *Democracy and Education.* New York: The Macmillan Company, 1916; *How We Think.* Boston: D.C. Heath and Company, 1933.
5. William H. Kilpatrick. *The Project Method.* New York: Teachers College Bureau of Publications, Columbia University, 1919.
6. *Op. cit., How We Think*, p. 116.

2. a data-processing stage
   Including collecting, organizing, and evaluating relevant information
3. an analytical-synthesizing stage
   Involving comparing, contrasting, inferring, speculating, and applying in hypothesis formation
4. a critical, testing stage
   Constituting probing the validity of hypotheses, reconstructing data, reaching plausible conclusions in the form of tentative principles useful in the next encounter

These ideas seem like old friends to many elementary school teachers who have long used problems as a means of getting their pupils to think critically. The current emphasis on inquiry, however, highlights interesting considerations about skills and the problems approach as a means for developing them.

Implications for Skill Development

Most important is the fact that the problems approach, as often interpreted, does not necessarily promote the goals of the inquiry method. The crux of the matter concerns the difference between inductive and deductive learning. Inquiry emphasizes the inductive process. Learning experiences set up in problem form may, or may not, call for inductive procedures, depending on the nature of the problem and what the learner is required to do. For example, if a problem is posed as "How do the religious beliefs of some people in India increase famine there?," the learner is pointed toward religion and hunger. The relationship is established; his job is to prove it with specific data. If the question is put a little less specifically, "Why does India continue to have a shortage of food?", there is no real change in the nature of the task especially if sub-problems are attached, such as, "What is the population of India?" "What methods of farming are used?" "What does India have to offer other countries in trade?" This learning experience is not designed to give pupils an opportunity to develop and test hypotheses; they are called on to proceed deductively. A corollary to this approach often is the use of materials that supply the answers organized in the same way the information is requested.

If, on the other hand, the problem is posed in a more open-ended way, such as "What accounts for problems facing India today?", and materials are provided that give data of various kinds—geographic, demographic, cultural, political—the task of finding, assimilating, evaluating, testing, rejecting, re-applying, deciding is left to the child. There is room for disagreement among pupils on the relative importance of causes and the effectiveness of possible courses of action. The learner is given the chance to draw relationships himself rather than to explain or support those made for him. The strategies employed by a child working inductively are revealing indicators of thinking style and intellectual growth.[7]

The emphasis, then, that will be dominant depends on the *nature* and *amount* of direction provided by the teacher. The need for guidance of learning, be it inductive or deductive, must, of course, be recognized. With children who are younger, less able, or inexperienced in inquiry procedures, the greater becomes the need for direction. Opportunities for structuring exist in the depth of the problems to be researched, the questions posed for discussion, the working definition used for an hypothesis, and the number of obvious cues contained in study materials provided. As pupil competency develops, the teacher can widen the horizons and plant fewer and fewer cues in the learning experience.

Gagné discusses the nature of direction as one of the conditions of problem solving along with contiguity of the elements involved and recency of recall. He observes—

> Guidance may vary in amount or completeness, always short of describing the solution itself. At a minimum, guidance of thinking takes the form of informing the learner of the goal of his activity, the general form of the solution; this amount appears to be required if learning is to occur at all. Greater amounts of guidance function to limit the range of hypotheses to be entertained by the learner in achieving solution . . . When these conditions are present, the learner is able to solve the problem, although the time required for this solution is likely to vary with the amount of guidance provided, as well as with certain innate capacities of the learner.[8]

The prime requisite for the teacher is the ability to distinguish between goals of various kinds and to identify the learning procedures appropriate for different ends. Important also is willingness to

---

7. For more detailed discussion of these aspects than is permitted here, *see* Fannie R. Shaftel, Charlotte Crabtree, and Vivian Rushworth. "Problem Solving in the Elementary School" in *The Problems Approach and the Social Studies,* edited by Richard E. Gross, Raymond H. Muessig, and George L. Fersh. Curriculum Bulletin No. 9 revised edition. Washington, D.C.: National Council for the Social Studies, 1960. pp. 25-47; Charlotte Crabtree. "Inquiry Approaches: How New and How Valuable?" *Social Education* 30: 523-525, 531; November 1966; J. Richard Suchman. "The Child and the Inquiry Process" in *Intellectual Development: Another Look,* edited by A. Harry Passow and Robert R. Leeper. Washington, D.C.: Association for Supervision and Curriculum Development, 1964. pp. 59-77; Robert M. Gagné. *The Conditions of Learning.* New York: Holt, Rinehart and Winston, Inc., 1965. Ch. 6.

8. (Gagné, *Conditions of Learning*), p. 163.

let pupils venture on their own, to elicit suggestions for new ways of proceeding to encourage differing opinions, and to respect pupil fumblings along the way.

Another implication concerns the relative importance of various classifications of skills. The prominence currently given to the inquiry method, with focus on cognitive skills, may seem in effect to dwarf the importance of other kinds of skills. Actually, the opposite is true because effective thinking is facilitated by competency in a variety of abilities somewhat less complicated in nature. The quest for information cannot proceed far without the ability to determine and find the kind of resource that will supply the data needed and know how to extract the information efficiently. Similarly, the organizing skills of notetaking, outlining, and reporting are steps along the way. In addition to such work-study skills as these, proficiency with the intake skills of observing, listening, and reading is basic to effective living today. The competencies to which social studies make a particular contribution—developing a sense of place and space, and a sense of time and chronology—provide perspective for decision-making. And the need for effective group-work skills, in school and in life, is apparent. In fact, at the primary level, this category of skills may well be not only basic to but also as important as the cognitive abilities.

Nothing in the current examination of learning in relation to thought processes contradicts either the principle of sequential development of skills (although stages cannot be expected to proceed neatly) or the concept of readiness (although time is subject to reinterpretation).

The need, then, is for thoughtful design and management of the learning environment to maintain balance both horizontally and vertically among the various kinds of skills needed for effective living today—and tomorrow.

SKILLS TEACHING
IN THE PRIMARY GRADES
by
John Jarolimek*

The term *skill* is applied to the ability to do something with some degree of expertness in repeated performances. To have a skill or to be skillful, however, is usually something of a relative matter. The kindergarten child is highly skillful in his use of language when compared with a two-year old. We would say that he is less skillful in most things he does when compared with an upper-grade pupil. Adequacy of skill development must not only take into account the expertness of performance *per se*, but the age and prior background of the learner.

When children enter the primary grades, they have already developed a number of skills. They can carry on conversations with others, follow directions, take care of many of their personal needs, play simple games; some can read. Such skills are essential for ordinary living. Left unattended and untutored, the child will improve these skills simply through continued use. The refinement of the skills the child has when he comes to school and the learning of others that are introduced as a part of the curriculum will be greatly enhanced through careful and systematic instruction. From the moment the child enters school, his continued success in the school environment will depend to a significant degree on the extent to which he is able to learn and use essential skills.

There can be no doubt that well developed skills enhance the ability to do other school-related tasks. Conversely, poorly developed skills result in arrested school progress. Pupils who are off to a poor start in their skill development in the primary grades fall farther and farther behind in their overall achievement. Eventually the deficit accumulates to a point that becomes overwhelming to the pupil and nearly impossible for him to overcome. School dropouts at the high school level invariably present histories of skill deficiencies that can be traced to the earliest grades in school. Skill competence strengthens the child's positive perception of himself, an important compo-

From *Social Education*, March 1967. Reprinted with permission of the National Council for the Social Studies and John Jarolimek.
*This article is a substitute for one of the same title that was solicited from another author but not received.

nent of school success. The child uses skills to deal with the social world confronting him, and consequently, skills contribute directly to his social competence. It would be hard to underestimate the vital role primary grade teachers play in ensuring a successful introduction of the child to the skills program.

In the primary grades it is almost impossible to separate social studies skills from the skills objectives of the total primary grade program. There is no particular reason to label certain skills as being the unique province of the social studies, providing essential skills get the instructional attention they deserve. The advantage of singling out social studies skills in the curriculum is to ensure that they *are* included and taught systematically. Moreover, skills presented in a social studies context can often be taught in a more realistic and functional setting than when presented either in isolation or in the framework of another curriculum area, as for example, in the reading program.

In the first article of this supplement, Professor Carpenter has noted that in spite of the concern for social studies revision in recent years, no new skills have been identified. Essential skills persist in their importance in modern programs even though there have been some shifts in emphasis. Uniqueness in skills teaching does not come through the discovery of some new skill but in imaginative approaches to the teaching of those that have always been regarded as important. The social studies skills with which the primary grade teacher is concerned are less complex variations of skills that continue to receive attention throughout the total program.

One large group of such skills deals basically with a variety of intellectual operations. Thinking, asking questions, using language, solving problems, interpreting stories and pictures, and making simple analyses are few examples of skills of this type. In most cases they are related to the informational content of the program. They do not deal basically with *getting* information but with interpreting, processing, and using information. In the following example, notice how the teacher is building thinking skills with her first graders:

> The teacher selected a picture from a magazine advertising a dishwasher. The picture shows a young mother removing sparkling clean dishes from the washer while her daughter (about a six-year old) looks on. One can see a bright, modern kitchen and the landscape greenery through the kitchen window. The teacher prepared the following questions in connection with this picture:
> 1. Is the mother taking the dishes out or putting them in the washer?
> 2. Is this a large or small family?
> 3. Does this family have a comfortable home?

4. What season of the year is it?
5. What might other members of the family be doing at this time?
6. Do you think the lady is the little girl's mother?
7. Is this a city home or a farm home?

The purpose of this exercise is not to establish right or wrong answers to the questions. Indeed, it would be impossible to determine precisely the rightness or wrongness of some of them. For example, one could not be sure about the size of the family by the number of dishes used; the family may have had guests, or the dishes may be an accumulation from more than one meal. Similarly, the season of the year could not be verified by the presence of greenery because some parts of the country are green the year around. Pupils could be expected to point out these possibilities, and while they may select what they think is the most likely answer, the door should be kept open to the consideration of other alternatives. In activities of this type, it is more important to consider a variety of possibilities and have pupils give reasons why a response is plausible than to agree on a right answer. (This degree of flexibility would not be acceptable, however, in considering factual questions where correctness can be established. Factual questions serve a different purpose from those designed to encourage reflective thought.)

Other examples of intellectual skills can be developed around such situations as these:

1. Identifying sequences—What happened first; what happened next; what happened last?
2. Considering alternative solutions—Can you think of another way to do it? What are some other ways the man could have solved his problems?
3. Differentiating between fact and fiction—What parts of the story are true and what parts are make-believe? How can we find out if something is true?
4. Developing sensitivity to words—Can you think of words that make you feel happy? Sad? Angry?
5. Predicting or speculating on outcomes of situations—How do you suppose the problem was solved? What do you suppose will happen next?

Telling pupils to think or admonishing them for not thinking are not effective methods for developing intellectual skills even though such practices in one form or another are fairly common. More productive approaches call for the pupil to respond to simple questions of the reflective type that may not have a single answer but force him to consider many alternatives, predict likely consequences of each, and decide the best course of action. There can be little if any thinking if the pupil does not have to consider alternatives in situations that involve choice or decision-making.

The importance of intellectual skills, and especially thinking skills, is often overlooked in the primary grades because of the widespread belief that one gains knowledge first and then uses that knowledge for thinking purposes at some later time. As a result the development of thinking abilities of young children has not always been the concern of primary grade teachers. Children at this level were expected to build literacy and work-study skills and expand their backgrounds of information. Thinking would come later. There is no evidence to support the notion that knowledge acquisition and knowledge use in the thinking process are separate and discrete functions. In fact, the practice of disassociating a skill from its functional context is rejected as unsound practice in most other realms of skill development. It is unfortunate that it should persist in teaching pupils the most important skill of all, namely, thinking.

A second large group of skills important to the primary grade social studies involves social relationships. They include ordinary social skills needed for harmonious living and working with others, as well as those more structured skills related to instructional processes, i.e., working on a small committee, contributing to a group project, participating in class discussions, and so forth. These skills are the concern of the total curriculum of the elementary school, of course, but the social studies provide excellent settings in which to teach them because of the nature of instructional processes associated with this area of the curriculum.

The most important point that could be made in connection with social relationship skills is that they *need to be taught.* It is often assumed that all that is required are activities in which pupils can apply and practice them. Consequently, pupils are forced to learn the skills of social interaction on a trial and error basis. In the process the teacher may become annoyed, isolate those pupils who were not "cooperative," and return the others to their seats to a more formal instructional posture. While there might be times when a child should be separated from the others, no child ever learned the skills of social interaction while he was in isolation. Neither do classes learn such skills in formal instructional settings where social interaction is not allowed or is discouraged.

A third category of social studies skills has to do mainly with the use of learning resources and tools including simple map and globe reading, knowing where to go for information needed, how to speak before the class, reading signs and symbols, and other similar operations. They are commonly called work-study skills. The need for instructional attention to these skills has been generally accepted through the years. Conventional reading programs ordinarily devote some instruction to work-study skills that are relevant to social studies.

It often happens that a specific activity can be used to attack several related work-study skills. For example, a third grade class may be collecting pictures that show the way of life in another country. Such an activity might be used to promote any or all of the following skills:

1. Locating appropriate pictures.
2. Explaining or telling the class something about the picture.
3. Classifying information—placing pictures in appropriate categories such as those that show home life, those that show work people do, holiday observances, or sports events.
4. Comparing information from one picture with another.
5. Learning and using new words and concepts represented in the picture.
6. Asking appropriate questions concerning picture content.
7. Planning and arranging an exhibit, such as a bulletin board.
8. Creating and writing appropriate captions and/or explanations to accompany the pictures.

Similarly, in the selection of activities for the development of work-study skills, the primary grade teacher can attend to intellectual skills and social relationship skills as well. For example, in teaching pupils how to use the school library, the teacher will undoubtedly stress such intellectual skills as listening to directions, observing carefully, asking questions, and knowing what information is wanted. If the activity involves going to the library as a class or in smaller groups, she will also use the experience as a way of teaching or reinforcing social behavior of pupils. Finally, in the process pupils will learn something about use of the library—how it is arranged, where to look for certain kinds of books, and how to check out a book. Although we separate these skills for discussion purposes and focus instruction on specific skills from time to time to ensure learning, the whole cluster of social studies skills is highly interrelated.

To a degree skill growth is related to the developmental pattern of children. Consequently, no matter how intensively skills are taught in the primary grades, there are definite upper limits on the level of proficiency that can realistically be expected of most primary grade pupils. It is advisable, therefore, to establish reasonable criterion levels of expectation and settle for those rather than to expend an excessive amount of instructional time in order to get small increments of improvement in performance. The growth curve on skills rises sharply to a point and then levels off; perhaps the optimum performance expectancy is just beyond the point where the curve begins to plateau. If adequate instruction on skills can be assured and reasonable expectancy levels set, there will be time to spend on other important dimensions of an effective primary grade program. Skills and skills teaching, while extremely important, should not entirely dominate the primary grade curriculum to the exclusion of art, music, poetry, literature, and other learnings vital to the total development of the young child.

USING LEARNING RESOURCES
IN SOCIAL STUDIES SKILL DEVELOPMENT
by
Clarence O. Bergeson

Developing skills for dealing with social and political problems must obviously be an important area of concern to teachers of the social studies. True, in the secondary school one might well expect that pupils will bring with them many if not most of the needed basic study skills. Elementary teachers, on the other hand, cannot ignore the important need for much basic skill development as younger children approach the task of understanding the people in their expanding world.

Admittedly this is both an extensive and complex task. Its complexity increases with each new communication, transportation, and political innovation. Technology, the handmaiden of the "progress," adds its own unique burden of change. However, for the teacher who is willing to explore these changes, help exists in the technology itself. It can provide effective learning through the use of new channels and more efficient means of using older channels. Such learning resources have many potential uses in developing social studies skills in young children.

Discussion of learning resources in this context needs to be based on the recognition that many of these materials are "newer media," and as "media" are themselves skills to be learned by the elementary school child. Teachers must systematically assess and prepare for such skill learning before any intelligent approach to using media for the learning of other skills can be successfully attempted.

What does the child see in the wandering lines on the pages of an atlas, lines that adults so quickly recognize as a map? What does a child understand in the varying shades of gray deep blacks and shiny whites, the straight and curving lines that modern adults so easily accept as black and white photographs?

How clearly does a child understand the implications of a graphic caricature of the president of the United States, the symbol of a foreign land, or the stereotypes of good and bad as used in cartoons and comic strip presentations? To what extent can a child "read"

From *Social Education*, March 1967. Reprinted with permission of the National Council for the Social Studies and Clarence O. Bergeson.

into a motion picture the intended passage of time between scenes, the rapid transpositions of location, the manipulated sequence of events punctuated with sophisticated cinematic techniques?

Would it not be fair to say that their ability in any of these media skills all too often develops without guidance and without any certainty that needed levels of proficiency exist?

These children live in a world that operates with many media, not just one. They are both a product of that multi-media world and its heirs. To be illiterates in any of these media when meeting that world is to court disaster. For their future and the future use of these learning resources in the school the children must learn a wide variety of modern communication skills.

Fortunately, literacy can often be taught by using the very media in question. A class and a teacher can look at a picture, not only as social documentation but also as a picture. How has the picture been distorted or determined by the use of a special lens, a special angle, a special frame? What does it say and what does it not say?

Who took the picture and what might have been his biases? After all, a picture is at most a very selected view, a momentary cross-section of a dynamic event. Even the singular aspect of size must be interpreted by both photographer and viewer. To a greater or less degree, then, the picture is an interpretation; it is not a fact. It is a medium that must be learned and can be learned through a critical approach by teacher and pupil.

Map "reading" skills, though universally recognized as important, still cannot be overemphasized. Most teachers know about the sand box or table-top display as possible beginning experiences with map meanings. A flannelboard or a hook-and-loop board provides a good surface for more abstract approaches. The overhead projector will present simple map materials as well as a large variety of commercially produced map transparencies. Kits demonstrating concepts of map projection and distortion give opportunities for developing more sophisticated understandings. Numerous commercially produced films and filmstrips help build skills in map meanings and map usage.

All media require an overt effort on the part of the communicator and the perceiver to understand the "grammar," the "rules of composition," before effective learning can be expected. This is doubly true in the social studies where the events of man and his world are no longer "documented" exclusively on the printed page, but where these events can be seen, heard, and felt through an expanding array of media and materials. The elementary teacher of social studies must be knowledgeable and sophisticated in using these resources. He must help pupils develop similar skills.

Having said that media are skills that one must learn and having recognized the multi-media world pupils must face, it becomes only natural to consider these media and related learning resources as teaching vehicles and techniques for learning other needed skills. In other words, these learning resources can act as tools for meeting effectively those principles of learning that are active in skill development.

Since all too often newer media and materials conjure up a passive role for the intended audience, it might be appropriate to begin this part of the discussion by remembering that pupils learn better or benefit more when doing the things they are learning rather than only witnessing a task. Of course, a motion picture documents an event. But as such the teacher should make certain it enters the learning situation as a result of the pupil's search or need for "evidence" on a topic, problem, or project.

Pupils can actively use modern media in a number of ways. Modern automatic equipment makes possible classroom produced motion picture—a summary report, an event recreated, a documentary of a field trip developed by the pupils and teacher. The chalkboard, and its modern counterpart, the overhead projector, can serve as a recorder of progress in pupil discussions or outlining the progress of group planning sessions.

Television production facilities (where available) can be a vehicle for class project reporting, for pupil interviews of local and visiting specialists not available at class time, for pupil-prepared dramatized social or historic situations, and for class directed current events presentations. Closed-circuit systems with video recording equipment bring to classrooms the opportunity to organize and deliver a report, interview, or presentation; view the product; criticize and refine the presentation in terms of content, organization, and techniques; and then record again.

Recording and editing audio tapes of a report and combining the refined version with slides offers similar possibilities for pupil participation. These experiences not only contribute to developing skills in each respective media but also build skills in locating and organizing needed information, in presenting such information through many media, and in viewing critically the work they and their fellow pupils have produced.

In building skills as in other types of learning, the need for the experience to be meaningful to the child is imperative. Of course, such meaningfulness should first reside in the overall curriculum, the course of study, and the assigned unit of work. Often, however, it becomes necessary to start with the "now" and work toward pupil understanding of larger goals.

Here, properly chosen learning resources can help. Of course, a diagram on a chalkboard may very well make the organization of a village or town perceptually tangible and possibly more meaningful. Motion pictures of past events in history, still pictures of the important cities of the world, bulletin board displays of community service agencies all have the possibilities of developing greater meaningfulness.

Perhaps teaching techniques are equally as important as the material one chooses. Why not include pupils in planning sessions? A small group can select a filmstrip for showing to the class. Let them prepare the introduction and lead the discussion. They are capable of some self-direction. And in the process they will generally expose that which is and is not meaningful to them.

Meaningfulness as a criterion for useful learning experiences leads directly to the principle that pupils tend to learn only that which they can perceive in a situation. Skill experiences too far beyond their present level become an enigma. Past experiences color and, in fact, control what pupil's learn.

Much is said these days of the culturally deprived. These and many other learners might more accurately be described as experientially deprived. Their home environment, their relation with parents, their community horizons, all tend to leave many children without needed experiential background for dealing with controversial issues, with newspapers and magazines, with using the library, and the like. Such deprivation poses a real problem for the teacher approaching social skill development in the elementary school child.

Modern media and materials can go far in remedying a dearth of experience in specific areas. The growth of 8 mm "single concept" loop films represents one channel for help. Remedial films, filmstrips, recordings, maps, charts, and diagrams all are as legitimate a part of the classroom as remedial reading materials.

The teacher might also provide an opportunity to "translate" from one media to another—a picture of the inauguration of a president changed into words, the data about population in a motion picture extracted and built into a graph or a diagram, or a word description developed into a chart or a drawing.

Building useful social studies skills does require meaningful, understandable, learner-involved experiences. But the child facing a need to learn a skill must have something more. How ought the pupil work with other children in a small group, on joint projects, in class activities? How should a democratic meeting be run? How does one develop an organizational outline for a topic summary? Guidance by the teacher becomes inperative.

Special step-by-step instructions become universally available when tape recorded and placed at a listening station at the back of the room, in the library, or in an independent study center. You can combine taped narration with colored slides in automatic projectors for pupils who need to see and hear about such things as example outlines or sample library cards.

Record those models of performance, of error, of excellence on audio or television tape needed as reference by class members, including such examples as proper parliamentary procedures and proper respect for fellow class members when developing group projects. Exemplify the usual steps in approaching a controversial social issue through a set of pictures. Emphasize the proper approach to reading a book by building a bulletin board display.

The teacher need not depend exclusively on himself for these models of skill performance. Commercially produced motion pictures review the steps involved in making a legislative bill into a law. Some films deal with proper and improper parliamentary procedure while still others explore good study habits closely associated to social studies skills. Filmstrips cover such topics as introducing the young pupil to the library and helping him understand the sequence of events in history, the interpretation of time, and the use of geographic tools. When programed into study tables or listening stations these materials become teacher-directed-activities delivered by remote control.

With thousands of motion pictures presently available to schools, multiple titles deal with each of the many social studies skills. One title might be used in a scheduled class discussion while another could be made available later to individuals or small groups. Where the children are very young or the school cannot provide individual pupil service, then multiple showings might satisfy.

Another technique would be to tape record small group discussions of a controversial topic. Play back these tapes for pupils to analyze the procedure used, to see if good evidence played a part in the discussion, to check if the assigned topic remained the center of attention, to notice if good social studies skills were used. Later pupils might listen to other groups, still trying to understand which procedures proved profitable for equitable group discussion.

In other words, modern media such as television, motion pictures, still pictures, and audio tape readily adapt to the need for varied replication of experiences when learning social studies skills. Once planned or prepared, these materials free the teacher for keener observation of all pupils in the class and for personal, individual help to a larger number of children.

This latter need to cope with each child as the unique entity that he obviously is, remains a major problem for the teacher. In skill development as in other types of teaching the modern and modernized types of learning resources are finally receiving recognition as potential avenues for meeting the individuality of children's needs.

A "library" of teaching/learning materials should reside in the classroom, the level varying within the collection. Introduction of concepts relating to time and the calendar, for example, may need first of all simple introductory manipulative materials—e.g. moving clocks of wood and clocks built on overhead transparencies. Single concept films can range from similar introductory material to the relatively sophisticated concepts of dates in history. A child can choose and study the material he needs whether he does or does not have the teacher's direct help.

Documentary films, recorded speeches, and photographs all provide individual study opportunities. Assignments to evaluate such materials as sources of information about historic events or social institutions and agencies can help the child who needs special experiences and provide expanded horizons for children especially motivated toward a specific topic.

Let some children, at least, design their own overhead transparencies, tape record dramatizations, and prepare feltboard presentations. If possible, arrange for small groups to take less difficult, more specialized field trips, even if it is only to nearby stores.

Learning resources are avenues for exploration and development of skills for each child in a class. They should not be thought of as mass presentation procedures or group techniques exclusively but as individualized resources for unique pursuits.

Many of the resource examples and approaches cited above serve more than those principles of learning and teaching already considered. Important to skill development are those characteristics of media that provide opportunities for the pupil to see himself as he appears to others. More to the point, these media confront him with an untouched, mirror-view of his actions and his skills for his own evaluation.

The television taping of reports by pupils, of classroom discussions, of small group activities, all provide the pupil with a look at himself. An audio tape narration together with still pictures requires that the pupil perceive his report on a topic very much as other children see it. Taking a field trip planned and prepared by pupils forces them to live and learn from situations of their own design.

Under such conditions the teacher frequently changes his role from dispenser of marks to sympathetic supporter and desirable guide. The child may very well become his own most severe critic. This becomes a uniquely gratifying position for the teacher since automatically his role is constructive.

Almost a corollary to the above, and certainly not to be overlooked, is the caution that success in learning generally breeds success, and failure can induce failure. Many apparent failures can more easily be pointed toward success and the experience can lead to greater maturity when the pupil is the evaluator and the teacher an empathetic, constructive guide.

Modern learning resources can help skill development in the social studies in many more ways than enumerated here. These examples merely indicate the special roles they might play. Having recognized their usefulness, a reminder seems in order. The teacher using learning resources must remember that the pupil generally experiences learning as a total human being. He makes an indivisible approach to any learning task.

Many learning resources, on the other hand, are mono-sensory—visual or auditory or tactile. The pupil is not. The motion picture and television, at least, deliver bi-sensory experience. Display boards can be made multi-sensory—visual, tactile, and even auditory—though all too often they are not designed by teachers to make full use of these possibilities.

Therefore, it behooves the teacher to plan carefully when using such learning resources. He must allow for broadening experiences through a wide variety of resources. He must plan for integration of these experiences into the total pattern of the pupil's development. And finally, he must allow the pupil to develop independence in using these media and materials. Then, modern learning resources will contribute greatly to the learning of social studies skills.

SKILLS IN THE ELEMENTARY
SCHOOL SOCIAL STUDIES CURRICULUM

by

Clifford D. Foster

Although skill development is generally conceded to be one of the major outcomes of social studies education, it is the exception rather than the rule to find a school with a well-planned and fully functioning skills program as an integral part of the elementary social studies curriculum. In an examination of statements of objectives in professional textbooks and in curriculum documents, one is led to believe that the learning of skills ranks equally in importance with the acquisition of concepts and factual understandings and with the development of attitudes and values. Some would insist that skills are even more important, because they constitute the tools for learning. A closer inspection of curriculum materials, however, reveals that the objectives dealing with social studies skills frequently are not accomplished by models for the teaching of these skills. Although skills are among those learnings that are the easiest to evaluate for mastery, skills programs are often not operational to the extent that a thorough-going evaluation is possible. The unfortunate status of skills teaching in many schools is due, in part, to the nature of the curriculum itself. This paper examines some of the curricular dimensions of social studies skills teaching and learning.

Curriculum workers and teachers must give thought to various philosophical and psychological implications for skill development in the elementary school social studies program. Philosophically, a sound program of skill development is based on the assumption that the child is a feeling, thinking citizen. The skills he needs, therefore, are contained in the various processes of instruction as well as in the content of the program. If the philosophical position is one that values the acquisition of factual information to the extent that processes involved in working together, accepting responsibilities, and cooperating with others are neglected, then the program is a narrow one indeed. Psychologically, a sound program in skill development recognizes that: (1) skills are learned most efficiently when a need exists, (2) direct teaching at the point of need is necessary to estab-

From *Social Education*, March 1967. Reprinted with permission of the National Council for the Social Studies and Clifford D. Foster.

lish mastery of many skills, (3) repeated opportunities are needed to practice skills in a variety of applications, (4) skills develop along a continuum throughout the elementary and secondary school program, and (5) differentiated instruction is necessary in order to meet the individual needs of pupils.

The social studies teacher must be given guidance in the selection and the teaching of skills. It is easy to overlook the importance of the need for *teaching* skills in the social studies. The teacher frequently assumes that the social studies program is one in which skills taught in reading, arithmetic, science, art, music, and related communication areas will be transferred automatically by children to social studies learning activities. This assumption belies the fact that unless those skills learned in the remainder of the curriculum are focused, with the teacher's help, on specific social studies learning tasks, most children will not transfer these skills as efficiently as would be possible. For example, the child who has learned to use the table of contents, the index, and the glossary in the reading class needs to be taught that these skills are *usable* in certain work-study activities in the social studies. A directed lesson in applying these skills in the social studies is necessary for many children.

Balance in the types of skills selected by the teacher is important in the development of an effective program. In order to achieve balance in the selection of skills, the teacher needs a classification system. One such classification system groups social studies skills according to *work-study skills* such as reading, outlining, map reading, and interpreting graphs; *thinking skills* such as critical thinking and problem solving; *group-process skills* such as those involved in leading or participating in other ways in group undertakings; and *social-living skills* such as acting responsibly, cooperating with others, and living and working in a group setting.[1]

It is not unusual to find that the work-study skills are emphasized to the virtual exclusion of the remaining three groups of skills. In the intermediate grades, group-process skills and social-living skills are taught only on an infrequent basis. The newer programs are stressing thinking skills; however, much needs to be done in order to give the group-process and social-living skills their proper place in the social studies program. On the primary level, the group-process and the

---

1. See John Jarolimek. "The Psychology of Skill Development in Social Studies," in Helen McCracken Carpenter, editor. *Skill Development in Social Studies.* Thirty-Third Yearbook, Washington, D.C.: National Council for the Social Studies, 1963. p. 18.

social-living skills are begun by conscientious teachers only to find that an over emphasis on content in the intermediate grades relegates these skills involving the actual processes of human relationships to a less important status. In the final analysis, the teacher who believes in the importance of helping children acquire competencies necessary for effective social living will see that a balance exists between these skills and those involved in acquiring and interpreting information.

A sound program for the development of social studies skills provides for continuity. Although there is no definitive research to guide the exact grade placement of specific skills, teachers need guidance as to the types of skills appropriate for pupils on at least three levels of emphasis in the primary and intermediate grades. The first level of emphasis provides for the introduction of a given skill, the second provides for the systematic practice of the skill through repeated applications, and the third provides for the maintenance and the extension of the skill. This approach suggests that it is not sound practice to identify specific skills peculiar to a single grade for any one of the three levels of emphasis. Rather, it is better for the teacher to be aware of the various sub-skills in the work-study, thinking, group-process, and social-living categories and to apply whichever level of emphasis is appropriate for the child's needs and to the topic of study. Skills should be introduced, developed, and extended when the maximum potential for learning exists. This means that for certain children a skill in the work-study category may be introduced appropriately at the first grade level. For another group of children, the same skill may be appropriate at the second grade level. It is important, however, that once the skill is introduced that it be maintained and extended from that time on. The third grade teacher may find that the same skill must be emphasized on all three levels of instruction in order to meet the diverse abilities of all of the children in the group.

A curriculum that provides for continuity in skill development not only classifies social studies skills according to major groupings, it also provides for the identification of the sub-skills in each major category. These sub-skills are then arranged sequentially in accordance with the three levels of emphasis discussed here. An excellent guide for the analysis and grade placement of social studies skills has been prepared in chart form for teachers by Johns and Fraser.[2]

2. See Eunice Johns and Dorothy McClure Fraser. "Social Studies Skills: A Guide to Analysis and Grade Placement," in Helen McCracken Carpenter, editor. *Skill Development in Social Studies.* Thirty-Third Yearbook. Washington, D.C.: National Council for the Social Studies, 1963. pp. 310-327.

Teachers need a curriculum guide that is explicit as to the objectives for skill development as well as useful in its provision of suggested teaching strategies. A curriculum guide that merely lists skills appropriate for the study theme fails to provide the teacher with a model for making the objectives operational. It is not reasonable to expect that the development of social studies skills should consume the bulk of the teacher's time and effort—there are other legitimate teaching tasks that require his attention. A useful curriculum guide, therefore, will identify those skills that are basic to the effective utilization of the learning activities suggested in it. In addition, the guide should provide suggestions from which the teacher can formulate a teaching strategy designed to implement the skill on one or more of he three levels of emphasis, i.e. (1) introduction, (2) systematic practice, (3) maintenance and extension.

In many curriculum guides there is a merging of learning activities and skills. It seems to be common practice in the typical curriculum guide to lump together these two aspects of teaching and learning. Usually skills and learning activities are combined in the curriculum guide under a heading frequently designated as "learning activities." This practice encourages opportunistic as opposed to systematic approaches to the teaching of skills. Its results are well known. In the first place, it encourages the indiscriminate use of learning activities that depend on the pupil's mastery of skills basic to the effective prosecution of the learning activities. Granted that a learning activity such as "map study" is built entirely on the pupil's general ability to study maps. Reference only to map study, however, does not identify the sub-skills that are necessary for the success of that learning activity. The same applies to a learning activity labeled "establish a committee to locate study materials." Again, numerous skills are involved, some of which are a definite responsibility of the social studies while others are not. Moreover, the relationship between the specific activity and the skill it is supposed to enhance may not be clear either to the teacher or to the pupils. More attention needs to be given to the relationship of social studies skills and learning activities by authors of curriculum guides. In order for the objectives in skill development to become operational, a methodical plan of reenforcement is needed. This can be accomplished by the inclusion of selected skills *throughout* the guide that are stated as expectancies for pupil growth.

Whenever a skill is identified, it should appear strategically at the place where various learning activities are appropriate both to the utilization of the skill and to the development of the main idea or concept to be learned. For example, on the primary level the ideas to be learned may be embodied in the statement, "Each member of the family does important work." During the study of this idea, certain skills are included as pupil expectancies in skill usage. The expectancy that the child should grow in he ability to share with others is a skill that is developed by giving the child an opportunity to explain to the group the type of work his father does. Another learning activity appropriate to the development of a second type of skill involves the child's ability to plan and to evaluate his learning experiences. This expectancy materializes as the child helps to plan a dramatic play activity based on the experiences of family life. What shall we play? How many will we need? How shall we play? What shall the rest of the group do? The child then participates in the evaluation of the learning activity. What did we do? How could it be improved? Finally, a third expectancy, that the child needs to grow in his ability to control bodily movement, becomes operational through learning activities in which he uses paint brushes and scissors in making figures of members of his family. The child may also participate in rhythms representing home activities such as working, ironing, baking, and sweeping. These activities are suggested within a meaningful context, not restricted simply to the idea to be learned, but requiring the application of skills basic to the learning activities.

Continuity in skill development can be illustrated in an example from the intermediate grades. The idea to be learned is summarized in the statement "pioneers moved west to improve their living conditions." Pupil expectancies in skill growth involve in the first instance the correct use of work-study skills. The learning activities include writing a story describing the depression of the late 1830's, making a population map of the United States in 1840, and writing a poem on pioneer love of open spaces. A committee is designated for each learning activity. These learning activities require the pupil to apply work-study skills involving the use of the book index and the table of contents to find information on the depression of the late 1830's in order to write the story and the poem. Making the population map, in addition to the mastery of map skills, requires the pupil to use study aids such as the glossary, pictures, charts, tables, and graphs. In each learning activity the skill of notetaking is basic. The study of the idea involves the group-process skills necessitated by working on a committee in which the pupil must help the group plan, knows what his specific job is, does the job within the time limit set, and respects the rights of others. Finally, the expectancy that the child continue his development of skills in motor coordination is made operational in a learning activity in which the child participates in folk dances similar to those done by pioneers. These examples from the primary and intermediate grade levels illustrate the possibilities to make skill development operational in the on-going study of the main ideas comprising the theme or unit topic. The strategic location of statements relative to skill teaching in the organization of a curriculum guide can do much to alert the social studies teacher to the importance of skills. A systematic provision for skill development helps to minimize the possibility that learning activities and skills will become merged to the point where skills lose their identity and thus are neglected altogether.

An effective program in the development of social studies skills provides for an ongoing evaluation system. If measurement of learning outcomes in the social studies is restricted to the determination of the amount of content that the pupil has acquired, then there is only an indirect feedback with respect to the pupil's degree of mastery in the four categories of skills. In order to have immediate feedback for teachers and pupils, the curriculum guide should provide suggestions for the evaluation of skill mastery within the context in which the skills are used. In the example of skills teaching provided earlier, the primary teacher should use several evaluation techniques in order to assess the degree of skills mastery demonstrated by the pupils. Observation in this situation would permit the teacher to determine how each child participates in group planning, contributes to the group and uses the various learning tools. The example that illustrated the application of social studies skills on the intermediate grade level contained numerous possibilities for the evaluation of skill proficiency. In this instance, teacher observation and the use of a check-list designed to evaluate pupil progress in work-study skills would be appropriate.

In the final analysis, a good program in skill development does not just happen. It is carefully planned and taught in a developmental, sequential, and systematic fashion. The time and energy necessary to develop an effective program will pay handsome dividends in providing pupils with the tools necessary for effective citizenship.

IX. Values and Attitudes

CAN WE TEACH VALUES?

by

Robert Botkin

In keeping with the perennial reticence to examine the presuppositions of one's own discipline, educators too seldom raise the question of the purpose and meaning of education itself. On the other hand, we certainly will make a serious blunder if we assume that a predetermined and unique function or goal for education must be uncovered before we can understand its meaning. A major thrust of contemporary philosophy is toward clarifying the idea that the meaning of a concept is determined by the way it is used in ordinary or technical discourse. Meaning is not established by a mysterious, metaphysical essence which the mind must discover. The classical search for underlying essences and substances that make a thing or an activity what it is, apart from its accidental qualities, is misleading and vacuous. Words and concepts derive their cognitive vitality from the myriad uses to which they are put; not from a *sui generis* essence which they signify. When we apply this insight to the concept of education, we discover that there is no one simple generic idea that categorizes the substance of the educational process.

From the kindergarten through the graduate school, education serves the purposes of the state. Modern culture could not long maintain itself without an educated populace. On the other hand, in non-totalitarian states at least, it is assumed that the processes of government, including education, not only seek to perpetuate and strengthen the society, but aim at enhancing and fulfilling the individual. While education is vital to the self-interest of the state, its purposes are not limited to that interest alone. Educational goals for which most Americans probably opt are to prepare a person for a vocation, to help him learn to cope with all aspects of his environment, and to guarantee as much as possible that he will be an asset to society rather than a liability.

The Moral Function

There is, nonetheless, another honorable tradition in the philosophy of education. In contradistinction to the more pragmatic empha-

From the *Educational Record*, Spring 1968. Used by permission of the American Council on Education.

sis just outlined, this tradition makes a fundamental distinction be-tween education and craftsmanship. The ends desired by most Amer-icans are more analogous to the practical goals of technology and craft than the veritable ends sought in the liberal arts. The liberal tradition implies that the educator who sees the student as a plastic material to be molded and conformed into a predetermined goal is morally reprehensible. This humanistic tradition emphasizes that the student is a person whose freedom for self-discovery must be respect-ed; he is not basically a social animal to be acculturated. The func-tion of education, liberalism maintains, is to inspire an inward trans-formation, deepened insight and sensitivity, a rational frame of reference and attitude, and an ever-widening appreciation of experi-ence. In short, the goal of education is self-realization and self-inte-gration. One recalls John Stuart Mill's transformation of the ethics of utilitarianism from social hedonism to self-realization with the classic remark,

> It is better to be a human being dissatisfied than a pig satisfied, better to be a Socrates dissatisfied than a fool satisfied.[1]

Just as there are qualitative as well as quantitative differences between pleasures, a liberal education ought to produce a certain liberating quality of life rather than developing vocational and politi-co-social skills that can be measured in quantitative terms.

Historical Consciousness

It is important to recognize that the varying emphases of the pragmatic and self-realization philosophies of education do not throw us into an either/or dilemma. To assume that they do is to be captivated once again by the essence-accident dichotomy in which a "valid" education must achieve one thing and one thing alone. The development of practical skills and theoretical understanding can co-exist with the liberal arts as complementing goals in the total educa-tional venture. There are genuine problems, however, even when this artificial one is set aside.

It would be a fatal error if we failed to understand the crucial difference between the task of modern education and that of pre-modern man. This difference is rooted in the more complete emer-gence of modern man's historical consciousness. What I mean by this is that modern man is more keenly aware of his separation from nature than any of his predecessors. It is not just a more intense

1. *Utilitarianism*, Ch. II

consciousness but self-consciousness that distinguishes man from other animals. Various degrees of self-determination, limited by the boundaries of our finitude, grow out of our self-awareness and are the mark of our historicity. The modern man's increasing awareness of his historicity means that he can and must accept responsibility for his world. It cannot be overemphasized that the secularity of modern life is rooted in this acceptance of our historicity. A consequence of this historical consciousness is that modern societies, founded upon secular and technological foundations, face a different educational task than those of the past. I am not referring here to the obvious fact that education today must be more scientifically and technologically oriented than in the past, but am observing that, as a result of our increased historical consciousness, the means by which we come to understand the values we hold and the meaning and significance we understand life to possess have been radically altered.

Formerly, cultural evolution took place so slowly it passed almost unnoticed. Values were passed on by oral traditions, puberty initiation rites, cultic myths, etc. One learned a vocation, perhaps served an apprenticeship, and upon cultic initiation. accepted one's social responsibilities. A radically deliberate attempt to reach self-understanding and a conscious choice of a value system were not called for or needed. Cosmopolitan skepticism and relativism in the Hellenistic period were abberations in the pre-modern world, and signified only a momentary loss of equilibrium. Social institutions were, generally speaking, so non-historically conceived that they were accepted as much a part of the natural order as the seasons. Government was rooted in the inscrutable will of God or in a metaphysical *logos* rather than in a social contract for which man must accept full responsibility. The exact areas in which and the extent to which modern man has a keener sense of responsibility for his world than his pre-modern counterpart may more safely be left to the research of the anthropologist and historian. But certainly our increased awareness that the environment is, to a great extent, subject to man's own lordship has created a crisis in the valuational and acculturational process that consciously (or unconsciously) is carried into the warp and woof of the educational enterprise.

Facing the Loss of Innocence

This childlike loss of innocence, the self-transcending of nature, has resulted in a twofold responsibility. Not only do we face the enormous task of plotting out the very quality of life we will seek to create, but we also face the collapse of any vital sense of social solidarity and sacramental union with nature and the past. If large segments of the younger generation seem crass and unappreciative of the tried and true ways of the past, we must recognize that a greater cultural evolution has occurred within this century than in the whole history of man combined. Not to mention the natural impetuousness of youth, is it any wonder that, in the fact of this cultural upheaval, the values of our fathers often seem nearly as distant to them as the values of the Middle Ages?

How long can a modern society vigorously maintain itself without raising the question of the meaning of that society? The pragmatically oriented educator tends to ignore this question. He is so deeply engrossed in fulfilling the vocational and other practical demands of the age that he fails to gain an overarching view into the existential meaning and significance of the culture itself. Certainly the instrumentalists and pragmatists are right in their affirmation that thinking and learning are goal directed and survival oriented. But man is also the animal who demands meaning and significance of life. It is right at this point that the problem of teaching values within the educational process comes into sharpest focus. In this highly developed and technical age, value problems need to be faced on a conscious level and made an integral part of curricular goals. If they are repressed because of an unarticulated realization that the values and traditions of this society have already been damaged or eroded away by the dynamics of history, or if they are ignored by the academic community as being too subjective, speculative, and unscientific for serious consideration, we may very well mesmerize ourselves into a kind of cultural nihilism that in the long run is fatally unpragmatic. Modern man's full acceptance of his historicity means, in the final analysis, that he must accept responsibility for his values and his gods in the very same manner that he has accepted responsibility for his natural and political environment.

This is the point at which the self-realizationist is apt to seek to call the plays. If the pragmatist fails, however, for not having an adequate world view, the self-realizationist fails for having too little empirical substance. One thing we will notice about all his talk concerning self-fulfillment, deepened insight, and broadened sensitivity is that the self-realizationist is given to excessive jargon and rhetoric. The pragmatist is quick to point out that he is bewildered about how one may translate this verbiage into action, or how appropriate methods for instruction and measurement of learning may be devised. Just how does the teacher build the character of his students? And where did the teacher gain some *a priori* insight into just what that charac-

ter ought to be? Must not his frame of reference be his own character, and, if so, what credentials may he present attesting to his authority to play God, to make students "in his own image and like-
ness?" The self-realizationist can easily become a propagandist in
spite of initially decrying those who would mold the mind of a
student toward a predetermined end in order to achieve some practical skill.

This then is our current dilemma. With the emergence of science
and its stepchild, scientific technology, the means by which man may
control and utilize his environment have been almost infinitely mul-
tiplied. These techniques may be taught and learned. Consequently,
the pragmatic and technical goals of our society have become the
fundamental concern and responsibility of the educational enterprise. Concomitant with the birth of science, and doubtlessly causal-
ly interrelated, is the increasing development of man's sense of his
own historicity. Modern man more fully realizes than his predecessors that he may, to a large degree, transcend his roots in nature, and
he may take responsibility for huge segments of his world.

A consequence of this new human understanding is a sense of
estrangement from the world and from the values of the past. The
transmission of values has been a special concern of the liberal arts
and the self-realization educational theory. I have rejected the self-
realization theory—at least in its classical form—for it inadvertently
invests the teacher with a kind of infallibility that I doubt he possesses. It has been the perennial temptation of self-realizationists from
Plato to Mill and beyond to believe that educated people's prejudices
are not really biases but are species of the truth. They too easily assume that value problems have answers that are like ready-made
gloves, with just one size to fit everyone. In spite of liberal disclaim-
ers to the contrary, the self-realizationist is apt to exert the most
stringent and arrogant particularism imaginable. In the remainder of
this paper, I shall seek to overcome this impasse by suggesting ways
in which we may responsibly approach the question of value as a
needed aspect of contemporary education and an important facet of
the liberal arts tradition.

The Life World

Culture, value, and choice are correlate ideas; hence it is impossible to conceive of man without a value system. Through introspec-
tion or from the data collected by the behavioral sciences, we know
that man may exert his freedom in the face of such fundamental
urges as sex and survival. This ability to transcend blind, instinctive

behavior reveals a hierarchy of values and indicates that values result from the interaction of maturation and learning. The idea of a *Naturmenseh* or the happy savage, unimpended by culture, is a myth. Man always appears enveloped in a natural and a cultural environment, and there is no compelling reason to reduce one to the other. However, values are not easily recognized or isolated. Rather, they are the basic assumptions and meanings that undergird the actions of a society or a personality. More often than not, they have never been consciously or clearly articulated. These assumptions are not merely the postulates on which actions are based, but are versions and visions of the world. In this immediate world of lived experience, the *Lebenswelt* or life world as Husserl and other phenomenologists have labeled it, there is no clear line between thought and action.

Unlike the older, Lockeian epistemology, we can now see that the mind is not a passive instrument—a *tabula rasa*—receiving sense impressions that faithfully record objective reality. The mind is selective, and it orders its data into *Gestalts* and meanings, bringing order and rationale into experience. What is the content of the mind's creation? Partial contents are a vision of the world, a system of meanings and values, life projects, and a self-image. The language used to express this world is not scientific and mathematical; it is mytho-poetic, metaphorical, and convictional. For this reason, both in philosophy and science, this world of lived experience has often been depreciated as subjective, irrational, and relative.

The charge of subjectivism is meaningless. If I am right in suggesting that the life world is the initial ground of all experience, then science is an abstraction—a removal of the mind from the most basic encounter with reality that it possesses. To be sure, science is justified in taking its objective stance in terms of its goals and methods, but to assume that science is thereby getting us closer and closer to the "really real," or that the life world is only a confused shadow of reality, is neither a conclusion of science itself nor one of its concerns. Such charges against the life world are unscientific and pejorative. One may be committed to science without being committed to scientism, the latter itself being a "subjective" version of the world.

It is also a mistake to call the life world irrational. When this world is explored, we discover that, as a creation emerging out of the mind's interaction with its environment, it always has a rational structure. Even a psychosis has rational structures, a *logos*, or else a psychiatrist could never deal with it. Something that is completely irrational defies understanding, but the life world can be understood. The charge of relativism is obviously true and needs careful attention. The accusations of subjectivism and irrationalism grow out of this realization. Ever since some of the ancient Greeks realized that one city's gods were not always homaged in another, it has been feared that the necessary outcome of relativism was skepticism and sophistry. Consequently, such thinkers as Parmenides and Plato equated becoming, change, and relativity with the irrational. Rationality's attributes—being, eternality, universality—were irrationality's opposites. Mathematics, with its proofs and certainties, became the ideal science, and the philosopher sought to rise above the flux of social change and personal experience by contemplating a deductive system of implicatory truths founded upon self-evident axioms and postulates. Individual, relative goods were depreciated and hypostatized into the *Good*, a supposed objective and rational reality that not only was as necessary as the truths of mathematics, but was also their ontological ground.

The Objective Order

The upshot of this bout with nihilism was the committing of Western culture to the belief that truth and value are objective, absolute, and universal. Christian theology captivated this Hellenistic outlook and added its own beliefs in a personal God and personal immortality. The fundamental notions on which Christendom was based were that objective reality was rational, good, and personal. While still with us, at least since the seventeenth century these beliefs have been held more and more tenuously. While modern science kept faith with the classical tradition by never questioning that the universe was rational, it repudiated teleology and final causality as unsuited to its method, maintaining that reality was impersonal and value free.

While unable to establish an objective Good or a personal God, the nonpurposive methodology notwithstanding, the new scientific intelligentsia were unable completely to shake Greek teleology or biblical eschatology. The concept of the "kingdom of God" was secularized into the beliefs in "utopia" and in the inevitability of progress through science. Even where faith in objective, other-worldly values was gone, seldom was it questioned that there were objective, this-worldly goals upon which all rational men agreed and that were capable of realization. By turning outward, first to the metaphysical and the supernatural, and later to the physical and the empirical, Western man was able to avoid academically the life world with its inwardness and projects, pregnant with risk, uncertainty, and relativism.

Many now believe, including many eminent scientists, that the objective order is not only impersonal but also not rational. Physicists like P.W. Bridgman of Harvard suggest that

> the structure of nature may eventually be such that our processes of thought do not correspond to it sufficiently to permit us to think about it at all. . . . The world fades out and eludes. . . . We are confronted with something truly ineffable. We have reached the limit of the vision of the great pioneers of science, the vision namely, that we live in a sympathetic world in that it is comprehensible by our minds.[2]

Hence, physical concepts are thought to be pragmatic, goal-directed operations rather than ideas passively corresponding to reality. From a scientific framework, belief in a personal universe and objective values seem now to be only pseudo-hypotheses, incapable of verification either way. Events within the twentieth century need not be catalogued to reach the conclusion that belief in the inevitability of progress is nothing short of inane.

Thus, we are led full circle back to the threat of nihilism against which Plato was reacting. Before collapsing in despair, however, we should reckon with the possibility that the exploration of the life world might lead to the discovery of an authentic meaning and value which objectivism never was able to disclose, and that relativism is not necessarily the bugbear we have contrived it to be.

Relativism and Authenticity

Relativism necessarily results from human freedom and historicity. The phenomenon we broadly designate as "culture" is rooted in man's self-transcendence. Man, to be man, must order his experience and choose a life's project. No two persons or cultures order their life world in the same way. While limited and conditioned by environmental and genetic factors, as far as we can tell, the life world is a creative act, unique and unpredictable. Hence, a more positive approach to relativism is to view it as "conditioned creativity" or "finite freedom." So understood, relativism is not an albatross around man's neck, but it is probably his greatest intellectual boon. Without this self-transcending capacity for relativism, we would not have cultures but merely animal societies, universally the same and unable to engage in purposive change. Without this capacity for change and culture—the capacity for historicity if you will—we could not recognize man as man.

The above paragraph itself is an aspect of our contemporary life

2. Quoted by Huston Smith, "The Revolution in Western Thought," *Saturday Evening Post*, August 26, 1961 (234), p. 59.

world, or, at least, the author's. When cultures were more isolated from one another than at present, this was not as obvious as now. On the other hand, the universality of anxiety growing out of a person's ontological commitments indicates that there is always some awareness that the life world is reft by uncertainty and risk. In fact, this ontological anxiety is another manifestation of our "self-transcendence-infinitude."

Life's basic task is to deal with this ontological anxiety successfully and creatively. Following the lead of existential thinkers, let us call this dealing creatively and honestly with our ontological anxiety "authenticity." Whether this is one of the tasks of education depends on how broadly education's goals are envisioned, and how widely the educator conceives his function and responsibility. It is through the category of "authenticity" that we can see affinities and differences between existentialism and pragmatism, on the one hand, and self-realizationist rationalism on the other. Since both of the latter philosophies have been utilized in the philosophy of education, there seems to be a possibility of utilizing existential categories.

The pragmatist maintains that the successful life is one able to cope with its environment. Values native to pragmatism include adaptation leading to survival and the enhancing of life with material prosperity and a sense of dignity and meaning. Both a physical and a psychological homeostasis are valued. In education, the pragmatist affirms that the curriculum is made for the student not vice versa. He wants to allow for each person's unique situation in life, and, therefore, his unique goals in learning. There is no absolute way everyone must deal with his environment for it is precisely *his* environment. Note how homeostasis or equilibrium is close to the existentialist category of authenticity. Also note that the pragmatist emphasizes with the existentialist that everyone's reality is unique and relative to him. On the other hand, pragmatism, especially Dewey's instrumentalism, seems to maintain that science and technology offer the possibility of gaining not only physical but also psychological homeostasis as well. The existentialist is not necessarily hostile to technology, but he maintains that authenticity is only possible when one freely accepts responsibility for his life with all of its risks and uncertainties. Nothing, not even science, can make this decision for persons who exist. In other words, the existentialist emphasizes inwardness, a leap of faith, and the anguish and risk accompanying the leap that are all aspects of the authentic life. Whereas the instrumentalist continues to structure his thought in the objective tradition, the existentialist is more conscious of the life world.

The Submerged Viewer

There are profound similarities and differences between the self-realizationist and the existentialist. The similarity between authenticity and self-integration and realization is obvious. However, the rationalistic tradition that gave birth to the self-realization ideal assumed that there is a rational, objective criterion of self-realization for all men—although only a few are able to attain it. While Aristotle made more room for idiosyncracies and differences in temperament than Plato did, both of these intellectual fountainheads of Western thought maintained that the highest realization of humanity is the theoretical speculation of the philosopher—the paragon of rationality itself. Contrarily, the existentialist maintains that because existence itself stands within reality and is enveloped by its mystery, he can never gain an objective view of that which infinitely transcends him. How can the fish ever gain a view of the pond as it is in itself when he is condemned to be submerged in the pond? As Kierkegaard suggested, a finite mind can never know the Infinite, but life can be lived and the Eternal can be pursued with an infinite passion. It is this infinite and passionate openness to life that the existentialist designates "authenticity" rather than the contemplation of a rational truth, the goal of Plato's realized self.

The openness of authenticity leads out in two directions. First, there is the acceptance of one's past. This means the acceptance of one's sex, parents, nationality, and all of the other contingencies that describe his "throwness" into existence. Some are able to accept the contingencies with gladness and thanksgiving; others do so grudgingly. Perhaps with most of us, there is a mixture of both. What is important is not one's emotional response to his past, but that he freely accepts it as his, as the past that allows him to be and that defines his unique existence and future possibilities. The authentic self also turns toward the future and projects itself into it. The past certainly dictates the limits of the future's possibilities, but an authentic self freely chooses and takes responsibility for that future possibility which he chooses for himself.

But how are we to decide what to choose? Is one choice better than another only because it is freely chosen? Perhaps this is implied in such works as Jean-Paul Sartre's play, *The Flies*. The first authentic act that Orestes, the protagonist, ever performs is the murder of his mother. Traditional values are suddenly reversed and turned topsy-turvy. While Orestes's previous actions had been mere responses to outside stimuli, detached and almost automatic, this act was freely and consciously chosen. "I have done my deed, Electra," he announces, "and that deed was good."

A moment's reflection, however, causes us to wonder how an act can be chosen at all unless one can give a reason for the choice. A non-purposive act is closer to instinct or impulse than it is to choice. The criterion necessary for choice is not just awareness that it is we who are choosing, but purpose-in-self-awareness. A moral choice is governed by two considerations. First, what is possible in terms of the situation? Facts in the situation determine the appropriate response just as much as any abstract theory of the good. Secondly, the choice is governed by our own self-image and evaluation of personality as such. Many existential thinkers believe that authentic personality is neither isolated in its own skin nor amalgamated in the collective. Rather, we are seen as potential personalities, persons who experience a "law of life" or a moral demand to become persons. This demand is always in a community context for we are essentially persons-in-community. The ability to enter into mature relations with others and to live our temporality as if it were a pilgrimage seem to be formal norms that govern the concept of authenticity itself.

The Catalytic Teacher

It should now be clear that the concept of authenticity deepens and corrects the pragmatic idea of psychological homeostasis and the rationalistic idea of self-realization. But can authenticity be taught? Yes and no. The most the teacher can do is to serve as a catalyst, making the student aware of his freedom and historicity. In this catalytic capacity, the teacher has two responsibilities.

The teacher, first, comes as a conveyor of information and as an authority in a discipline. While the life world is bound to be relative, we seem to be forced to conclude it is always a vision approximating *the* world. Some of these visions speak more completely to the facts of our experience and contemporaneity than others. It is assumed that the teacher, in the pursuit of his discipline, can offer the student new dimensions and harmonies to his life world not previously there. Starting class by sitting on the edge of the desk and cheerfully asking, "Well, kids, what do you think of your old life world today?" is neither teaching values nor practicing scholarship. While it is important to realize that the student must always learn from his situation, it is equally true that the academic setting itself is a part of that situation. The student is not before the academic community to keep his old situation intact. It is to be judged and refined by the academic community.

Secondly, the teacher must nurture a climate of devotion rather than fanaticism.[3] A fanatically held life world is closed and inauthentic. Fanaticism is an effort, in the name of righteousness, to deny the risk and uncertainty that is integral to human existence. Guised as faith, it is the supreme manifestation of suppressed doubt. Faced with threat, it becomes demonically hostile and self-righteous. Refraining from fanaticism is not necessarily refraining from convictions held with integrity. Devotion is a deeper and more sincere form of conviction. Without deception, it confesses the way the world appears, steps into dialogue with the other, and holds its ground with creative insecurity. Academic freedom is a farce and sham unless this academic devotion is maintained so that an idea can be entertained without fear or presented without propaganda.

When teaching is understood in the above manner, there is no reason to fear the teaching of values. The goal of the teacher is to lead the student to the threshold of maturity, authenticity, and self-determination. This is as far as the teacher can go if the student is to be respected. Anything more would be paternalism, propagandizing, and conditioning. The university cannot function as the university unless the falue of authenticity is nourished. It is both the means by which the academic community operates and the end it pursues. Philosophy and the liberal arts in particular, and the university in general, are the guardians of human freedom. Without it, the scientific method is sterile and lifeless. While science may have a corner on scientific method, it has none on scientific attitude, for it is the attitude of authentic humanity itself. Democracy is dependent upon this posture. Where it is absent, the masses will soon be victimized by tyranny. Plato saw this, and preferred a benevolent despot, a philosopher-king to the Athenians democracy. Yet a democracy committed to the task of achieving *human* freedom, as well as a political and economic freedom, is one of our greatest hopes for the future of man. Paternalistic despotism and authentic freedom are contradictions in terms.

When we clearly understand the difference between teaching and propaganda, and are unconditionally committed to the former, we not only can teach human values, we ought to teach them. To fail to do so is to imperil the human spirit.

---

3. See John Wild, *Existence and the World of Freedom* (Englewood Cliffs, NJ: Prentice-Hall Inc., 1963), pp. 167-77 for an enlightening comparison of devotion and fanaticism.

VALUES HELD BY TEACHERS

by

James T. Hamilton

The investigation was designed to provide an insight into some of the current values that experienced teachers hold. As Rich[1] has said, "Values set the tone and give meaning in the life of the individual." The values which teachers were asked to analyze dealt with selected concepts of liberty, justice, middle-age, sex, war, and alienation. Furthermore, the study was undertaken during the 1967-1968 academic year—a time in which the involvement of the United States in Vietnam was questioned by a large segment of the population, a time when two national leaders were assassinated (Dr. Martin Luther King and Senator Robert F. Kennedy), a time of racial disturbances in our cities, and a time of student and faculty unrest in our schools and universities.

Subjects

Fifty-two elementary and secondary teachers participated in the study. All of the teachers were studying for their Master's degrees at the University of Bridgeport. Moreover, the teachers had earned their Bachelor's degrees from thirty-four different institutions and were teaching in school systems that extended from New York City to New Haven. The average number of years that these teachers had taught was 3.2 years.

Procedure

Each teacher that engaged in the study was given a questionnaire that contained six propositions that focused upon current values. These propositions in the main were extracted and formulated from an article by Harry Broudy[2] in the *Phi Delta Kappan*. Upon receipt of the questionnaire, each teacher was asked to indicate whether he agreed, disagreed, or was undecided with regard to the central idea contained within each of the six propositions. A tabulation of these responses was made; next, the chi-squared test of the divergence of

observed responses from those that would be expected under the
hypothesis of equal probability was undertaken.[3]

The Findings

Both verbal and tabular representations are used to clarify the
findings of the investigation. In turn, the remainder of this section is
devoted to an analysis of the responses that teachers made with
regard to each of the six propositions.

Proposition #1

"Most students are unwilling to accept real liberty to shape their
own studies or their lives—especially when the price of liberty is
accountability for the wrong choices."

Of the respondents to this proposition, 32 agreed, 14 disagreed,
and five were undecided. The data are shown in Table 1. Since P is
significant at the .01 level, we must reject the null hypothesis and
conclude that the teachers sampled favor the proposition.

TABLE 1
Responses to Proposition #1

	Agree	Disagree	Undecided	Totals
Observed	32	14	5	52
Expected	17.3	17.3	17.3	51.9

$x^2 = 18.12$ df = 2
P = .01

Proposition # 2

"Once technology makes social justice possible, we cannot get by
with good intentions."

Of the respondents to this proposition, 42 agreed, one disagreed,
and nine were undecided. The data are shown in Table 2. Since P is
significant at the .01 level, we must reject the null hypothesis and
conclude that the teachers sampled favor the proposition.

TABLE 2
Responses to Proposition #2

	Agree	Disagree	Undecided	Totals
Observed	42	1	9	52
Expected	17.3	17.3	17.3	51.9

$x^2 = 54.53$ df = 2
P =   .01

Proposition #3

"The half-hearted virtue of the middle-aged is almost correctly diagnosed by the young as complacency, indifference, hyprocrisy, and perhaps even cowardice."

Of the respondents to this proposition, 33 agreed, 13 disagreed, and six were undecided. The data are shown in Table 3. Since P is significant at the .01 level, we must reject the null hypothesis and conclude that the teachers sampled favor the proposition.

TABLE 3
Responses to Proposition #3

	Agree	Disagree	Undecided	Totals
Observed	33	13	6	52
Expected	17.3	17.3	17.3	51.9

$x^3 = 22.70$ df = 2
P =   .01

Proposition #4

"The moral dimensions of sex now has to be sought in personal relations and individual character rather than in social consequences."

Of the respondents to this proposition, 46 agreed, three disagreed, and three were undecided. The data are shown in Table 4. Since P is

TABLE 4
Responses to Proposition #4

	Agree	Disagree	Undecided	Totals
Observed	46	3	3	52
Expected	17.3	17.3	17.3	51.9

$x^2 = 71.25$ df = 2
P   =   .01

significant at the .01 level, we must reject the null hypothesis and conclude that the teachers sampled favor the proposition.

Proposition #5

"That art has been unable to glorify the modern soldier is a better sign of the bankruptcy of war than any logical argument."

Of the respondents to this proposition, 13 agreed, 18 disagreed, and 21 were undecided. The data are shown in Table 5. Since P lies between .30 and .50, we must retain the null hypothesis and deduce that the deviation of observed answers from expectation might easily be a matter of chance. Therefore, we have an indeterminate situation with regard to the responses of the teachers sampled.

TABLE 5
Responses to Proposition #5

	Agree	Disagree	Undecided	Totals
Observed	13	18	21	52
Expected	17.3	17.3	17.3	51.9

$x^3 = 1.89$ df = 2
P lies between .30
    and .50

Proposition #6

"In this time of trouble not all shouts of alienation, lostness, and meaninglessness are equally significant. For the virtues that define humanity can give us direction and purpose and identity, if we stop making believe that we no longer believe in them."

Of the respondents to this proposition, 50 agreed, one disagreed, and one was undecided. The data are shown in Table 6. Since P is significant at the .01 level, we must reject the null hypothesis and conclude that the teachers sampled favor the proposition.

TABLE 6
Responses to Proposition #6

	Agree	Disagree	Undecided	Totals
Observed	50	1	1	52
Expected	17.3	17.3	17.3	51.9

x^2 = 92.52 $\qquad\qquad$ df = 2
P = .01

Summary

What implications can be drawn from the study? First, it is evident that teachers do not believe that students are ready to accept liberty in its fullest sense if it carries the requirement of total accountability. Second, the teachers are concerned with social justice and maintain that we should eliminate the inequities that exist in our society, for it is technologically possible to achieve this goal. Third, many of the teachers feel that young people regard middle-aged people as complacent, indifferent, hypocritical, or perhaps as cowards, for the virtues which the middle-aged supposedly espouse seem to be only half-heartedly followed. To the young there seems to be a major gap between the conceived and operative values of the middle-aged. Fourth, the teachers regard sex as a personal matter which is no longer constrained and structured by social consequences. Fifth, the teachers are uncertain whether to regard war as a bankrupt operation or not. They seem to be in a major quandary with regard to this proposition. Sixth, the teachers still believe that there are universal virtues that transcend the shouts of alienation, lostness, and meaning-lessness that can provide life with a purpose.

REFERENCES

1. Rich, John M. "Misconceptions Concerning the Teaching of Values," *Improving College and University Teaching*, (Summer, 1968).

2. Broudy, Harry S. "Art, Science, and New Values," *Phi Delta Kappan*, (November, 1967).

3. Garret, Henry E. *Statistics in Psychology and Education.* New York: David McKay Company, Inc., 1966.

LITTLE LESSONS IN SPIRITUAL VALUES
by
Augusta Graham

Our nation is morally bankrupt!! At least, so run the headlines and titles in many a newspaper or magazine today. By moral bankruptcy the writers mean the forsaking of responsibility, the absence of ideals and standards in both youth and adults, and the demise of wonder and reverence for anything. Yet with all this word-commotion and emotion, one is hard put to find any suggestion on how the situation can be helped.

The sorry part of all this is that it *can be* helped, and primarily by parents, especially parents of young children. That's where it all begins—in childhood and at home. And what is it that we want begun? In sum, we want children to learn a love of life and people, an understanding of the function of families, a reverence for faith, and a respect for the riches of wisdom and the treasures of knowledge, the beauty of friendship, and the importance of graciousness, courtesy, consideration, and truth.

Catalogued like that, it's a large order, and one that takes a long time to fill. It's not, however, an impossible one—that is, if considered rightly and undertaken seriously and hopefully. Let's say you agree. What then do we start with? Perhaps it's best to start with teaching the nature of families, since families are what most children are born into and intimately a part of.

To start children on a true knowledge of family life, parents need more than a layette for a new arrival. The expenditures of money I would suggest—and there are only three—are for a clock that is not electric but ticks, and preferably strikes as well (a grandfather or a grandmother clock would be ideal); a family Bible, certainly to read but also a place in which to record births and marriages and deaths; and a blackboard, which I'll explain later. In addition, and this doesn't cost a penny, every family should have a small collection of anecdotes about ancestors who were "characters," the more eccentric the better, and a few songs or poems about them such as:

> *My grandfather's clock was too tall for the shelf*
> *So it stood for ninety years on the floor.*

Reprinted from *The PTA Magazine*, December 1968. Used by permission of the publisher.

It was taller by far than the old man himself,
Though it weighed not a pennyweight more;
But it stopped . . . short,
Never to go again
When the old man died.

Even babies enjoy that song and unconsciously adopt its owner,
the old man, who could have been their grandfather too. They learn
quickly that Mama and Daddy used to have brothers and sisters like
themselves—now Uncle John and Aunt Jessie and the rest—and that
the children of these relatives are called cousins. This enlarges the
family group, and if they have a grandfather and grandmother still
living, it is enlarged still further. If they have not, let them pretend:

Over the river and through the wood
To Grandmother's house we go;
The horse knows the way to carry the sleigh
Through the white and drifted snow.

Out of such simple beginnings does a child begin to grasp the
miracle of life. Crying is a reflex, the first act the infant performs.
Next comes the smile we so eagerly await, and what fond parent
hasn't mistaken a faint grimace for Baby's first smile, or a burp for a
laugh? As someone has said so well, the joy of the cosmos lies in a
child's laughter. Nothing on earth is more tragic than a child who
never smiles—and unfortunately there are such children in the world.
But ours do smile and laugh because we give them cause for both.
And if babies could express their feelings, they might say something
like this: "What a happy introduction to the world! Thanks for
making us love to be alive and for being part of your family." They'll
have ample time later to learn to cope with hate. Now is the time to
begin learning infinite sweetness of love.

However we conceive of God, there is no easier way to teach
reverence for the rights and customs we consider sacred than to refer
these things to him. Nearly all prayers for little children are beautiful
and winning. Your minister, priest, or rabbi will gladly make friends
with your children and help to lead them from a notion that God is
an old man somewhere in the sky to the concept of an all-embracing
force that ennobles not only their lives and Mama's and Daddy's but
those of all mankind. Would that our children's minds received as
much drilling on this concept as on the alphabet and the multiplica-
tion tables.

Children brought up lovingly in a home where the sight of friends
is no rarity are usually not slow in finding friends when they go to
school. By that time they should have been taught, not just some-

thing but a good deal, about the importance of graciousness, courtesy, and consideration for others. It's a commonplace fact that children learn or fail to learn these things from us.

Granted it isn't easy for parents to exhibit them at all times. Certainly we get angry; we like some people better than others and show it; and being human, we are often selfish, putting our own needs and desires above those of others. But this is a far cry from speaking ill of strangers or of friends. It's a far cry from being rude to people who wait on us in supermarkets or the hardware store. What if they *are* rude to us? We use this behavior to underscore how unpleasant rudeness is. This is all the more reason why we shouldn't be mean or rude. Let's never underestimate our young children. They may not yet be able to tie their shoelaces or blow their noses but they can pierce ideas so profound that it seems all but miraculous.

I remember hearing a mother tell a story on herself that illustrates this beautifully. At dinner one evening she noted that her youngster seemed rather despondent. When pressed about why he wasn't his usual self, he confided that Jack, his best friend, has told a falsehood about him in school that day. Since this wasn't the first time Jack had played him false and his perfidy had been overlooked, the mother in righteous indignation said, "Why do you bother with Jack? By now you ought to know he's not your friend." After a moment's silence, he replied, "Yes, Mother, but I'm still *his* friend." The mother, shaken by the boy's capacity for friendship and chagrined by her own impatience with human frailty, could only nod and go on to some other topic of conversation.

Never will there be a better time to teach children respect for all people than in the preschool years. Children, as we know, have no class consciousness. Left to themselves, they would find friends just as readily in slums as in suburbs. They are practically the only group that looks at people as people, without regard to where they live or work or worship. To be sure, children soon become aware of the color of a person's skin, but it makes no more difference to them than the color of his eyes or size of his ears.

How significant that God sends children into the world with a built-in affinity for all human beings. Give a preschool child an "Are You Prejudiced?" test and he would take highest honors. Only later, after he's been exposed to our so-called civilizing influence, is he in any danger of flunking such a test.

Once one could say almost with certainty that a child reared by bigoted parents would turn out to be a bigot. This is no longer true. Many young people are today teaching their parents that prejudice has no place in modern life and that where it persists we have social dynamite as explosive as the bomb. Some adolescents have become alienated from their parents because of this very issue. How much better for both if parents and children *grow together* in truth and consideration for all human beings.

One of the most enduring gifts given me in my childhood was antipathy toward prejudice of any sort. The gift came from my father, whom I considered the gentlest and most just man in the world. Hence the shock of witnessing his wrath for the first time and realizing that it was directed against me.

The incident that sparked his anger occurred when I was about six. Because Mother was ill, my father and I went alone to buy me a much-needed winter coat. Gladly would he have bought his only child the best to be had, but money was scarce and I well recall how anxiously he looked at the price tag of each coat I tried on. Finally we made our purchase and set for home. On the way we met a little girl, shabbily dressed and unkempt, who warmly greeted me by name. Instead of returning her greeting I turned my face away and hastened my step.

I don't know what my father said to the spurned little girl, but I shall never forget what he said to me: "Do you think God tags people as if they were coats? And what makes you think that he would put a higher price tag on you than on another human being? Nothing makes him sadder than what you did today, for everyone is precious in the sight of God. Never are you to forget this. Do you understand?"

I understood this little lesson in spiritual values, and I could not have forgotten if it I had wanted to. To this day, many years later, whenever I feel a momentary twinge of superiority, my father's words quickly bring me to my senses: "What makes you think God would put a higher price tag on you than on another human being?"

In general, however, young children are affectionate and outgoing. They have no critical sense and are bewildered when for their own good we must teach them not to talk to strangers or ever to go anywhere with them. Seldom will even the most shy or fearful child fail to respond to a tender gesture or a soothing word. For all their infighting and occasional cruelty toward each other, children can never match the ruthlessness of man's inhumanity to man.

For building immunity to senseless hate and prejudice there are no better years than the preschool years. They are also the best years for instilling in children a sense of God's goodness. The sad mistake some of us make is to put creed before grace in our spiritual curriculum.

Children should know that God, like their parents, will not hate or reject them no matter how naughty they have been.

"I would teach a child, in defiance even of reason," says the noted English essayist, C.E. Benson, "that God is the one Power that loves and understands him through thick and thin; that He punishes with anguish and sorrow; that He exults in forgiveness and mercy. . . . This, it seems to me, is the gospel teaching about God, impossible only because of the hardness of our hearts."

Mindful that some may think I am defying reality, I would still express my belief that the hardness of our hearts is dissolving. And not alone because this generation of adults is beginning to learn its nuclear lesson—that no people can live severed or estranged from other members of the human race. Undoubtedly self-survival is a factor. But so is an awakening of man's spiritual kinship, which is another way of saying men's dependence on one another. So also is our fervent hope that mankind may at last create a peace that no tyrant can threaten.

All the peace-building and peace-protecting machinery in the world, indispensable as it is, will not work without the friendly heart and understanding mind. Since we have programed instruction for everything from science to sex education, perhaps the day will come when we can also program peace education.

But that time is not yet. Moreover, such a program will be meaningless without a background of spiritual values that must begin in toddlerhood. The cost of a peace-education computer is minimal. All it takes is the investment of a few hours a week on our part. There are many ways to fill that time so that it will yield little lessons in spiritual values.

None of us of course wants to throw children into premature experiences and fretful anxieties. We can, however, begin to exercise their conscience and compassion by enabling them to contribute something to the less fortunate. One family I know has a tradition of stopping on the way home from church at a children's hospital or a home for the aged, there to leave a toy or a book or a flower to brighten someone's life. The youngest child struck up a friendship with a woman in her eighties—and what a joy to hear them exchange thoughts and fancies. We who have seen friendship grow between a very young child and an elderly person are aware that it can be as warming to both as any hearth fire.

Now what about that blackboard I left hanging a while ago? Few of us have the time or inclination to embroider samplers with maxims as did our grandmothers. But we can write little words and sentences on a blackboard. When my children were growing up, there was no material possession that they prized as much as our blackboard. Even the three-year-old would come running into the kitchen in the morning to see what the blackboard said. I heartily recommend such simple words as "Good morning, dear," or "Thank you for being so helpful yesterday." And above all else there is the sentence, "Mother and Daddy love you." For love is both the essence of spiritual values and the vehicle by which they are best transmitted.

Something happens to a child brought up in a home where love and kindness prevail and spill over into the outside world. Each day he stores his mind with new treasures. He is already rich in his family, which has given him so much of affection and interest and stimulation. He can look forward to new riches in the world before him, riches of human contact and concern and the satisfaction of sharing. He will win these riches because of the permanent spiritual gifts his family has bestowed upon him. They procure for him admission to the greatest of all fellowships—the people who serve God and their fellowman, and see no inconsistency in so doing.

X. Curriculum

SOCIAL STUDIES INTERESTS
OF THE PRIMARY-GRADE CHILD

J.D. McAulay

What interests related to the social studies do children in grades
one, two, and three seem to indicate through oral conversation? This
was the concern of a study with 315 children attending schools in
eastern Pennsylvania in the spring of 1960. The children were organized in small groups about a tape recorder, and the first and second
graders were asked to discuss (1) people of long ago, (2) people who
live today, (3) people they like, (4) places in this land, (5) places in
other lands, and (6) places they like. The third-grade children were
instructed to discuss: (1) places they would like to visit in other
countries, (2) things they would like to know about one country
which they would like to visit, (3) places they would like to visit in
the United States, (4) times of long ago when it would have been
exciting to be alive, and (5) things they would like to know more
about in the social studies. The study took place during the social
studies period each day for a four-week period.

The topics were analyzed and the interests organized under four
headings: historic, those interests which seemingly were concerned
with the past; geographic, those concerned with space, location, details of the earth's surface; social, those concerned with mores, folkways, and the interaction of people; and general, which included
those interests that could not be classified under any of the other
three headings.

The social studies interests of first-grade children seem to center
about the following areas:

1. First-grade children seem to be interested in the days of the
past, particularly cowboys and Indians. The influence of TV may
have produced this interest. Ancient days—the days of the gladia-
tors—are of concern to children at this grade level. This interest was
probably due in large part to the fact that the movie, *Spartacus* was
being shown in the local theaters at the time of the study.

From *Social Education*, April 1962. Reprinted with permission of the National
Council for the Social Studies and J.D. McAulay.

In response to numerous requests for further details about the report he published in the December 1961 issue of *Social Education*, the author has prepared
this and a companion article, which will appear next month. Dr. McAulay is
Associate Professor in the Department of Elementary Education of the Pennsylvania State College.

2. The geographic interests of first-grade children are concerned with environments different from the immediately known environment. The beach was of common concern to several groups of children, probably because of the coming summer vacation when many of them might expect to visit the ocean. Several groups talked about a visit to Texas, perhaps because of the influence of certain western TV programs popular in the community. Speaking more generally, however, it might be said that at the conclusion of their first year of school, first-grade children seemingly are interested in dry lands (the desert), wet lands (the jungle), hot lands (lands of the elephant), and cold lands (the country of the reindeer).

3. First graders are interested in social processes—how clothes are made, how milk is produced, how stone houses and paper are made. They are interested in where the trucks go, how people live on the prairies, why stone is used to build houses. They are concerned with the sleeping habits of other people, the games and toys of children in other countries, how other people tell time, the housing of other lands.

4. Under the heading, "general," it should be noted that first-grade children have social studies interests beyond the immediate community. These interests are broad and fluid. They embrace peoples and countries, climates and topography, cultures and processes different from those with which they are immediately acquainted. Their interests emerge from the immediately known, such as houses and games, clothes and milk, home and neighborhood, and move into the larger sphere of contrasting and different homes, neighborhoods, and communities.

The following discussion of Mr. Eisenhower's Gettysburg farm is typical of the recordings made during the study. Nine first-graders took part in this conversation.

Child A: My Dad was in the town where the President lives.
Child B: You mean the White House town;
Child C: No, she means where all the people are.
Child A: No, I don't, I said his farm. (Five children talked about farms they had visited or seen.)
Child D: Did your Dad see Ike?
Child E: He is the President.
Child B: My grandmother says Ike.
Child F: Does he make laws?
Child A: Not on the farm. He just lives there.
Child F: Are there chickens there?
Child C: Sure, of course a farm has chickens.
Child A: My Dad says there are some good cows on the farm. When he came home he brought . . . .

Second-graders seem to have the following social studies interests:

1. They want to know the historical detail of their national environment—why our country is called America (or the U.S.A.), why we have a President, why we have a Statue of Liberty.

2. Africa, Japan, the North Pole—all seem to hold a fascination for second-grade children. They are interested in environments removed and different from their own.

3. At the second-grade level children seem to be aware of social differences. They ask why there are differences in skin color, in religions, in nations ("How are the Russians different from us?"). They are aware of and curious about social customs—why we salute the flag, why the law helps us, why the Negroes are treated differently. Seemingly, they are interested in social living which contrasts with their own—a cowboy in Wyoming, a silk-maker in Japan.

4. In general, second-grade children are eager to gain a broader and deeper understanding of places that differ from their own immediate environment and of the people who live in those places.

The following discussion of Holland carried on by a group of nine second-grade children is typical:

> *Child A:* Is Holland larger or smaller than our country?
> *Child B:* It is smaller because most of the people travel by bicycles.
> *Child C:* That country has a queen instead of a president.
> *Child A:* What is their weather like?
> *Child C:* It is something like ours because they grow many, many tulips.
> *Child E:* Do they have bull fighting there?
> *Child B:* No, they live like us.
> *Child E:* In what kind of houses?
> *Child B:* Brick houses.
> *Child F:* Do their homes look like ours? I think we're better.
> *Child B:* The houses are clean.
> *Child C:* I know something we get from there—like clocks and dolls.
> *Child D:* What crops do they have? I don't think they have farms.
> *Child B:* Oh yes, there are farms.
> *Child C:* Big farms?
> *Child B:* I don't know—flower farms, I guess.
> *Child H:* I suppose everybody goes to school.
> *Child A:* I wonder if the children look at TV?
> *Child H:* Why do they have a queen?
> *Child E:* Japan doesn't have a queen—my Dad was there.
> *Child F:* Japanese kids don't wear wooden shoes.
> *Child G:* My Dad was there and he said . . . .

The social studies interests of third graders seem to focus upon the following concepts:

1. The historic interests of third-grade children are broadly allied

to the beginnings of settlements, of transportation, of social differences between sections of the nation. The children seem to be interested in the historical beginnings of their own state, or of neighboring states. Thirty children discussed the topic "why we have states." Five children wondered what Gettysburg looked like after the War Between the States. Three children discussed the appearance of the capital city of Washington at the time Lincoln was President. Three children discussed the disappearance of John Wilkes Booth after Lincoln's assassination. Early transportation seems to hold a fascination for third-graders.

2. Third-graders also seem to have interests largely related to geography. They want to locate the large land masses. They are inquisitive about the climate, the flowers, the animals of the continents. They want to know about the people who live on them—their homes, their eating habits, their games and dances. Eighteen children were interested in the kind of food Africa produces; sixteen children wondered what Africa sent us; fourteen children were concerned with India's lack of food. Third-grade children seemingly have broad interests in the location, the general physical features, and the peoples of the continents of the globe.

3. Wide interest in how the peoples of the earth differ from one another is evident in third-grade children. One group of ten third graders carried on a lively discussion of how the people of Japan manage chopsticks. Another group of nine children discussed the ricksha. Still another group of six wondered if the country of Turkey looked like a turkey. Sixteen children discussed what children in other countries might study in school.

4. Third-grade children seem to have some understanding of the broad differences between the U.S.A. and the U.S.S.R.; between the colored and the white in American society; and, in some small degree, between the more developed and less developed nations of the earth. It would seem that third-grade children have some interest in the current international scene.

It might be of interest to note here some of the topics discussed and the comments made by several groups of third-graders involved in the study. Three groups discussed how far Australia was from the U.S.A. Using the globe, they looked at the "big" ocean that separates the two nations. Locating Africa and Asia on the globe, the children in one group commented, "There's not as much water between these places" (as between the U.S.A. and Australia). One child was interested in "How far around is Africa from where we live?" Included in the discussion of these continental islands were such comments and questions as, "Do they have schools?" "What animals are there?" "I know it's hot there." The children were also concerned with what the people of these continents ate and wore, grew as crops, how they were housed. They discussed the games the children would play in this place (Africa). One group of children discussed the army Africa might have. One child volunteered that they wore short pants and long hats.

In seven groups, historic interests centered about the discussion of people. The interest in locomotives revolved about the children's concern with the men who stoked the wood and coal on the old steam engine—where did they stand? Did they have much rest? Two groups discussed the Revolutionary War—or the beginning of our country. The children in these groups were concerned with how the soldiers fought, how they dressed, what weapons they used, on what side were the Indians?

One group discussed who might have discovered Alaska. Members of this group were concerned with the hardships of the first explorers—were they cold, hungry, and lonely? Did the explorers use a ship or horses to reach Alaska?

Third-grade children seem to have broad general interests concerned with large land masses. One group of children discussing the location of Africa, indicated such divergent interests as what animals are found there, what is the weather like? Do people use gasoline there? Do the people look like us? Do they have planes as we do? Do they have Christmas and Easter at the same time we do?

Units in the social studies for grades one, two, and three must not revolve entirely about the social interests of children in those grades. Consideration of the structure of the social sciences and of the social scene in the immediate community must also be included in the structure of a unit. It would seem, however, that there should be some first-grade units built about trips or journeys to the bizarre and different—a trip on an elephant in a hot land, a trip on a camel in a dry land. Second-grade children might study a unit centered about a trip to Japan or the North Pole. For the third grade, a unit might be structured about the animals and people of Africa or South America.

These are days of crisis. The continuation of the democratic way of life, the very survival of mankind may well be decided within the next decade. To meet the challenges of society, the child must experience a social studies program that has vitality, breadth, and pertinent meaning. There is no better place to begin the revision toward such a program than in the primary grades.

ENCOURAGING CREATIVE PUPIL BEHAVIOR
IN ELEMENTARY SOCIAL STUDIES

by

Mary Lee Marksberry

Creativity—what is it and how can it be developed? Is it a magical quality given to only a few fortunate individuals, or is it something that can either be increased or allowed to atrophy, depending upon the nurture that is given it? These and similar questions are the concern of many people in many occupations at the present time. The reason is simply that creativity, more than any other human trait, is basic to the shaping of man's future.

Creativity has been defined in various ways, but for those who are interested in its development in children and youth, one conception is generally accepted: an individual has created if he has an experience which results in a sincere, straightforward invention, new and fresh for him. It does not depend on producing a product that has never been produced before. Rather, the point is that it be first-hand for the individual, not taken second hand from someone else. Another important point is that every curriculum area offers opportunity for creative thinking and the products resulting from it. These products vary. They may take one of three forms: that of unique communications such as pictures, stories, or characterizations in creative dramatic productions; that of plans or proposed sets of operations such as plans for testing hypotheses, plans for organizing a group to gather data, or plans for evaluating an endeavor; or, that of sets of abstract relations such as the formulation of hypotheses, or the discovery of generalizations.[1]

The question of who is creative is so closely related to what has just been said that it is almost repetitive to say that psychologists are convinced that all people are to some degree potentially creative. Individuals differ in their degree of potential for creativity in various fields of activity and in the modes and expression of their creative-

From *Social Education*, October 1965. Reprinted with permission of the National Council for the Social Studies and Mary Lee Marksberry.

Mary Lee Marksberry is Professor of Education at the University of Missouri in Kansas City. This article is based on an address she gave at the Annual Meeting of the National Council for the Social Studies held in St. Louis last November.

1. Benjamin S. Bloom *et al. Taxonomy of Educational Objectives, The Classification of Educational Goals. Handbook I: Cognitive Domain.* New York: Longmans, Green, 1956. p. 163-164.

ness. But creative thinking is made up of the same basic ingredients at all levels. Extremely creative people just have more of all or some of these ingredients. The solving of everyday problems is very likely a part of the continuum of creativity which extends from expressions having relatively little originality to those having a great deal.

Having established this much of a conceptual background, we can now turn to the question at hand: What are some principles of instruction for encouraging creative pupil behavior in the elementary social studies? Selected findings from the growing body of research in creativity can give some help.

In the first place, research has identified some of the characteristics of creative people. One study which compared the achievement of a high creative group and a high intelligence group found a relatively low relationship between the IQ metric and measures of creativity.[2] Despite the 23-point difference in IQ, and no difference in achievement motivation, there was equal superiority between the high IQ group and the high creative group in scholastic performance as measured by standardized tests. These results were replicated by another researcher with six different samples.[3]

These same researchers also found that the high IQ students were better known and better liked by their teachers than the highly creative students. Both groups (the high IQ's and the high creatives) felt that the traits the teachers valued and those predictive of success in life were moderately related, and the high IQ's valued these traits for themselves. There was no necessary relations, however, between the traits valued by the high creatives and success in adult life. The traits they valued were somewhat opposite to those their teachers valued.[4]

Other studies show that creative people are flexible and original, curious about the environment, open-minded, objective, indifferent toward conformity to many cultural stereotypes, willing and eager to try new ideas, willing to work long hours over long periods of time, confident in their own ability, willing to be alone both figuratively and physically, and sensitive to various sensory stimuli. They have high skill in the problem-solving abilities of conprehension, applica-

2. Jacob W. Getzels and Philip W. Jackson. *Creativity and Intelligence.* New York: John Wiley and Sons, 1962. p. 24-25.

3. E. Paul Torrance, "Education and Creativity." In Calvin W. Taylor, editor. *Creativity: Progress and Potential.* New York: McGraw-Hill Book Company, 1964. p. 53-54.

4. Jacob W. Getzels and Philip W. Jackson, *op. cit.,* p. 30-37.

tion, analysis, systhesis, and evaluation; have a wide knowledge of vocabulary, facts, generalizations, and methods in their specific fields, as well as in related and general areas; and have the psychomotor skills necessary to use the tools of their particular area of interest.

The findings suggest several principles or guidelines for encouraging creative behavior.[5]

> We need to recognize that creative children tend to be penalized by the two most common criteria for evaluating scholastic aptitude—measures of the IQ test and teacher evaluations of student characteristics. Students who may potentially be the most creative, by current test criteria may be labeled "over-achievers" with all the unfavorable connotations such a term has come to suggest. We must be cognizant of this danger and avoid it.

> We need to make a distinction between independence and obstinateness and between individuality and rebelliousness. Creative students may be harder to get along with but it must be recognized that their behavior likely has its roots in independence of thought. Since their values differ from the values of their teachers and less creative students, they are likely to view the world about them differently. Creative students should probably be given greater autonomy, and perhaps rewarded for behavior that fails to correspond with behavior we intended to reward.

> Able students should be encouraged to work on their own interests even if it means working alone.

> We should provide opportunities for discovering as well as for remembering, for playing with facts and ideas as well as for repeating them, for finding different interpretations and solutions to problems.

> We need to differentiate between evaluation and censorship, between judging and prejudging.

> Emphasis should be placed on discovering rather than repetition as the instructional method, and upon evaluating the ability to use knowledge rather than to give back memorized facts.

> We need to distinguish between creative behavior which meets standards of intellectual merit and behavior which is merely "cute." Only that which has intellectual merit should be rewarded.

A second group of selected findings from research might be classified as characteristics of creativity and the creative process.

Creativity, like intelligence, is not an entity in itself. Rather, it is thought to be a constellation of behaviors—knowledges, attitudes, intellectual abilities and skills, psychomotor skills and habits. Furthermore, these behaviors vary with different spheres of activity.

A close look at the behaviors which make up creative thinking reveals that they are the same ones involved in thinking that is

---

5. Some of these principles were suggested by Jacob W. Getzels and Philip W. Jackson, *op. cit.*, p. 123-132.

termed critical or reflective. In both creative thinking and reflective thinking the intellectual abilities and skills are the ability to interpret with a high degree of accuracy, the ability to analyze, the ability to evaluate, and the ability to apply what is known. Thus the difference in creative thinking and critical thinking appears to be primarily in degree rather than in actual make-up. Creative thinking puts more emphasis on imagination and intuition and less on predetermined, correct, and conventional solutions bounded by rules and conventions.

The creative process is a problem-solving process. It is made up of a series of experiences or part processes, each of which continues what has gone on before and leads directly into other experiences so that there is a continuous merging of the whole. Each of these experiences is a problem-solving situation in itself making its contribution to the over-all creative process.

The creative process is believed by many to be made up of four stages. The first is a period of intense, routine work characterized by trial and error. It is concerned with inspection of the problem and collection of information and is called the preparation stage. The second is called the incubation stage. It is a period of quiesence out of which a new idea will come if the process is successful. The third is illumination, during which insight comes. And the fourth is verification, which is concerned with elaboration and revision.

These characteristics and two mentioned earlier—that there are gradations of creativity in problem solving and that creativity in the classroom may result in three types of products—reinforce some of the principles already mentioned and suggest others:

Learning experiences to develop creativity, like learning experiences to develop any other type of behavior, must give the learner opportunity to practice the behaviors which compose it at a level commensurate with his maturational level and in such a way that he gets satisfaction from it.

Since creativity is a constellation of behaviors, learning experiences to develop it must incorporate the principles for developing these separate behaviors. We must incorporate what is known about the development of knowledges, attitudes, intellectual abilities and skills, psychomotor skills, etc.

Children should be provided opportunities to solve various types of problems (intellectual, interpersonal, and practical) in group problem-solving situations, on an individual basis, and in discussion situations.

We need to encourage original and free thinking in the problem-solving process. This can be done especially during the formulation of hypotheses and when plans are made to test the hypotheses.

We need to prepare children for the first and last stages of creativity, by teaching industry, regular study habits, intellectual skills, and critically controlled attitudes.

Since insight into a problem situation comes when the learners have sufficient background and preparation, when they are able to see the realtionships in the total situation, and when opportunities for change of activities are given if they reach an impasse, the teacher needs to see that these conditions are met.

Teachers need to allow for unplanned and irrelevant happenings in the classroom so insight can be caught when it comes.

We need to be respectful of children's questions but seldom give answers which can be discovered by children themselves. The teacher's role is to help them find answers to their questions and to make the effort worthwhile by rewarding their efforts.

We need to ask provocative questions—questions which require children to interpret, to apply, analyze, and to synthesize and evaluate.

Reports, stories with a historical setting, dramatics, pictorial illustrations, murals, dioramas, panoramas, and the like (growing out of questions and problems in social studies) should be the children's own interpretations after thorough research. They should never be pattern or copy work.

Opportunities for children to make their own formulations of generalizations after careful gathering and study of facts must be provided.

The last group of selected findings to be considered here give insight into some of the forces that inhibit and promote creativity.

One report lists six inhibiting factors.[6] The first is the success orientation of the United States. This dictates that children must not be frustrated and that failures must be avoided. As a result children fear to try new things or to tackle problems that are difficult. The chance of failure with its resulting price is too great.

Second, the United States, according to anthropologists, is the most peer-oriented culture in the world. The inhibiting effects that peer pressures toward conformity exert on creative thinking have been very evident when researchers observed children, when they conducted experiments, and when they studied the creative writing of children.

Sanctions against questioning and explorations also work against creativity. The child who is constantly questioning and exploring poses a threat to many teachers in terms of the teacher's breadth of experience and in terms of smooth-running, teacher-dominated conforming classrooms. Teachers have many devices for putting the curious child in his place—insisting on one way to solve problems, insisting that every child use the same methods of study, insisting that all children complete their work within the same time limit, rewarding conformity, emphasizing giving back ready-made answers instead of answers the child has discovered for himself, and others.

6. E. Paul Torrance, *op. cit.*, p. 98-102.

Overemphasis or misplaced emphasis on sex roles is a fourth force that inhibits creativity. By its very nature, creativity requires both sensitivity and independence of thinking. Sensitivity, in our culture, is regarded as a feminine virtue and independence as a masculine one. Thus, highly creative boys are likely to appear more effeminate than their peers and highly creative girls more masculine. This results in pressures to conform to the accepted sex virtues.

A fifth force working against creativity is equating divergence with "abnormality." Although the belief once held that "genius" and madness were associated has been discredited, the belief has persisted that any divergence from behavioral norms must be corrected at all costs because it is an indication of something abnormal. The pressures of society to rid children of divergent characteristics are relentless.

Another restraining force is the work-day dichtomy in our culture. One is supposed to enjoy play and do dislike work, and something is wrong with the person who doesn't conform with this expectation. Also, there is supposed to be no playing in work. This appears to be one reason why teachers do not more frequently allow children to learn through dramatic play, through "fooling around" with maps, globes, books, and other materials and equipments, through informal discussions with their peers, and through satisfying their own curiosity by individually initiated projects.

On the positive side, biographical studies of creative people (scientists) indicate that some experiences may increase a person's chances to be creative while other experiences may decrease his probabilities. An early broad interest in intellectual things appears to be positively related to later creative performance.[7] The more creative scientists reported that they learned more about things which curiosity prompted them to study on their own than they did from classroom work or assigned homework.[8]

These findings reinforce many of the principles already given, and in connection with findings previously reviewed suggest four basic principles for providing an environment to further creativity:

1. Provide a physical environment which stimulates curiosity and invites experimentation.
2. Provide conditions where children can work with a minimal encroachment of interests.

7. Calvin W. Taylor and Frank Barron, editors. *Scientific Creativity: Its Recognition and Development.* New York: John Wiley and Sons, 1962. p. 386.
8. Calvin W. Taylor. "Clues to Creative Teaching: Developing Creative Characteristics." *The Instructor* 73:100; May 1964.

3. See that every individual is accepted and provided an emotional environment in which external evaluation is absent.
4. The classroom, since it is an important part of a child's culture, must tolerate deviations from the traditional and the *status quo* and permit freedom within the individual and between the individual and his environment.

In summary, if creative behavior in the social studies is to be promoted, we must put emphasis on discovery rather than repetition as the instructional method. This presupposes an informal, permissive, yet supportive classroom climate, a physical environment that invites both group and individual exploration and experimentation, many opportunities for original thinking and problem solving, honest appreciation of creative behavior that has intellectual merit, and a recognition and cherishing of individual ways of learning and responding.

WHY INQUIRY FAILS IN THE CLASSROOM

by

Martin Laforse

Modesty, common sense and a "decent respect to the opinions of mankind" compel even the marginally reasonable writer on education to shrink from confidently asserting why inquiry fails in the classroom. The over-inflated rhetoric characteristic of many of our contemporary social critics has been commonplace among educational commentators for generations. A sense of our own limitations, therefore, seems to be the best frame of mind in which to approach this topic. Since this article is not founded upon exhaustive scientific research studies based on matched random behavior samples, its main thrust will be historical and philosophical. This writer is convinced that a historic and social sense and a philosophic understanding of inquiry are most pertinent to a clarification of the issues. Accordingly, the question of why inquiry may fail in the classroom is viewed here not so much as a problem of how to improve teaching technique—although that, to be sure, is important—but, rather, as an attempt to clarify our use of words and concepts and identify those forces which make an impact on educational policy and, ultimately, teacher behavior.

The new emphasis on "inquiry" or "discovery" or "inductive" teaching—not so new an idea really—has manifested itself in the midst of the crystallization of powerful historical forces which combine to make ours one of the great watershed periods in the history of this species. We may be in the midst of the transition from civilization to post-civilization as Kenneth Boulding has persuasively argued. In view of this kind of transcendent outlook, the inquiry approach as presently advocated seems to lack a sense of change being undergone and of the fix in which the species finds itself. Judging by the kinds of concerns deemed worthy of the discovery efforts of children, the new advocates are at some remove from where the children are and have a paucity of imagination in forecasting where they might have to go. Their underlying world view is static, still evoking success and

From *Social Education*, January 1970. Reprinted with permission of the National Council for the Social Studies and Martin Laforse.

Martin Laforse is an Associate Professor of Education at Ithaca College, Ithaca, New York.

achievement in the manner of our Protestant heritage. Not considered is the possible dysfunctionality of the anxiety achievement mode not only for the future but the immediate present.

A Look at the Past

Unfortunately, there is nothing new about this kind of unreflectiveness, and the history of education in America may be viewed, after all, as a series of missed opportunities. The record of educators and social scientists as forecasters and relevant policy planners is not encouraging. What, for example, were our young students "discovering" about the Black experience in America in our schools in 1954? Our traditional school history, for example, not only seems to have left the ideas out, it also omitted phenomena which later, ironically, surprised us by the suddenness of their importance.

An assessment of the outcome of past educational reform movements is small comfort to those of use pondering the impact of the present inquiry mania on the classroom. That Herbart's proposals in American hands hardened into the rigid five step pattern of instruction ought to give us pause. No less relevant is the transformation of John Dewey's formulations by those who romanticized the raw impulse of the child. These dogmatic progressives so sentimentalized the child that Boyd Bode was moved to warn them that progressive education would come to little unless its proponents got their minds off the child long enough to work out a thorough democratic philosophy. Well might we now ponder how absurd became the attempts of some progressives to act on their own slogans. In the pages of the house organ of the Progressive Education Society, for example, children never seemed to "listen" to music or "read" books or "draw" graphs; they were always "experiencing" them.

The glorious and evocative word was "experience," even as the words "inductive" and "discovery" and "inquiry" seem now to adorn all new textbook materials, program packages and pronouncements of state education departments. Despite the shift in language, the beholder sometimes gets the feeling that little of fundamental importance has changed.

If the fate of the so-called "life adjustment" movement is yet another unpromising example from the past, there is a parallel movement to the inquiry enthusiasm that might well require scrutiny. One cannot help suspecting a certain element of dysfunctionality in the current interest in the non-graded elementary school. Advocates of this type of organization tend to exhibit a zeal to fix each child at just the right level of achievement in each and every aspect of his school experience. As a result, they may be engaging in a flurry of measuring which could yet make the non-graded school the most graded educational institution yet conceived.

The saddest aspect of these examples is that they contained much that was sound and held out great promise when first proposed. As a matter of fact, the contemporary discovery approach seem to embody an elaboration of John Dewey's original notions, which tends to slight his great concern for the vital facts of child development. It is as if process has now overwhelmed person. It is sad to note that a rereading of Dewey's writings of fifty years ago and more moves the reader to the rather puzzling conclusion that little of what he advocated has as yet been tried out in our schools. In the rush to obtain certainty, the discovery advocates may have neglected some essential elements of discovery—suspended judgment, an attitude of searching and a spirit of excitement.

The cultural phenomenon which originally leads us astray and then provokes a defensive attitude which can preclude reassessment may be the peculiarly American necessity for obtaining premature closure and hard feedback. Inside the classroom and out we Americans have not been noted for tolerance of ambiguity. This characteristic may help to explain the fads which periodically sweep our educational establishment in response to environmental pressures. Our high demand for answers is reinforced by the efforts of vested interests which present certain commercial programs to teachers and administrators as the answer to their social and political needs to appear innovative.

It sometimes seems that it is almost a sin in our culture to suspend judgment, to admit that we are not really sure in any given instance. Teaching is particularly prone to ambiguities. Moreover, it may well be that we are only in the very early stages of attaining some reliable understandings of the outcomes of the teaching act. For many years to come adequate feedback may be difficult to come by and it is this kind of indeterminacy, particularly in a product-oriented society, that frustrates the human being.

It is in this context that the impact of the work of people like Skinner and Bruner on the education of teachers becomes understandable. Rather than promoting a devotion to open-mindedness, the work of these behavioral scientists and others often has been seized upon in an effort to obtain positive classroom procedural justification. The hard science emphasis in social and behavioral science tends to dominate at this juncture, aided by hard research dol-

lars from the United States Office of Education. No one would deny
that the work of these men has a place in the preparation of teachers.
Perhaps, we ought to approach their findings, however, in a spirit of
inquiry rather than as dissemination of a gospel. Catching the tides in
the affairs of men can be dangerous for the work of seminal thinkers
as the fate of the ideas of Dewey and Herbart attests. Well might the
original thinker exclaim, "God save me from my disciples!" And well
might the teacher-in-training or in service agree as he faces the disciples. The current proliferation rate of ideas makes it imperative that
we adopt an attitude of sensible skepticism before we find ourselves
overwhelmed by fixed dogmas.

The Values of Freedom of Inquiry

The vision of the teacher as heroic figure may be relevant to
genuine inquiry. For to take inquiry seriously, he and his pupils must
examine ideas in the classroom including the teacher's and those of
his pupils and their parents. Even in elementary grades this can raise
the issue of academic freedom. Examining issues that people may
care something about is, like democracy itself, a risky business. Yet,
teachers on the firing line probably will have to face the consequences. For inquiry must have the freedom to move explorations in
directions which may produce unpredictable outcomes. Can teachers
construct a hospitable environment in which to function? They may
be the only ones who can and in so doing they have to instruct a
reluctant community in the values of free inquiry if that is demanded. However, they cannot do this unless they themselves understand
these values and internalize them. Moreover, the young people with
whom the teacher interacts probably have to share in these decisions
increasingly as they progress through school. As if this were not
enough, there is still that uncertainty which an inquiry approach will
probably only exacerbate. Consequently, the teacher may have to
learn to live without the kinds of visible returns on efforts which
lend meaning to the lives of salesmen, engineers, electricians, micro-
biologists, and the stray published poet.

However, rather than viewing this as a lamentable situation, we
could see unusual opportunity in it. We might even decide to depart
from the humorless and pedestrian discovery materials now flooding
the education market. For example, we could put affect first, deciding that pupil self-involvement and excitement ought to be our chief
concern. We might even start by admitting that what we mainly
know about the teaching act itself is that it can be enjoyable, excit-

ing and compelling and that discovery may be relevant to this. However, the old social studies dominated so long by narrative history seems now about to be replaced by a concept of discovery which almost by design kills off pupil initiatives which generate excitement. Well might we recall how John Dewey, years ago, wondered why children were so full of questions outside of school and so silent within. The problem with many pre-packaged materials is that they abstract out the burning cares of youth while failing to generate new concerns. While they may simplify the task of the teacher, these materials and an excessively mechanical conception of inquiry can reduce the whole procedure to a ritual.

In summary, what I am suggesting is that we teachers ought to view the programs of the exponents of inquiry as a fit subject for discovery. We need to understand the social, historical and economic movements which propel us toward discovery methodology. We ought to be self-aware and socially aware. Teachers must have a philosophy of society, a sense of where the action and the concerns are, a chance to prepare carefully and back off, a sensitivity to where the children are burning and a cautious effort to help them find the flame, a due regard to the growing processes in the child, a perception of the values which have propelled us in the past and an assessment of their appropriateness in the future life of our children. This list is not exhaustive, but its realization may be exhausting. Perhaps, what we can best do is to resist the tide—as tide, and skepticism and a touch of irony might help. After all the fuss and fume, the notion of induction is not new. After all there once was a fellow named Francis Bacon, and it was he who formulated four reasons for human error. The last of these he called the "Idols of the theater," which, he noted, were those fads and fashions of the time which can lead us into error.

PROJECTIVE EDUCATION
FOR THE CHILD'S NEED TO KNOW

by

Barbara Ellis Long and David Wolsk

The following article is the work of two experimental psychologists who are researching the use of projective techniques in the elementary classroom. BARBARA ELLIS LONG *is a psychologist at the Saint Louis State Hospital, and* DAVID WOLSK *is associated with the Denmark Pedagogical Institute in Copenhagen. An outgrowth of their international collaboration is the development of an experimental curriculum whose central core is the child's "... recognition of his own uniqueness and identity, and his legitimacy as a real person...." This approach, point out the authors, enables one to enjoy the existential fact that each child is a research scientist and philosopher in his own right. They believe that a child is capable of identifying his own learning objectives, and therefore it is unnecessary for others to specify these for him.*

This article is an attempt to formulate a model of the processes of education and learning which has emerged during several years of research and development of a curriculum in the behavioral sciences for children of the upper elementary and secondary years in American and Danish schools. Recent findings in neurophysiology and the social sciences tend to support indications from the present program for a specific approach to how a child learns and how to help him do it. The roots for much of this approach can be found in Dewey and Piaget and a whole host of like-minded educators. What we have added to a child-centered approach is a foundation of child-centered information and concepts—information and concepts about human behavior developed within a particular kind of classroom milieu. This approach may well be useful in the other parts of the school day as well as the specific curriculum in the behavioral sciences.

The Data Base

It is becoming clear to us, on the basis of our research as well as that of many others, that the basis of a child's learning is himself and his own need to get new information about his world, so that he can manage his own life more and more. He takes in new ideas, new bits of information, fits them into his existing frame of reference, reorganizes that, and goes on to the next moment of need. This is an

From *Social Education*, March 1971. Reprinted with permission of the National Council for the Social Studies, Barbara Ellis Long, and David Wolsk.

active seeking process arising from a personal need and carried out in an idiosyncratic way.

There is a kind of rhythm to this process. First, there seems to be the "itch" to learn something for a reason. It is a kind of anxiety for learning, one could say. The searching takes place in order to scratch the itch, relieve or resolve anxiety. There is connection, if the child is lucky or aided in his search. He makes the fit. The itch is relieved for that particular place in his schema. That particular anxiety is relieved or resolved. He reorganizes his existing matrix of ideas and information that relate to that topic and equilibrium is restored for a time.

This description begins to sound like Cannon's ideas about physiological equilibrium or homeostasis.[1] It should. Thinking and learning are done by the brain and all of the body. We know that now. As physiological processes, thinking and learning are an inseparable part of the total system of homeostatic mechanisms within the body. Emotions and muscles as well as the cortex are usually involved.

The rhythm of the itch and then the scratch is becoming well documented by neurophysiologists and experimental psychologists.[2] Much of the theory and supporting data are found in work being done with information theory, the concepts of measured amounts of information called "bits," and the ensuing information processing that is done by the brain.[3,4] "Brain" in this context really means *all* the person, since his gut, his muscles, his hormones, and all the rest of him feed information to and are controlled by that strange evolutionary phenomenon—his human brain. The brain functions in a constant feed-back and feed-forward system with the subsystems of both its "own" body and the outside environment. From this viewpoint, the changes in the nervous system which we call learning are mechanisms of adaptation.[5]

The notion of classification appears in all of this research. It is becoming very clear that our visual and auditory systems as well as our other input systems do not work as passive recorders of our environment. Rather, they reduce the total stimulus array, the "blooming, buzzing confusion," according to classification schemes already existing within the brain. The actual process that operates with the input of information is more on the order of active construction of meaning—a kind of reorganization for the purpose of fitting.[6]

This information processing is part of an immense, ongoing decision-making process of the awake brain. The primary business of the brain—of thinking—seems to be decision-making. Millions of decisions or choices are made each day regarding raising or lowering blood pressure, sleeping or waking, opening or closing windows, walking or driving the car, etc. Some are conscious, some are not. Growth and development of the brain and the maintenance or disruption of homeostasis are largely governed by the negative or positive consequences of all these choices made each day.[5]

Decision making depends upon information; the more the better. There is also evidence from neurophysiological research which implies that we actively scan the environment continually for new information to maintain ourselves.[7,8,9] Eyes continually move. The brain depends upon change or new information in order to process it. In addition, deprivation of stimuli or temporary paralysis results in feelings of panic.[10] As soon as available information is inadequate for ongoing decision-making processes, anxiety results.[11]

The child often tries to predict his future needs for information. He role-plays the future. The information-gathering process is frequently an attempt to forestall future anxiety. He "plans ahead," and in order to do that he needs all kinds of data. He is, in a way, "anxious" to avoid future anxiety, so he gathers data now for future use. Clinicians and philosophers have based much of their work on the notion that we role-play the future. Current theories of brain functioning lend support to this.

The same kind of thinking seems to be done by the child, primitive man, the scientist, or any human when going about daily problem solving or decision making.[12] The only difference seems to come when reasons are assigned. The reasons or explanations may come out differently, depending upon the amount of information available. The process remains the same. Primitive man may have to resort to magic for his last great reason. Children do all sorts of things, including asking the teacher or even reading. Scientists may have access to a great wealth of scientific literature distilled from the experience of many preceding investigators, and great quantities of sophisticated hardware to help them. But we all go about it the same way, because that is the way our brains work.

The Child's Own Behavioral Science

The child is *first* interested in things and ideas as they relate to himself; he makes decisions and then goes out to actively seek information that will help him grow and learn how to deal with his world. His world includes the people around him and his interactions with them. He is intensely interested in learning all he can about human behavior. He must know what to expect in thousands or millions of institutions with others. He more or less learns "on the job," and must use the objects of his curiousity—other people—to teach him what he must know.[13] He finds models—all kinds—and literally develops his own private science of human behavior, based upon observations done by observer (himself) over one lifetime. He observes, records in his memory, makes some generalizations and predictions—which will be of use in the future, perhaps.

This is an extremely active information-seeking process. All kinds of bits of information go into the hopper, to be connected and interconnected and reorganized with existing matrices of concepts for present and future use. He knows there will be a tomorrow; a tomorrow full of both certainties and uncertainties, and so he plans ahead. He can be depended upon to seek information that he sees as relevant in any way to his own needs.

We need only cooperate with the child's obvious interest in human behavior, and both a curriculum and a method of presentation result. Some rather remarkable side effects began to appear. The child's view of himself, the school, his teacher, and his relationships within the classroom all begin to change in some very dynamic ways.

A Behavioral Science Curriculum

Our experimental curriculum is still being evaluated and changed as the children and the teachers using it indicate. It was based upon he premises and evidence outlined above:

1. The child needs information for growth: information about human behavior and the world around him as it relates to human life.
2. The child actively seeks this kind of information both for present and future needs; he ruminates over the past and role-plays the future.
3. The child structures the information content of new experiences according to his own existing classification system. Each child must use the system that is uniquely his own, based upon his own experiences, and his own needs.
4. That system is first based upon his interest in "me" and then other topics as they relate to "me."
5. The child needs adults and other children around him as support and stimulation for growth and change.
6. Nothing makes an idea stick better than experiencing the conditions that give rise to it.
7. Children are all different and all pretty much the same. They enjoy finding this out; and a curriculum on human behavior can be based upon it.

The curriculum consists of a collection of experiements, games, a few stories, and a number of open-ended activities which are designed to demonstrate one or more principles of human behavior. These are presented by the teacher as she feels the class is ready for them. Some are borrowed from classical psychological research and all of these experiments are simple to work and simple to set up. There are experiments for the children to try out that they see as games. These are probably not real games. It never really matters who wins or loses. There is always a hidden agenda. They are experiments that demonstrate some aspect of human behavior. The children become involved because it is fun. They literally fall for the fun of the game. A session typically begins with one of these group activities, and is followed by a general class discussion of their observations and research findings. The general plan in the discussion is to work from the self, to the group, to the world out there. In addition, control is gradually handed over to the children so that, eventually, they decide what they would like to study next, and also end up designing many of the experiments by the end of the year, in order to find out more about what interests them.

As the children investigate the science of human behavior by studying their own behavior as a group in various contexts, as they discuss their findings and work out general principles of behavior for themselves, they not only pack away a great deal of useful information about people for present and future use, they also find needs for all kinds of other information. Each child takes in the group experience in his own way. This is expressly recognized and encouraged by the teacher. The child continues his own zigzag path to his own goals, integrating new findings and searching for new information. His horizons widen, and his search widens as well.

As the child is encouraged to go on with his information-seeking in relation to human behavior, he finds that he has use for other "subjects" in the general school curriculum. He finds real, compelling reasons for increasing his skill in reading, or writing, or arithmetic. He becomes curious (he is anxious for information) about topics from history, economics, chemistry, and all the other "disciplines." His own personal need to find out has been recognized, and he begins to organize his learning for himself. He begins to understand that the classic and fragmented academic disciplines and knowledge are manmade. They are all different views of man's universe, and are all ways of gathering information for his own personal use. After having some fun with visual illusions, the student may follow this up by finding out how the eye works, which leaves him with questions about photochemistry, the physics of light waves and the mathematics which relates wave frequency to wave length, or he may pose the philosophical question: "What is real?"

He begins to set short-term objectives for himself in relation to skills he would like to acquire, or ideas he would like to explore. He might or might not verbalize these. Creative thought and learning are highly idiosyncratic in both direction and duration.[14,15,16] He is never sure where his interests will take him. The teacher cooperates with him in his search, and supports him as he works alone or with the group. She recognizes that it may be a class of 37, but it really consists of 37 brains working in 37 private searches for information and meaning.

An important part of the behavioral science curriculum/projective education method is the discussion by the children of their experiences, and of their experimental findings within the group. It is becoming clear, both as a result of our present research and that of others,[17] that the child must have a way to verbalize his findings. He seems to need to play with his experiences in words before he can really put them together into concepts for classification, reorganization, and retrieval for future use. He needs to articulate his findings, and in so doing, he recognizes himself.

This recognition of himself, his own uniqueness and identity, his legitimacy as a real person in the classroom and school is the central core of the curriculum and method. The program is explicitly structured around what he and the other children may want to learn concerning human nature. Emphasis is on general principles of human behavior, either singly or in groups. He is helped to see that a specific experiment can lead to general possibilities—even probabilities, and may be concerned with several aspects of the human experience. There will be some applications of these salient principles of behavior to real life, as recognized by the children. In talking about human behavior as a phenomenon which can be observed objectively, and even predicted to some degree, the child finds a way to place himself in relation to the scheme of things. He finds a way to deal with his major interest—himself, and his relationship with his world— that is useful and comfortable. He can withdraw temporarily to the objective view and re-enter the system more efficiently. Talking about it is a way to handle his discoveries with less heat of emotional bias and loneliness. He does not have to talk about "me." He can talk about "we." His own search for meaning and identity is implicit and is officially recognized. School becomes of value because he and his interests have become of value. This discovery is as dramatic as a thunderclap at times, and often comes about as suddenly.

The Method of Projective Education

If we accept the research evidence that the child is actively seeking all kinds of data for use in the evolution of his own private epistemology,[18] then we need no longer concern ourselves with specifying behavioral objectives for the pupil to justify or evaluate our own work as teachers and administrators. We can turn our attention from the responses we hope to get from him and the frustrating search for means to these ends. We can enjoy the existential fact that he is a research scientist and philosopher in his own right, aged 8 or 12 or 18. We can concentrate on providing provocative stimuli and materials for his use in his own information-seeking and processing. We only need cooperate with his search. Implicit in this is our recognition that he will take and use data in line with his own perceptual system and needs. Our concern about his responses is wasted, regardless. We are also relieved of the enormous burden of being the expert on everything in the classroom. We need only point to the library, the laboratory, and the world out there.

However, we who are older and more experienced in the business of living and observing can make some fairly useful predictions about what stimuli he will choose to respond to and to what degree of complexity he can go. Education of each child becomes an administrative possibility. Luckily for us, we have the recorded observations of generations of educators, developmental psychologists, psychoanalysts, anthropologists, parents, and many others to help us guess what stimuli (lessons, learning materials, topics, etc.) will be of interest to a budding thinker, aged 11, from a particular culture. We do not stand alone, any more than the child does. We can depend that he will search, and that we can help him find—usually on these topics, in these fields—relating to these principles. We need only keep our attention focused on the children, not the materials.

Contrary to the fears that "individualized instruction" can be chaotic, we find that most children aged 11, for example, will respond with interest to *these* ideas, in *this* way; so we find we are dealing with individuals in groups. We have simply recognized that groups are made up of people.

The projective approach has been used for years in diagnostic psychological testing. Projective techniques all depend upon the premise that each person takes and uses data according to his own perceptual framework which he has built up from his experiences and active data-gathering over his lifetime. No one is a *tabula rasa;* not even a baby. Each person will project himself and all that he has experienced into his responses. Each person's response to a given stimulus (his learning) will be slightly different from that of the next person, because of this. However, there are general similarities between people of the same age, sex, and culture. There is some order. People are not as wildly different from one another or as unpredictable as one might expect when we consider their individual backgrounds.

Traditional education begins with the response and tries desperately to work back to a specific stimulus. Projective education begins with some stimuli that probably are related to a general idea, and then deals with the responses when they turn up. It is a one by one approach—one step at a time, and one individual or class at a time. Each time, the stimulus is introduced, and responses can be infinite. A branching set of follow-up stimuli have been provided for the teacher, and she can choose from these the appropriate next step. The next array of infinite possibilities of response comes out, and she is free again to choose the appropriate stimulus.

For the word stimulus, in the context, read *lesson*. Another better word would be *experience*. There are many ways to drop the pebble in the pool. One can read a story to the children, or one can lecture, or one can even tell them to go read something in the textbook. These are all experiences for the children. However, they are pretty weak stimuli. No muscles have been used. No hormones are running around. We are not even very sure that the brain has been engaged. The view out the window may be much more of a stimulus.

Why not provide stimuli or experiences for the children that really mean something? Why not real pebbles in the pool instead of figurative ones?

Why not real experiments with real things, real muscles, real hormones, real emotions? Why not a slice of life in miniature? Educators have been talking about ideas like this, but they have been coming around from the wrong end. Provide the experience, the stimulus, the lesson which could lead to many ideas, and then hang on tight to see what happens next. However, in this case, one had better make very sure it's a strong stimulus, or there won't be much of a response (learning).

The most important point to make here is that the content of the course is the behavior of the children. They literally study their own behavior. The children become motivated to find out—no matter what—and will read, or listen, or watch. They have now experienced a small contained bit of some aspect of life. They have probably already experienced other bits of it out there in the real world. They have learned (remembered) a few things about human behavior from their cumulative experiences. But, their learning has not been structured or meaningful in most cases. They are not able to predict as much as one would hope, because they do not have the broad view which comes with structure.

So, we talk about it. It is as simple as that. Projective education would ask, "Why did that happen? Why did you do that? Why do people behave that way? Did you ever notice?. . . ." The questions can lead the children on to the next step, which is integrating their findings. The teacher helps them articulate what they discovered.

After the stimulus or lesson or experiment or experiences or pebble has been dropped in the pool, the children *must* talk about it. They must be helped to articulate, to organize, to generalize, and to attach what they have experienced to the other parts of their lives. This is an active process, not a passive acceptance. No one can give it to them, or lecture it into them. No one can predict where they will take all their experiences. However, the teacher can stand by with questions and suggestions. This seems to be a direct application and extension of Piagetian techniques and theory to the classroom.[19],[20]

The teacher is relieved of the necessity of "stuffing it in their heads," which she cannot do anyway. The fallout after exam week, if visible, would make Krakatoa look silly. She is relieved of the responsibility of defining objectives, since they are not hers anyway; they belong to the children. She need not worry about evaluating her work except in the eyes and progress of the children toward what *they* want and need. She shifts her attention from the books to the children—who are more interesting anyway—and helps them as an active assistant in their search. She probably comes home far more exhausted after a day at school; but she probably has more fun and a lot less guilt about "covering the material." *She* can not cover "it" anyway, unless she likes talking to herself.

Summing Up

When a course of study is based upon the theory that the child is actively seeking information and processing it constantly, that he *needs* information to help him grow to his fullest and that he will fit new data into his own perceptual framework as it presently exists, then the entire method of presentation and eventually the philosophy of education in that classroom (and later, the school) begins to change.

The child becomes the center of attention, not the "course of study." The sciences concerned with human behavior become important elements of the general curriculum, because we have recognized the child's own insistence on learning about himself, and his past, present, and future relationships with other people and the world, in about that order. The other subjects of study become of interest to the child, as he learns more about himself and others. They take on practical meaning. The fragmented nature of the disciplines disappears as he begins to form relationships between his need to know and the various parts of the general curriculum. The curriculum and method of presentation become so intermixed that it becomes impossible to separate them.

Something quite remarkable begins to happen in that classroom. The children and the teacher all come together as Martin Buber and David Hawkins have both described it,[21],[22] within the framework of *I* and *Thou* relating to one another about *It*. In this case, *It* is that body of knowledge available in the school which now has great meaning for all parties to the transaction.

Concepts are handy baskets to carry information around in.[23] The important thing to remember is that we must all build our own. Also, we must build our concepts around our own perceptual system built upon our own experience and needs.

If this is a defensible approach, and present neurophysiological and clinical evidence indicate that it is, then this is the way the management of learning in schools should be arranged.

In that case, then the projective education approach of providing stimuli and information for the child's own processing will tend to get us the long-term goals we have been trying to reach. We need not specify objectives. The child will do that for himself. We need not worry about specifying responses and then search for adequate stimuli. We can provide stimuli and rest assured that the child will take and use them for his own growth as a self-actualizing human being.[24] His biological design will have it no other way. We will be more likely to reach our long-term goal of developing healthy, civilized, and responsible citizens. We will have less need to worry about the slow dance on the killing ground of our present educational methods. They don't work very well, anyway. We can build upon the very human need to know, which is part and parcel of every child's basic biological equipment.

REFERENCES

1. Cannon, Walter B., *The Wisdom of the Body.* New York: W.W. Norton, 1932.
2. Grastyan, Endre, "Towards a Better Understanding of Human Emotion." *Impact of Science on Society*, 28:187-205, 1968. (Special issue on "What brain research reveals about learning and behavior.")

3. Reitmen, Walter R., *Cognition and Thought*. John Wiley and Sons, 1965.

4. Uttley, A.M., "The Transmission of Information and the Effect of Local Feedback in Theoretical and Neural Networks." *Brain Research*, 2:21-50, 1966.

5. Ashby, W. Ross, *Design for a Brain*. London: Chapman and Hall, 1960.

6. Gibson, James J., *The Senses Considered as Perceptual Systems*, Boston: Houghton Mifflin, 1966.

7. Festinger, Leon, *et al.*, "Efference and the Conscious Experience of Perception." *Journal of Experimental Psychology*, 74: #4, Part 2, 1-36, 1967.

8. Bizzi, Emilio and Schiller, Peter H., "Single Unit Activity in the Frontal Eye Fields of Unanesthetized Monkeys during Eye and Head Movement." *Experimental Brain Research*, 10:151-158, 1970.

9. Yarbus, A.L., "The Perception of an Image Fixed in Respect to the Retina." *Biophysics*, 2:683-690, 1957.

10. Solomon, Philip and Kubzansky, Philip (eds.), *Sensory Deprivation*, Cambridge: Harvard University Press, 1961.

11. Wolsk, David, "An Information Processing Model of Anxiety," Unpublished manuscript.

12. Levi-Strauss, Claude, *The Savage Mind*. London: Weidenfeld and Nicolson, 1966.

13. Hayward, Ruth, Personal communication.

14. Ericksen, Stanford C., "The Science of Teaching, the Art of Learning." In T.S. Krawiec (ed.), *Teaching of Psychology Newsletter*. (Division 2.) Saratoga Springs, New York: American Psychological Association, 1968.

15. Mager, Robert, "On the Sequencing of Instructional Content." *Psychological Reports*, 9:405-413, 1961.

16. Mager, Robert F., "Explorations in Student-controlled Instruction." *Psychological Reports*, 13:71-76, 1963.

17. Bruner, Jerome S., *On Knowing: Essays for the Left Hand*, pp. 81-96. New York: Atheneum, 1967.

18. Campbell, Donald T., "Evolutionary Epistemology," in Schlipp, Paul A. (ed.), *The Philosophy of Karl R. Popper*, a volume of *The Library of Living Philosophers*. LaSalle, Illinois: The Open Court Publishing Co. In press.

19. Kamii, Constance, "A Sketch of the Piaget-derived Curriculum Developed by the Ypsilanti Early Education Program." Ypsilanti Public Schools, September, 1970.

20. Sinclair, Hermina, "Some Implications of Piaget's Theory for Teaching Young Children." *School Review*. 78:169-183.

21. Buber, Martin, *I and Thou* (trans. by Ronald Gregor Smith). New York: Scribner's. 1958.

22. Hawkins, David, "I, Thou, It." *Elementary Science Study*. Reprint of a paper given on April 3, 1967 at the Primary Teachers' Residential Course, Loughborough, Leicestershire, England, Mimeographed.

23. Bruner, Jerome S., *The Process of Education*. Cambridge, Massachusetts: Harvard University Press, 1960.

24. Maslow, A., *Toward a Psychology of Being*. Princeton, New Jersey: Van Nostrand, 1968.

SELECTING SOCIAL STUDIES TEXTBOOKS:
THE CHALLENGE OF CHOICE

by

Ralph Adams Brown

Marian Brown

RALPH ADAMS BROWN, *Professor of History at the State University of New York College at Cortland, is an experienced scholar, a dedicated teacher, and a productive author. For years he and his equally talented wife,* MARIAN, *have formed a team to provide teachers with solid information and sound analysis of social science issues. They are the editors of the forthcoming NCSS publication* The American History Booklist. *As they did several years ago in* SOCIAL EDUCATION, *they examine the complicated problems involved in selecting textbooks.*

The mid-twentieth century is truly a time of educational change, of experimentation, and of controversy. Programmed learning, gamesmanship, new materials, and new techniques all clamor for attention. Teacher shortages, teacher strikes, new certification requirements also plague and perplex us. Yet amidst this ferment the textbook remains one of the most important basic tools for social studies teachers.[1] Sternig has pointed out that "For the immediate future textbooks will be a necessity . . . ,"[2] and this despite the many weaknesses in texts. For example, it is often suggested that textbooks tend to reflect the demands of the average teacher, and that authors, as a general rule, tend to write for the average teacher rather than the creative one. Publishers, as businessmen, naturally produce textbooks that they feel will be used by the greatest number of teachers or school systems. This, too, can only mean that they tend to cater to the average rather than to the superior teacher's desires. When minority or pressure groups in the community are organized and vocal, their demands often curtail change or improvement of textbooks. In some instances, textbooks that "please" the public rather than the professional staff may be chosen.[3]

From *Social Education*, March 1969. Reprinted with permission of the National Council for the Social Studies, Ralph Adams Brown and Marian Brown.

1. See, for example, Eleanor Peterson, *Aspects of Readability in the Social Studies.* New York: Teachers College Bureau of Publications, 1954. p. 1.

2. John Sternig, "How to Select New Textbooks," *The Nation's Schools,* 77:114, 152, March 1966, p. 114.

3. Donald R. Taft, "History Textbooks and Truth," *Proceedings* of the Association of History Teachers of the Middle States and Maryland, No. 24, 1926; quoted by Robert Bierstedt, "The Writers of Textbooks," in Lee J. Cronbach, editor, *Text Materials in Modern Education.* Urbana, Illinois: University of Illinois Press, 1955, p. 128.

Despite these drawbacks, however, there have been encouraging signs in the area of textbook construction, signs that have been increasingly apparent in the past decade. Publishers frequently provide innovations in make-up and even in interpretations. Today's textbooks are often written by teams of teachers and scholars with differing areas of specialization, rather than by one person. Teaching aids, suggestions, and bibliographies are produced by individuals particularly skilled and able in these areas. The best of these books reflect the latest interpretations and research in the field rather than merely reorganizing the old data.

Believing that textbooks are still "essential to good instruction," Pershing Vartarian wrote that "The responsibility for the selection of good textbooks is enormous."[4] Miller and Berry are even more emphatic in their insistence on the importance of careful selection of texts.[5]

> The effectiveness of the teaching-learning situation depends to a large measure upon the instructional materials that are employed. All too often inadequate consideration is given to the various textbooks available for a course or subject area. Seldom are textbooks carefully analyzed in the light of established selection criteria. Many textbooks are chosen with less investigation than is employed in the selection of a case to house them.

Increasingly the choice of a textbook is left to the classroom teacher rather than to the school board superintendent, or supervisors. Chabe quotes the opinion that ". . . whether a textbook committee is large or small, formal or informal, for elementary or high school, classroom teachers should have the primary responsibility for making textbook decisions."[6] Equally important, perhaps even more so, there is evidence that with increasing frequency the final selection is based on "analytical, comparative studies of the books to be considered."[7]

The trend toward teacher involvement in textbook selection is rewarding. Even more important than the recognition of teacher ability to make wise selections, is the in-service training or growth that

4. Pershing Vartarian, "Criteria and Techniques for Textbook Selection." *The Social Studies*, 53:127, April, 1962, p. 127.
5. W.R. Miller and Robert H. Berry, "Adopting the Right Textbook." *Clearing House*, 37:18-25, September, 1962, p. 18.
6. Alexander M. Chabe, "Evaluating Elementary Social Studies Textbooks." *Education*, 86:302-307, January, 1966; quoting an article in the *Instructor*, 67, March, 1958, p. 85.
7. Ivan R. Waterman, "When You Choose A Textbook." *The Phi Delta Kappan*, 33:267.

can be realized through this process. Anderson has pointed out that evaluation of textbooks by a teacher or a group of teachers "focuses attention on present practice, recent research, and changes made in other communities."[8] Thus it calls not only for evaluation of what is being done but gives teachers an awareness and insight into what can be done.

Granted that the selection of a textbook should be made by, or at least with the active participation of, those teachers who will use it, several very important questions must be answered. Must every teacher in the same grade of a school system use the same textbook? Must every teacher who will use a given book participate in its selection? What are the advantages or disadvantages of selection by a committee? Should such a committee contain supervisors, administrators, laymen, and even pupils, as well as teachers? If a committee is used, should it select a single textbook or prepare a list of acceptable or recommended textbooks?

The above questions are not easily answered. It is true that in some school systems every teacher is supposed to use the same basic textbook, although the use of supplementary materials is often the prerogative of the individual teacher. In other systems three or four different textbooks are approved and a teacher may use one or more of them.

Spaulding strongly supports the idea that each teacher should select his or her own book, arguing that "The requirement that teachers use books which they have not individually selected is not justified by arguments related to the improvement of education."[9] Few systems, however, demand that all teachers participate in textbook selection. Even fewer allow each teacher to select his or her own book. Many systems ask all teachers for suggestions concerning a textbook, and then turn these comments and opinions over to a committee. Any report from the committee must then be accepted by the majority of the teachers before going into effect.

The advantages and also the disadvantages of committee versus individual selection are worthy of note. Anderson believes that "To serve on a committee to select teaching materials is a challenging professional opportunity."[10] Certainly a group brings a wider variety

8. Paul S. Anderson, "How Teachers Share in Textbook Selection." *The Nation's Schools*, 60:57, September, 1957.
9. Willard B. Spaulding, "The Selection and Distribution of Printed Materials," in Lee J. Cronbach, editor, *Text Materials in Modern Education.* Urbana, Illinois: University of Illinois Press, 1955, p. 174.
10. Paul S. Anderson, *op. cit.*, p. 59.

of interests and competences to the process of selection than can any one individual. There is less likelihood that a glaring weakness or inaccuracy will be overlooked. A group approach means that more "areas of special competence" will be represented than when selection is done by any one individual. Such group interaction, moreover, is a learning experience in analysis and evaluation. Group selection also, in many cases, will increase rapport, confidence, and group morale. There is general agreement, as stated above, that teachers are able to and should play the dominant role in any choice of basic texts. The time when School Board members administrators, supervisors, or lay groups arbitrarily choose textbooks has long since passed.[11] In some instances, however, representatives of such groups serve on selection committees along with classroom teachers.

Selection by a committee, however, has some disadvantages. It is time consuming. The need to reach a compromise may foster the choice of an average rather than an outstanding textbook. Unless the school system is small, not every teacher participates and those not included may feel that their wishes are not considered. Such teachers may tend to blame personal ineffectiveness on the committee's failure to select an "adequate text." Thus the widest possible teacher participation in textbook selection seems indicated.

While there exists basic and not easily resolved differences of opinion between the proponents of adoption by individuals or by groups, the actual process is much the same. There must be the same careful examination of books and the same consideration of advantages and disadvantages, of strengths and weaknesses. Textbook selection is a many-pronged responsibility. The teachers must keep informed concerning new books, must gain access to them, and must find time to read and analyze them. Annotations of textbooks, such as those prepared annually by the National Council for the Social Studies, will help teachers. Such listings, however, cannot release the teacher from he responsibility of seeking out and reviewing new publications in his field.

Regardless of how the teacher is to participate in textbook selection, whether individually or as a member of a group, he must have some basis for making a choice. Mellott has pointed out that few teachers have been fortunate enough to receive, as part of their training, help with solving or even with anticipating the problem of text-

11. See "Desirable Procedures in Selecting Textbooks." *Elementary School Journal*, 52:497, May, 1952. See also: Willard B. Spaulding, *op. cit.*, p. 170.

book selection.[12]   Spaulding writes of "The vagueness of ideas about what constitutes a good text," and laments the commonly held opinion that a textbook chosen in a "good" manner (i.e. democratically chosen) must be a good textbook.[13]

Selection as a Process

It is obvious that the ultimate objective of a process of textbook selection is the choice of a new basic text or texts. Yet the people involved in this selection need, also, to think of their assignment as a significant process. In fact, in a period when most textbooks are "good," and are similar in some respects, the process of selection becomes as important as the final selection.[14]

In emphasizing the importance of textbook selection one must think of it as "a continuous process during the school year."[15] We have come to accept the fact that curriculum construction and change is a continuous task. It has been pointed out repeatedly that this study and construction, or reconstruction, of the course of study should "go hand in hand" with the process of textbook selection.[16]

Such a continuous activity needs guide lines or directives in order to be effective. Waterman has suggested four steps that should be taken in any textbook evaluation.[17] First, he states, must come the formulation of criteria or standards for selection. Even if worked out by a committee, these should be brought back to the teachers, discussed, changed, added to, and approved by the entire group. Only in this way will all the teachers understand and appreciate the analysis and evaluation which is being done. Even though the standards or criteria for evaluating a basic textbook are adopted by all the teachers, an effort should be made by any committee to acquaint all teachers with the progress of the group and to gain general acceptance if not enthusiastic endorsement for any new book that the committee chooses.

12. Malcom E. Mellott, "What to Look For in Choosing a Textbook." *NEA Journal*, 44:158, March, 1955.

13. Willard B. Spaulding, *op. cit.*, p. 177.

14. Guy McNeil and D.H. Wilkinson, "Operation of a Textbook Selection Program," *The National Elementary Principal*, 36:26, September, 1956.

15. Charlotte D. Davis, "Developing and Applying Criteria," *The National Elementary Principal*, 36:38, September, 1956.

16. "Desirable Procedures in Selecting Textbooks." *Elementary School Journal*, 52:499, May, 1952.

17. Ivan R. Waterman. *op. cit.*, p. 267.

Secondly, Waterman suggests the construction of a score card "based on the assignment of numerical values to the several items of the criteria in accordance with their relative importance." Having constructed a score card or sheet, he believes the third step is to make a comparative evaluation of the textbooks under consideration. (Another writer has suggested that in this phase of the selection process, the textbook or textbooks currently being used should be reevaluated along with the ones being considered as possible replacements.[18]) Waterman lists the actual scoring of the textbooks and the selection of the "winner" as the fourth and final step in this procedure.

The first of the above mentioned steps in the evaluation of textbooks dealt with the development of criteria or standards. It is elementary that in the formulation of such standards any teacher, or any group of teachers, must think in terms of student development and the goals of the course, or the teaching aims they feel should be achieved. A text which would interest sophisticated, intelligent youth from an urban area might not meet the needs of equally intelligent young people in a rural school.

This same emphasis on meeting aims and goals appears over and over again in the literature of textbook selection. Pearson and Spaulding say, "Look first for the book or books whose teaching aims are in harmony with your own."[19] Mackintosh and Tandler say those making a selection should "Analyze the merit of individual texts in relation to the goals and programs of their school."[20] Leitch comments, even more definitely, that "A textbook is of value in a social studies program only to the extent to which it assists in the achievement of predetermined goals."[21] King puts it this way: "From the individual teacher's standpoint, textbook selection is a matter of finding the book or books in harmony with her own teaching aims."[22]

Thus a teacher of American history who believes that one of the

---

18. Neil L. Gibbins, "A Different Way To Select a Textbook," *Ohio Schools*, 36:42, March, 1958.

19. Richard M. Pearson and William E. Spaulding, "Textbook Publishers Look at Selection." *The National Elementary Principal*, 36:22, September, 1955.

20. Helen Mackintosh and Fredrika M. Tandler, "Textbooks for the Elementary School: Production-Selection-Utilization." *School Life*, 41:8, May, 1949.

21. F.A. Leitch, "The Place of Textbooks in the Social Studies Curriculum." *The Instructor*, 62:14, March, 1953.

22. Lloyd W. King. "The Teacher-Publisher Team in Textbook Selection." *The Instructor*, 67:84, March, 1958.

primary aims of his course is to develop critical thinking, and an analytical attitude on the part of his students, may well question the value of a textbook that encourages the reader to accept, unthinkingly, what he reads. Such a teacher will check any new book to see if the student is encouraged to evaluate and to question judgments, and if it sends the student to source materials and to other books for comparison.[23]

There is a considerable literature dealing with the "items to look for" in the making of a score card for selecting a textbook. Different writers have suggested, for example, that one may use "ten areas for evaluation," or eight areas for those "charged with a responsibility of selecting American history and civics textbooks," "five questions a parent must answer if he is selecting a textbook," or "seven criteria for selection."[24] It has been pointed out that nearly a quarter of a century ago Clement "developed one of the most complete instruments for analyzing and appraising textbooks as he attempted to rate quantitatively thirty different factors which were grouped under four major divisions."[25] Three years after Clement's suggestions were made, Williams constructed a similar score sheet that consisted of only twenty items.[26]

Through the years many people have felt that textbook selection could be implemented if a proper score sheet was developed. Three years ago Chabe wrote, "Through application of formulated guidelines and recommended procedures as heretofore described, textbook selection becomes a scientific process based on objectivity and sound judgment."[27] Unfortunately, at least in the judgment of the present writers, textbook selection can never be so completely objective or so accurately measured, as some people have hoped or asserted.

23. For a good discussion of this point, see: "Six Tests of Textbooks." *American School Board Journal*, 122:25, June, 1951.

24. See, among many: Guy Wagner, "Textbooks Can Be Evaluated by 10 Areas of Information." *Midland Schools*, 70:17, May, 1956; "Criteria for Textbook Evaluation." *Bulletin* of the National Association of Secondary School Principals, 35:10, October, 1951: "Johnny's Textbooks, How Good Are They?" *National Parent-Teacher*, 47:7-10, June, 1953; Dorothy McClure Fraser, "Improving Social Studies Textbooks." *Journal of Education*, 137:16-18+ March, 1955; and Malcom E. Mellott, *op. cit.*, pp. 158-59.

25. See John A. Clement, *Score Sheet for Analysis and Appraisal of Textbooks*. Champaign, Illinois: Garrard Press, 1942; referred to by Miller and Berry, *op. cit.*, p. 19.

26. See Amos G. Williams, "Choosing Your Textbook." *Industrial Arts and Vocational Education*, 34:344-348, October, 1945; quoted by Miller and Berry, *op. cit.*, p. 19.

27. Alexander M. Chabe, *op. cit.*, p. 306.

Areas for Investigation

The above statement does not imply, however, that *all* aspects of textbook selection defy attempts to be accurate, scientific, objective, or definite. Some characteristics or qualities of a textbook can be evaluated as definitively and checked as closely as an experiment in natural science. All of the suggested areas for investigation and evaluation can be grouped into two categories. For want of better terms these two categories may be titled *"definites"* and *"indefinites."* The first includes those that can be accurately measured, counted, or recorded. In regard to the evaluation of these points there is little or no element of subjectivity involved, little or no chance for argument. The "indefinites," on the other hand, involve opinions or value judgments; they are items or areas in which two teachers or two groups of the teachers could very easily disagree. To illustrate, the number of maps in a book, their size, and the colors used are all "definites." No two persons inspecting a book would disagree in regard to such items. In sharp contrast, the quality and the usefulness of the maps are "indefinites." Two teachers or two committees might very well look at a series of maps and disagree on their worth or value.

A list of some "definites" and "indefinites" follows. Individuals or committees may wish to curtail or expand this list to meet their own particular needs.

"Definites"

1. Title
2. Date of publication
3. Number of units—chapters—pages
4. Cost
5. Type size and type faces
6. Page format
7. Binding
8. Inclusion of a preface and/or an introduction
9. Table of contents
10. List of maps and illustrations
11. Complete index
12. Inclusion of material in appendices
13. Availability of a teachers' manual
14. Availability of a workbook for pupils
15. Availability of supplementary materials—records, films, filmstrips, maps, sources, etc.

"Indefinites"

1. Style
   a. Vocabulary—interest appeal—readability—reading level (are these based on an understanding of the intellectual and psychological development of the children for whom this work is intended?)

     b. Clarity of expression
     c. Proportion of generalizations to specific examples—use of incidents
     d. Technical terms—methods of use—explanation of terms
     e. Use of illustrations to increase interest or understanding

2. Scholarship
     a. Selection of material
     b. Areas and topics emphasized
     c. Analysis of data
     d. Awareness of and coverage of new interpretations

3. Organization
     a. Is sequence and development adequate?
     b. Are chronological and geographical balance maintained?
     c. Is there continuity between chapters? between units?
     d. Are political, economic, social, and cultural factors all developed?

4. Teaching aids
     a. Type and quality of exercises, questions, activities
     b. Their relationship to: (1) text, (2) aims of text, (3) goals of teacher
     c. The quality of illustrations and maps
     d. The relationship of illustrations to text—to teaching aims
     e. Reference to other materials such as book lists, library resources, visual aids, etc.

5. Philosophy
     a. What is the philosophy or point of view of the author or authors?
     b. Is the actual philosophy of the book clearly set forth in the introduction or preface or manual?
     c. Is this philosophy acceptable to the teachers who are to use it?
     d. Is it acceptable to the community?
     e. Is "slanting" held to a minimum and prejudice acknowledged?
     f. Is the book written out of an awareness of current issues and problems?

The evaluation points that have been labelled "definites" should require only limited explanation. This does not, however, mean that they are unimportant, but rather that in most cases they are self-explanatory. For example the *date of publication* of a text needs to be checked carefully. Many so-called "revised editions" are almost identical to previous editions; a few minor changes are made, and then a new date is placed on the title page.

It is not essential that a teacher be adept at identifying either type face or type size. Any teacher is able to make a judgment on the general appearance and typography of a book. Page formats vary and there is, for example, no definitive research to show that a two-column page is any more or less readable than a one-column page. The chief point here would seem to be, is the format attractive? Eye-catching? Is the page easily read?

There is much similarity in the durability of binding or cover used by major publishing companies. Yet it is important to check the type of binding to make sure that when the book is opened and laid flat, it will remain open on a desk or table.

The "indefinite" evaluation points have been grouped under five headings. *Style* is important. It is also difficult to measure or define. We may ask of any book, is the writing sharp, vivid, dramatic? Is the style or presentation predominantly exposition, description, or narration? Yet we all know that little if any textbook writing is truly exciting. The necessity to be logical, to explain, to cover so many aspects of so many themes, makes it difficult to write a really exciting textbook.

While it is possible to check vocabulary against word lists, this is not very meaningful. Every teacher of experience knows that children will read and enjoy one book with a difficult vocabulary while disliking another book on a much easier word level. The organization, the material, the illustrations, all are important in gauging readability. So, too, is the paragraph structure. Most important of all, perhaps, in measuring readability is the matter of concepts. How many new concepts are offered, per chapter? How often are concepts repeated or reintroduced? Are the concepts developed logically and carefully? The role of the new concept in measuring readability is one of the areas that has been last explored by educational researchers, one that needs attention. By using a vocabulary suitable to an age level, by developing new concepts carefully, by the gradual introduction of technical terms, and by the use of interesting illustration, social studies may become a continuing story rather than the mere development of facts.

Another major division under "indefinites" is *scholarship*. Scholarship, good, bad, or indifferent, reveals itself in the author's selection of material and in the emphasis he gives to ideas, events, or persons. It can be assayed in terms of the author's handling of data. It is especially noticeable in the acceptance or avoidance of new interpretations, new conclusions, recent research. Authors, at every grade level, have been notoriously remiss in their failure to include the results of recent research in their textbooks.

Polos recently wrote that "Not only do many of our textbooks in social science avoid coming to grips with important issues, but they also fail to take into consideration recent historical scholarship."[28] A bit earlier, Noah and his associates concluded that "The world

28. Nicholas C. Polos, "Textbooks—What's Wrong With Them?" *Clearing House,* 38:451-57, April, 1964, p. 453.

inhabited by the compilers of high school history textbooks tends to be black and white, stereotyped, suitable for perpetuating the myths which pass for history, but unable to provide students with contrasting interpretations of events and policies."[29]

Important as is the area of scholarship, its adequate and accurate appraisal is not easy. There is probably no better way to do this, however, than the method suggested to his students by Henry Johnson in the first quarter of the present century. Every teacher, Professor Johnson used to say, has, or should have, at least one area or period in which he feels competent to judge the organization, the emphasis, the statements of fact and interpretation, and the inclusion of recent research. Professor Johnson believed that when any teacher was confronted with a new or unknown textbook, he should turn to that chapter or section where his own scholarly competence was greatest, and read critically and carefully. The resulting evaluation is, of course, partial and subjective. It is, however, the best that one can obtain. With a committee or group of teachers, such individual spot-checking would result in a more complete evaluation of the scholarship of a book.

Organization is another major area for textbook evaluation. The evaluator must be concerned with what is included and what is left out, with what is emphasized and what is treated casually. He may ask such questions as: Is the sequence and development adequate? Is chronological and geographical balance maintained? What of the continuity and transition between chapters? Between chapters and units? Are political, economic, social, and cultural facts all developed without undue emphasis or important omission?

Teaching Aids seem important to most teachers, especially the inexperienced, the insecure, and the less creative. It is fairly easy to check the type of teaching aids, list their inclusion by chapter or unit, or even to obtain the total number of pages devoted to such aids. But the evaluation of the quality of these aids is a more difficult matter.

A teacher may well ask if such teaching aids as activities, reading lists, topics for discussion, review questions, vocabulary lists, research problems and projects are practical at the designated grade level. Are they related to the body of the text? Are they useful in terms of a teacher's goals? Are they designed to encourage the pupil to explore

29. Harold J. Noah, et al, "History in High School Textbooks: A Note." *The School Review*, 70:415-436, Winter, 1962. *passim.*

other materials and gain new ideas, concepts, and skills or do they merely drill on the facts found in the text itself?

Modern social studies textbooks are literally splashed with color. Both teachers and pupils are accustomed to a profusion of picture, cartoon, chart, and map. One even gets the idea that some publishers are determined to use color and picture regardless of their value or usefulness. Yet illustrations can be of vital importance as teaching aids. They can clarify and make the text more interesting. They can be used in the identification of the historical process.

Stutz is one of the many who have pointed out that the real purpose of illustration is to help pupils learn.[30] He has indicated four characteristics of "good" illustrations: (1) skillful reproduction; (2) located near the text they are to clarify or explain; (3) accompanied by meaningful captions; and (4) designed to make a maximum contribution to the learning process. Stutz concluded that "One part of an effective job of teaching the social studies would seem to be the ability to select well illustrated texts, to recognize good illustrations, and to use efficiently available visual materials."[31]

When examining illustrations, then, one may well ask these questions: Are they accurate? Do they clarify concepts? Do they depict real-life situations? Do they serve edicational aims, or are they purely decorative? Are significant items of content illustrated? Are illustrations in close proximity to the text they illustrate? Do the captions catch attention and produce thought? Do the captions lead to critical thinking and the development of understanding?

Maps also deserve consideration. Sica suggests the following questions in evaluating maps in a textbook: (1) Is there at least one map for every important area considered in the textbook? (2) Are there maps that show small sections and others that cover broad areas? (3) Are different types of maps utilized for specific purposes? (4) Is there a progressive development of map skills?[32]

Another important "indefinite" in selecting a social studies textbook consists of the evaluation of the *philosophy* of the author or authors in the light of the system's aims and goals. (Rather than putting this "indefinite" first, the present writers have left it until

30. Fred Stutz, "Textbook Illustrations—A Neglected Opportunity," in William H. Hartley, editor, *Audio-Visual Materials and Methods in the Social Studies.* 1947, pp. 88-93.

31. *Ibid.*, p. 88.

32. Morris G. Sica, "Do You Understand Your Social Studies Textbook?" *The Social Studies*, 50:148-50, April, 1959, *passim.*

last because the true measure of an author's philosophy can be gauged only after reading and analyzing a text.)

The present writers have suggested, in their checklist,[33] six questions that should be helpful in assessing the philosophy of a textbook. The matter of agreement between the expressed philosophy of the textbook and the actual content is important. An author might indicate, in preface or manual, that his book was written out of a firm belief in the democratic process. Yet if the textbook itself was authoritarian, seemingly reluctant to present differing points of view, the author's expressed philosophy would be worse than meaningless—it would be downright dangerous. One method of checking on this is to have the teacher or selection committee work through the textbook before reading the author's statement of philosophy. Then the degree to which the author's work supports his stated philosophy can be determined.

Many students are attracted by definite characterizations or strongly supported points of view in their textbook. One of the major appeals of the old Muzzey, probably the longest and largest seller of all history textbooks, was the fact that its pages were liberally sprinkled with heroes and villains. Yet the judgments of history are often elusive. These present writers are not opposed to the expression of definite beliefs and points of view; they do believe, however, that a teacher, and through him the students, should be made aware of such emphases.

Committees, as well as individual teachers, should not hesitate to seek advice in the appraisal and selection of textbooks. It is well to remember that there are many degrees of "expertness." To the teacher without experience, another teacher who has taught but a single year, or served on but one textbook selection committee, becomes an expert. A selection committee might well seek out teachers, perhaps in neighboring school systems, who had used a particular text or texts. Sternig advocates listening to publishers' representatives in the selection process. He notes that,[34]

> Most of the representatives are more than willing to meet with selection committees and to present their materials in a professional manner. They know that their influence will be no greater than their ability to interpret the strong points of their product in relation to the needs of the curriculum. Instead of fearing the publisher's representative, schoolmen ought to welcome him as a specialist in the task of choosing the tools of teaching.

33. See above.
34. John Sternig, *op. cit.*, p. 152.

Listening to the representatives of a large number of publishers will provide a basis for wide comparison

Additional materials and suggestions concerning the selection of
textbooks can be found in the literature. Price, for example, has
written a provocative article about textbook selection in which he
recommends the use of "five basic criteria"—(1) appeal, (2) interest,
(3) difficulty level, (4) realism, and (5) depth.[35]

Making a Final Judgment

After teachers have read and evaluated various textbooks, the final
step is the cooperative rating of the books. This is frequently done,
as mentioned above, by means of a score sheet or score card. Sometimes it is done by having each teacher or committee member list the
textbooks in order of preference and then assigning a predetermined
point score for each preferential listing. A better decision can sometimes be reached after general discussion and compromise.

Score cards with a numerical value are an attempt to make evaluation more objective. Whether this can be done successfully is questionable. A textbook may rate high on many points and accumulate
a fine score on any rating card, and still be dull, pedantic, and even
deficient in terms of scholarship.

Davis and Houtz both suggest that the chief value of a score sheet
is in its preparation, and that the purchase of commercially prepared
forms removes one of the chief values of textbook selection—the
process by which are decided the qualities that are most desirable in
a text.[36]

Other writers have criticized the idea of check sheets. Waterman,
though favoring their use under certain conditions, points out that a
text might achieve the highest score and yet be completely inadequate in one major aspect.[37] Spaulding says the score card formula
is[38]

> over mechanical and substitutes analysis of parts for understanding of the
> whole. The score card theory assumes that a good text can be chosen by
> examining texts. It gives little more than lip service to the ultimate criteri-

35. Robert D. Price, "Textbook Dilemma in the Social Studies." *The Social
Studies*, 57:21-7, January, 1966, pp. 26-7.
36. Charlotte D. Davis, *op. cit.*, p. 38; Harry E. Houtz, "Teachers Can Evaluate
and Select Textbooks." *Elementary School Journal*, 56:254, February, 1956.
37. Ivan R. Waterman, *op. cit.*, p. 270.
38. Willard B. Spaulding, *op. cit.*, p. 177.

on, the extent to which the text contributes to the education of the student.

It would seem that rating sheets are most helpful as a basis for initiating discussion of a book or books. The best decision or selection can then be reached only after the give and take of general discussion and a carefully considered compromise.

As long as social studies teachers make extensive use of textbooks, the basis on which such books are selected will remain crucial. Furthermore, the worth of any evaluation will be proportionate to the time spent, to the training and experience and the breadth of interest of the individuals participating in the textbook selection. Thus the ability to analyze, critically evaluate, and help select a textbook is an important part of the overall criteria by which a social studies teacher, himself, should be evaluated.

TOWARD RELEVANCY, CURRICULUM, AND THE SOCIAL ORDER

by

R. Neil Reynolds

One characteristic of a modern industrialized society is that it predetermines the nature of personal needs. Social needs and individual needs become so thoroughly integrated that any difference between them seems singularly academic. As a result, the individual is forced to find his identity in an existence imposed upon him by a society whose principal concern is the perpetuation of its own economic base, rather than the inherent needs of the individual.

The overriding design of education in such a society has been to mold the individual to function effectively in the role he is expected to play later in society. Higher education has not been spared this condition; in fact, it well may owe its central position in society to this extension of post-Marxian alienation and false consciousness. Whether by intention or not, our educational result has been the reproduction and refinement of the existing social structure. The perpetuation of this structure is dependent upon the individual's satisfaction with economically derived and predetermined alternatives conceived within the societal framework.

Taylor has pointed out that we never have taken seriously John Dewey's proclamation that the central method of social reform and social change lies in education.* This idea of social reform through education is reflected often in the literature of education, but, by and large, American education has failed to give leadership to the community and society. Education has not changed society so much as it has become another element in our money-culture serving to promote the social structure to the detriment of the individual.

The function of education should be to help the individual reassert himself as the center of a compassionate whole. In order to maintain control of his own essence, the individual must gain awareness of himself as a functioning entity with responsibility for choosing his own life. The mere fact of choice and awareness of choice are not the ultimate factors in determining man's freedom, however. Education

Reprinted from *School and Society*, January 1971. Used by permission.
*Harold Taylor, "Peace, War and Education," *Social Education*, 30:7-12, January, 1966.

must focus on the considerations of what man has to choose from and the source of the range of his choice. It is the nature of these possible alternatives and their sources that constitutes the essence of the educational procedure.

The role of the educational institution is to provide a setting. The role of the educator is to manipulate occasions and circumstances to lead the individual toward the realization of his own responsibility for himself in his relations with others in the social order.

The first step toward leading the student to this realization is for the instructor himself to be aware of his responsibility to himself and his environment; that is, to place his own life and ideals as if on a pedestal for others to see and emulate. In so doing, each student will be accepted by the instructor as an integrated being constituting an end in himself. Teaching must be geared to the individual, rather than to the subject matter—as with the Experimentalists—or to the group—as with the social psychologists. Truth, tradition, and all *a priori* facts will give way to the concept of intellectual relevancy. The student, in order for his education to have real meaning for his life as he will live it, must be involved in the learning/teaching process—not in order that he somehow will learn better, but in order that what he does learn will become a part of his own personal existence.

Of course, value judgments play an important part in this process. It is only by mixing one's own value judgments with subject matter that it comes to be truly known to the individual. A subject matter, or a body of knowledge, can not remain objective. For it to be known, it must be subjected to the personalizing processes of the individual learner. He must give it meaning in terms of his own existence. If there is nothing within his existence with which he can relate it, then he can not know it truly.

The actual content of a subject matter becomes less important than its position in the curriculum and the intellectual relevancy of the content to the lives of those who are to involve themselves with it. If we are to accept the premise that the individual, being aware of his own freedom in the world, and being free, thus chooses his knowledge, then the range of choice does not become the important factor for the chooser-student. What can be chosen and what is chosen become decisive factors in the exercise of freedom. Hence, the importance of the educator as a manipulator. His concern in the university setting is to create situations and circumstances designed to intensify the individual's awareness of personal responsibility.

The curriculum of higher education must not be so well-defined as to predetermine what is to be learned. The subject-content of curriculum is of much less concern than the learning goal desired. Ideally, the curriculum itself is an abstraction coming into existence only when the needs, interests, cares, and circumstances of the students' lives are known to the extent that they can be applied to the content of the curriculum to give it the breath of life. The inference here is, perhaps, that a problem-centered curriculum should dominate higher education. Students in the presence of a real problem can observe, participate, and assist the educator in the application of discipline-content to the solution of a real problem. The student learns on his feet, not from the seat of his pants. He takes hold of his knowledge, he works with it, he changes it, he makes it a part of his subjectivity. He is not a receptacle designed to receive so much information.

XI. Media

UNDERSTANDING TECHNOLOGY AND MEDIA: A CURRICULUM IMPERATIVE

by

O.L. Davis, Jr.*

Before he left for school today, one second grader saw on television a search and destroy mission in Viet Nam, an excerpt from a UN Security Council debate, and a demonstration for open housing. His eighth grade brother, switching on his transistor radio when he awoke, heard before breakfast three hit tunes, the day's weather forecast, and a political analysis of a presidential primary contest. Both boys did not walk to school; one rode his bicycle and the other took a school bus.

Technology and communications media are so much a part of their lives—and have been ever since they were born. To attempt the task of identifying how these giants of modern society effect the lives of these boys—and the millions of youngsters in this world— would surely yield a bulky catalog. Such an enterprise seems somehow unnecessary. The pervading essence of the relationships is insistent and known. Yet, the schools to which these boys go—and most others in the land—appear to ignore intellectually both the existence of technology and media in the culture and their relationships to people's lives.

To be sure, the decade just past has been a time of truly phenomenal expansion in the acquisition and use of certain technological hardware and media in schools. Television receivers and antennae, overhead projectors, film and filmstrip collections, cartridge loading projectors, and materials centers dot classrooms and schools which before knew only chalkboards, an intercom "squawk-box," and an alphabet chart.

Television cameras and recorders, computer installations, and teletype communication links, still generally rare, are not as awe inspiring as before; "have not" schools feel confident that they will be "haves" only a few budgets from now. In-service programs have "upgraded" and "retolled" thousands of teachers. Use of the obtained

From *Educational Leadership* 26(1), October 1968. Reprinted with permission of the Association for Supervision and Curriculum Development and O.L. Davis, Jr.

*O.L. Davis, Jr., Associate Professor of Curriculum and Instruction, University of Texas, Austin.

machines and materials, while not as high as enthusiasts dare dream, has been obvious and, in some systems, dramatic.

Opportunities and Ignorance

These years of bustle and rush about technology and media may be viewed, nevertheless, as tragic times. Two counts comprise the major observations.

First, the period has exemplified a packrat opportunism. Money was available; if unused, it would be "lost." So, the operational concern was conceptualized as "What can we get?" "Let's have an overhead projector in every room, at least one television set for every corridor or floor." And, "Who would like to spend six weeks in New York, Nashville, Boulder, or Los Angeles at a media institute?" A substantial residue is evident. Much equipment is now in schools. Many teachers are using the equipment.

But the *technologies* seem not to exist. A technology is not a machine; it is a social system in which machines and technological processes are related to people and their actions and other features of a society. Systems of relationships between machines and people— adults and pupils—in spaces and times have not been built.

A few primitive technologies have "happened." For example, overhead projectors and screens have displaced chalkboards in many classrooms; the teacher now sits, instead of stands, and the pupils look up rather than out. Too, the television set is pushed into the classroom for the 15-minute Spanish lesson on Tuesdays and Thursdays and quickly wheeled out in order that another group may have science.

Simply put, appropriate technologies—the system of relationships—for use of the new equipment in schools are not operational. More important, serious attention to this necessity is encumbered by matters seen as having higher priority, by issues involving how teachers want to work, by the relentless press of clock and calendar (school must be kept going), and by widespread ignorance of the basic problem.

Second, and a critical tenderness, technology and media as dimensions of culture are not taken seriously in curriculum. For the most part, indeed, they are not even treated casually. A kind of romantic, if harsh, analogy of present school programs to that well-known curriculum described by my teacher, J. Abner Peddiwell, is possible. The "fish-grabbing" program of the present does not recognize the existence either of fish hooks or available food supply from the saber-toothed tigers nearby. Some specific instances are illustrative.

Instance: Industrial Arts

Industrial arts, maintaining its legacy of the manual training movement, still is too much characterized by projects and vocational concerns. The tie-rack and shoeshine kit may have given way to a handsomely turned lamp or inlaid table. Many junior high shops use "home-type" power tools. Major goals are seen as skill development on special machines, some contributed by local industries. Uncommonly present in the program is a rational, even appropriate, conception of the worker in modern industrial society and of the processes of industry.

One uncommon program has these major features. An IA course, and the environment—the shop—was reorganized to stress the relationships and interactions of an industry in contemporary society. An industry is characterized by economic, political, and personal relationships with divisions of responsibility and power. So, the class group confronted, intellectualized, and lived with organization and its problems not just at the first of the year but throughout the course. The teacher was not a foreman nor were pupils "laborers" or "independent piece manufacturers." A product was chosen for production—for mass production.

Design, prototype development, and tool making were necessary. So were plans and trials for organization of machines in the production and assembly line. Studies were made of man-machine operations, including work efficiency patterns using photographic procedures. Marketing and advertising campaigns were detailed. And, of course, the product was made. But not many products.

The course was attending to industry in society, its relationships and actions, to people and their ideas in the processes. This type of program takes responsibility the charge to understand, intellectually and personally, the modern world in which pupils live. Not at all incidentally, girls are attracted to such a program and so are boys not wanting, necessarily, training for a marketable skill.

Instance: English

English throughout the school program defines appropriate communication as writing and reading the disciplined and artistic products of written composition. Only grudging attention, if any, is awarded speaking and listening. And almost none is given to viewing and to its prerequisite construction of viewable forms. New language grammars are not uncommon, but rare is attention to the language and grammar of film and television. Forgotten, if once realized, is that many literacy masterpieces were never intended for reading. Certainly not *Macbeth* or *Our Town* or *The King and I*. The purposes of *Common Sense* and *Macbird* are ill-attended if only known by reading for asserted artistic merits outside the context of the passions which produced them.

Pupil construction of responses to emotions and ideas lightly grasped or deeply sensed are limited now, to essay, poem, or other print-type form. With movie and television cameras so accessible, both in schools and in many homes, production of artistic, creative, even "literary" communications in non-print media should be encouraged. The critical success of the blossoming art of film making by children and youth is heartening. Yet, for the most part, such developments are independent of schooling, "underground," testifying to the one dimension universe understood by professional educators. The serious study of the film in schools seems to be gaining increasing support in certain quarters, but its legitimization in the curriculum is not at all secure.

In one sense, many of the enthusiastic attempts at reform in the English program unfortunately may be seen as a kind of intertribal warfare. Some authors are replaced with others currently enjoying more favor. A few works emphasizing pastoral and rural values, images, and messages are replaced with selections reflecting some of the tenseness, pitch, and rhythm of living in a technological, industrial, urban milieu. Some stimulating materials, if not too offensive to sensitivities and norms, are substituted for some rather stale, remote materials. The difference is real enough. But more is expected from such an important field. The curriculum must be a part of present reality—in particular, its technology and media—as well as the artifacts of the past. Isolated practices in some schools indicate that the vision is seen. Pressures for quite radical reform seem to be mounting.

Instance: Social Studies

Recent ferment in social studies has yielded some rather potent programs and materials. The impact of technology and media, however, seems slight. Possibilities for access to original sources—through microfilm processing, for example—are not realities in most schools. Use of the newer media as both source of data and vehicle for organization, generalization, and report, is not common. How convenient it is to take a small audio tape recorder to interviews with local candidates, to edit the material, and to develop a presentation to a larger group. Surely possible is the use of a portable video camera to record living conditions in various neighborhoods or a session of the traffic court or the arrival in town of a national figure. Now easy to have available is a video-recorded set of the President's State of the Union messages.

Somewhat as in the field of English, however, the curriculum revisionists in social studies have restricted their efforts to modification of emphasis and sequence in the conventional program. Reform has not included substantial moves to incorporate the serious study of all that which is social. In such efforts, surely to be made in years ahead, attention will be focused on man's ways in a technological society, on the impact of technological forces on societies emerging from preindustrial eras, and on the ways life has changed and the accompanying fallout of values, ideas, and materials resulting from technological innovations. The programs will take seriously the processes and consequences of media bombardment and citizens' necessities to think reflectively and creatively about the messages in their media environment.

Opportunities: Viable Inputs

So many other instances might be included. These few serve to illuminate the problem: that school curriculum, in the main, has not seized technology and media as viable inputs into the system.

These observations are not an indictment. They are advanced as opportunities. Such matters, when spotlighted, do acquire a sense of urgency. And they should. There is no neutrality here.

Technology and media are in our society and they must be in the substances and forms of our schools. For them to be excluded from curriculum, like lepers from those who are clean, is for the school to become increasingly remote and probably irrelevant to society. Or the prospect seems real enough that society, through its private and public agencies, will enforce attention through cruel excess with some valuable although never clear ends being swallowed up by the means.

The hopeful alternative, on the other hand, is to serve society well by vigorous, responsible action. In so doing, boys and girls now in school and those to enter will be inducted more appropriately into their culture. They should, as an accompanying attribute, understand this culture more intimately and more fully.